Living Trust Maker™

2.0

THIS BOOK INCLUDES:

USERS' GUIDE
by Albin Renauer

LEGAL MANUAL ON LIVING TRUSTS
by Attorney Mary Randolph

NOLO PRESS  BERKELEY

Your responsibility when using a self-help law book

We've done our best to give you useful and accurate information in this book. But laws and procedures change frequently and are subject to differing interpretations. If you want legal advice backed by a guarantee, see a lawyer. If you use this book, it's your responsibility to make sure that the facts and general advice contained in it are applicable to your situation.

Keeping up-to-date

To keep its books up-to-date, Nolo Press issues new printings and new editions periodically. New printings reflect minor legal changes and technical corrections. New editions contain major legal changes, major text additions or major reorganizations. To find out if a later printing or edition of any Nolo book is available, call Nolo Press at (510) 549-1976 or check the catalog in the *Nolo News*, our quarterly publication.

To stay current, follow the "Update" service in the *Nolo News*. You can get a free subscription by sending us the registration card included in your *Living Trust Maker* package. In another effort to help you use Nolo's latest materials, we offer a 25% discount off the purchase of any new Nolo book if you turn in any earlier printing or edition. (See the "Recycle Offer" in the back of the book.)

This book was last revised in: **September 1994.**

VERSION 2.0	September 1994	Software Design	MARY RANDOLPH
Book Design	TERRI HEARSH		ALBIN RENAUER
Package Design	TONI IHARA		MICHAEL SEXTON
Box Photo	RICHARD BLAIR	Programming	MICHAEL SEXTON
Illustrations	MARI STEIN	Testing	XAVIER GEORGE
Index	MARY KIDD		LESLIE NORWOOD
Proofreading	ELY NEWMAN		ADAM STANHOPE
Editors	STEVE ELIAS		EDDIE WARNER
	RALPH WARNER		ALBIN RENAUER
	DENIS CLIFFORD	Printing	CONSOLIDATED PRINTERS, INC.

ISBN 0-87337-275-1

Printed on paper with recycled content
Printed in the USA

Acknowledgments

This project, even more than other Nolo undertakings, was a group effort. It's no exaggeration to say that it would have been impossible without the tremendous energy and work of editors Jake Warner, Steve Elias and Denis Clifford every step of the way. Half a dozen opinionated people, one small office—who would have thought it would work so well?

It was the ingenuity of Albin Renauer, who spent countless hours on the program, that let us make a working prototype of the software. He also contributed good ideas, solved design problems and kept the whole project moving.

Michael Sexton creatively and efficiently turned the overweight, slow prototype into a sleek, fast commercial program. Special thanks for patiently accepting myriad last-minute editorial "improvements."

The crisp design of this manual is due to Terri Hearsh's inspired and efficient efforts. Thanks to Magdalen Gaynor, an estate planning attorney in White Plains, New York; Marilyn Putnam, a San Francisco estate planning attorney; Tony Mancuso, Nolo's corporations expert; Dale Ross, who carefully combed through every screen; Lisa Rose, who shared insights into interface design; and insurance expert Mike Mansel of Pleasant Hill, California.

For help with the painstaking legal research this project required, heartfelt thanks to Cora Jordan, Annie Tillery and Lisa Guerin.

On the software side, thanks to Mick Radtke, who helped design the program's data structure and offered constructive suggestions on project management. Many people at Nolo Press helped test the program in different stages of development: David Cole, Sandy Coury, Ann Heron, Monica Kindraka, Dave Middleton, John O'Donnell, Barbara Kate Repa, JoAnne Skinner, Jennifer Spoerri, Adam Stanhope and Marcia Stewart. Eddie Warner would get a special beta-testing merit badge, if there were such a thing. We also appreciate the help of other beta-testers, too numerous to mention individually, who spent so many hours pounding on the program.

Living Trust Maker License

This is a software license agreement between Nolo Press and you as purchaser, for the use of the *Living Trust Maker* program and accompanying manual. By using this program and manual, you indicate that you accept all terms of this agreement. If you do not agree to all the terms and conditions of this agreement, do not use the *Living Trust Maker* program or manual, but return both to Nolo Press for a full refund.

Grant of License

In consideration of payment of the license fee, which is part of the price you paid for *Living Trust Maker*, Nolo Press as licensor grants to you the right to use the enclosed program to produce living trusts for yourself and your immediate family, subject to the terms and restrictions set forth in this license agreement.

Copy, Use and Transfer Restrictions

The *Living Trust Maker* manual and the program and its documentation are copyrighted. You may not give, sell or otherwise distribute copies of the program to third parties, except as provided in the U.S. Copyright Act. Under this license agreement, you may not use the program to prepare living trusts for commercial or nonprofit purposes, or use the program to prepare living trusts for people outside your immediate family.

Commercial Use of This Product

For information regarding commercial licensing of this product, including use by educational institutions and nonprofit organizations, call Nolo Press at (510) 549-1976.

Limited Warranty

As to the original purchaser only, Nolo Press warrants that the magnetic disk on which the program is recorded shall be free from defects in material and workmanship in normal use and service. If a defect in this disk occurs, the disk may be returned to Nolo Press. We will replace the disk free of charge. This limited warranty gives you specific legal rights. You may have others, which vary from state to state.

Customer Remedies

Nolo Press's entire liability and your exclusive remedy shall be the return of the price paid, provided that Nolo Press may at its option and your agreement attempt to repair or replace the software or diskette that does not meet Nolo Press' Limited Warranty and that is returned to Nolo Press with a copy of your receipt. **These remedies are not available outside of the United States of America.**

No Other Warranties

Nolo Press disclaims all other warranties, either express or implied, including but not limited to implied warranties of merchantability and fitness for a particular purpose, with respect to the *Living Trust Maker* software, the accompanying written materials, and any accompanying diskettes.

No Liability for Consequential Damages

In no event shall Nolo Press be liable for any damages whatsoever (including, without limitation, damages for loss of business profits, business interruption, loss of business information, or other pecuniary loss) arising out of the use or inability to use the product covered by this license, even if Nolo Press has been advised of the possibility of such damages. Because some states do not allow the exclusion or limitation of liability for consequential or incidental damages, the above limitation may not apply to you.

Your Responsibilities for Your Documents

Although our best efforts were devoted to making Living Trust Maker useful, accurate and up-to-date, please be aware that state laws and procedures change and may be interpreted differently. Also, we have no control over whether you carefully follow our instructions or properly understand the information in the Living Trust Maker disk or manual.

Of necessity, therefore, Nolo Press does not make any guarantees about the use to which the software or manual are put, or the results of that use.

Any documents you make using *Living Trust Maker* are yours and it is your responsibility to be sure they reflect your intentions. Have your *Living Trust Maker* documents reviewed by an attorney in your state who specializes in living trusts, wills and estate planning if you want a legal opinion about the effect of the documents or their legal interpretation.

Term

The license is in effect until terminated. You may terminate it at any time by destroying the program together with all copies and modifications in any form.

Entire Agreement

By using the *Living Trust Maker* program, you agree that this license is the complete and exclusive statement of the agreement between you and Nolo Press regarding *Living Trust Maker*.

Governing Law

This License Agreement is governed by the laws of the State of California.

Users' Guide
Table of Contents

1 Welcome

2 Installing and Starting Living Trust Maker

3 Working With Your Trust Data File

4 Using Online Help

5 Creating a Living Trust, Step-By-Step

Legal Manual
Table of Contents

1 Before You Begin

2 About Living Trusts

3   A Living Trust as Part of Your Estate Plan

What Kind of Living Trust Do You Need?

Creating an Individual Trust

6 Creating a Shared Marital Trust

7 Signing, Storing and Registering the Trust Document

8 Transferring Property to the Trust

9 Living With Your Living Trust

10 After A Grantor Dies

11 If You Need Expert Help

USERS'
GUIDE

Welcome

W elcome to version 2.0 of *Living Trust Maker*. With this program and your computer, you can create a legally valid revocable living trust, and maintain and update it in the years to come.

This product is the work of a team of lawyers dedicated to making the law accessible to non-lawyers. Every effort has been made to make the program and manual thorough, accurate and easy to use. It has been refined through hundreds of hours of testing and use by non-lawyers to be sure you don't need a law degree to understand the information presented here.

A. If You Never Read Manuals

If you're the kind of person who never reads users' manuals, you should *at least* take the time to read the Ten Essential Tips in the Appendix of this Users' Guide. These ten tips highlight unique aspects of this program. Even if you are an experienced computer user, you should still look at this list.

Of course, the rest of this manual also contains important information everyone should know, and you should read it, too—especially the Legal Manual, which is the second half of this book.

B. Our Guarantee

If for any reason, anything you buy direct from Nolo Press does not meet your needs, we'll cheerfully refund your purchase price and we'll pay for your cost to return it to us via U.S. Mail (Priority). No ifs, ands or buts.

C. *Living Trust Maker* Package Contents

This is what you'll find in the *Living Trust Maker* package:
- the *Living Trust Maker* Install disk
- this manual, which explains how to use the program, and covers important legal and practical information about making a revocable living trust, and
- the registration card.

D. About This Program

What does *Living Trust Maker* do?

Living Trust Maker is two kinds of software in one.

First, it teaches you about living trusts and how they fit into an overall estate plan. Online help throughout the program explains, step-by-step, the legal and practical aspects of making a living trust.

Second, the program assembles and prints out a document that creates a valid living trust. You can use this trust to transfer property to your loved ones at death while avoiding probate. You can also use the program to amend or revoke your trust at any time.

What kinds of living trusts can it make?

The program makes two kinds of revocable living trusts: One for married couples, and one for individuals.

How will I know what I'm doing?

The program will take you through seven steps to create your trust document. As you go through each step, you'll find a full explanation of what you are doing. In addition, at each step, you can refer to online help that answers particular questions you may have.

How long will it take to make a trust?

Creating your trust document can take as little as half an hour, depending on how complex you make it. But you should probably set aside more time, perhaps an evening or two, to fully use the online help and the manual and to become familiar with the law of living trusts. This will better prepare you to make knowledgeable choices along the way.

E. About This Manual

The manual is split into two parts.

The first part is the Users' Guide, which explains the technical side of running the program—menus to select, buttons to click and keys to press.

The second part is the Legal Manual, which explains the legal and practical aspects of making and maintaining a revocable living trust.

I'ts easy to distinguish the two parts, as well as their respective indexes, by looking at the edge of the book.

Cross-Reference Conventions

Cross-references from one part of the Users' Guide to another, or from one part of the Legal Manual to another, are expressed simply as "Chapter #, Section X."

Cross-references from the Users' Guide to the Legal Manual are written as "Chapter #, Section X of the Legal Manual."

Likewise, cross-references from the Legal Manual to the Users' Guide are noted as "Chapter #, Section X of the Users' Guide."

Typeface Conventions

To make the Users' Guide instructions easier to follow, we use the following typeface conventions:

- Keys you're supposed to press appear in small capitals; for example, CTRL and SHIFT.
- Key combinations you're supposed to press are linked by a plus sign; for example, ALT+F4 means "hold down the ALT key and press the F4 key."
- Buttons you're supposed to click with the mouse appear in small capitals and bold type; for example **CONTINUE.**
- Names of menus, menu items and list selections appear in bold type, with hot keys (if any) underlined; for example **File** menu or **Print Options.**
- Field names are italicized; for example, the *Name* field.

F. Register Your Copy

Registered owners of Nolo products receive a variety of free services and benefits.

But to provide these services, we need to know who you are. *Please take the time now to complete and mail the registration card.* You'll find it in the package this product came in.

No postage is necessary; just complete the card and mail it in. We also would appreciate any comments you have on our product. We read every comment on every registration card.

G. The *Nolo News*

As a registered user of a Nolo Press product, you will receive a free two-year subscription to the *Nolo News*, our quarterly publication.

The *Nolo News* contains:

- articles on estate planning, consumer law, personal finance, small business law and other topics of interest
- the latest product news
- significant law changes that affect living trusts (if any)
- Nolo's famous lawyer jokes column
- a complete catalog of all our books and software.

If you buy other Nolo products or upgrade this product in the two-year period, you get two more years free. If your free period runs out, you can pay $12 for another two year subscription.

And, to save the trees and to save you from piles of junk mail, we promise never to give your name to any other organization.

H. Customer Service

Phone: 510-549-1976
Hours: 7 A.M. to 6 P.M. Pacific Time, Monday through Friday
E-Mail: NoloInfo@aol.com

Nolo Customer Service representatives can answer questions on product availability, prices, software upgrades, product features, customer registration, policies, procedures and other non-technical topics.

Change of Address

If you move, please send Customer Service a letter with both your old and new addresses and, if possible, the mailing code on your *Nolo News* mailing label.

Users' Guide

Here's the address:
Customer Service
Nolo Press
950 Parker Street
Berkeley, CA 94710-9867
ATTN: CHANGE OF ADDRESS

Defective or Damaged Products

If you are a registered user and your disk is damaged or defective, we'll replace it free of charge. Send the defective disk and a brief explanation to:
Customer Service
Nolo Press
950 Parker Street
Berkeley, CA 94710-9867
ATTN: REPLACEMENT DISK

I. Technical Support

Phone: 510-549-4660
Hours: 9 A.M to 5 P.M. Pacific Time, Monday through Friday
E-Mail: NoloTec@aol.com

If you have technical questions or problems operating your software, contact the Nolo Technical Support Department.

Before you call, please take a moment to check the following items:

1. Does your hardware meet the minimum system requirements for this software? These requirements are listed on the box and in Chapter 2, Section A. Check memory, disk storage, operating system type and version.

2. Have you checked to see if the problem or question you have is explained in this users' guide or the online help?

3. Are your hardware and peripherals set up according to the documentation that came with them? Are all cable connections secure?

4. So we can answer your questions more quickly, please complete the following form and have it available when you call.

Software _____   Version _____

Computer type _____   Model_____

RAM (memory) _____   Hard disk_____

DOS version _____   Windows version _____

Printer (make/model) _____

Graphics card and resolution_____

Expansion boards (if any) _____

Is your computer on a network? _____

Installing and Starting Living Trust Maker

A. What You Need to Run *Living Trust Maker*

To run *Living Trust Maker*, you need the following:
- an IBM compatible 286 or higher computer with at least 2 megabytes (MB) of RAM (Random Access Memory) and a hard disk with at least 2 MB free space
- a printer (to print out your final documents)
- Microsoft Windows 3.1 or later
- one floppy disk drive (for installation).

B. Installing *Living Trust Maker*

1. Start your computer and start Microsoft® Windows™. For more information about running Microsoft Windows, see the users' guide that came with it.
2. Open the Program Manager.
3. Insert the *Living Trust Maker* Install disk into a disk drive.
4. Choose **Run** from the **File** menu of the Windows Program Manager.

```
┌─────────────────────────────────────────────┐
│ ═              Run                           │
├─────────────────────────────────────────────┤
│  Command Line:                    ┌───────┐  │
│  a:\install                       │  OK   │  │
│                                   └───────┘  │
│                                   ┌───────┐  │
│  ☐ Run Minimized                  │Cancel │  │
│                                   └───────┘  │
│                                   ┌───────┐  │
│                                   │Browse.│  │
│                                   └───────┘  │
│                                   ┌───────┐  │
│                                   │ Help  │  │
│                                   └───────┘  │
└─────────────────────────────────────────────┘
```

5. If the Install disk is in drive A, type `a:\install`. If the Install disk is in drive B, type `b:\install`.
6. Click **OK** or press ENTER.
7. Follow the instructions that appear on the screen.
8. When the installation is finished, you will have a *Living Trust Maker* Program Group on your desktop with the *Living Trust Maker* application icon and a Read Me icon.

Living Trust Maker program group

9. Double-click the Read Me icon and read its contents. It contains important information that didn't make it into this Users' Guide.

WHAT GETS INSTALLED ON YOUR HARD DISK

For you techie types, here's a list of the files that get installed on your hard disk:

ltm.exe	the *Living Trust Maker* application
ltmres.dll	"resource" file that contains much of the *Living Trust Maker* screen and document information
ltmlegal.hlp	the *Living Trust Maker* Legal Help (a Windows Help file)
ltmprog.hlp	the *Living Trust Maker* Program Help (a Windows Help file)
xvt320.dll	resources used by the program
xvt320te.dll	more resources used by the program
readme.wri	the Read Me file

C. Starting *Living Trust Maker*

Once you've installed *Living Trust Maker* on your hard disk, you're ready to start the program. You can start *Living Trust Maker* by double-clicking the *Living Trust Maker* icon or by using the **Run** command.

1. Starting *Living Trust Maker* With the Mouse

The easiest method of starting *Living Trust Maker* is by double-clicking its icon.

1. Start Microsoft Windows, if it is not already running. For more information about running Microsoft Windows, see the users' guide that came with it.

2. Open the Program Manager.

3. Find the *Living Trust Maker* program group and open it. See the Microsoft Windows users' guide for instructions on how to find a program group in the Program Manager.

Living Trust Maker program group

4. Double-click the *Living Trust Maker* icon.

If the program fails to start correctly, consult the Chapter 8, Troubleshooting.

2. Starting *Living Trust Maker* From the Keyboard

If you can't find the *Living Trust Maker* program icon, you can start the program as follows:

1. Start Microsoft Windows, if it is not already running. For more information about running Microsoft Windows, see the users' guide that came with it.

2. Open the Program Manager.

3. Choose **Run** from the **File** menu.

4. Type c:\ltm2\ltm

Note: If you installed *Living Trust Maker* in a directory other than the default \LTM2 directory, substitute that directory name in Step 4. For example, if you installed the program in the \trust directory of drive D, you would type d:\trust\ltm to start the program.

5. Click **OK** or press ENTER.

If the program fails to start correctly, consult Chapter 8, Troubleshooting.

3. What You Should See on Your Screen if the Program Starts Successfully

If the program starts correctly, you'll see the opening screen.

Living Trust Maker opening screen

The title bar of the window reads "*Living Trust Maker.*" If this is your first time running *Living Trust Maker,* a new, untitled trust data file will be created. The title bar of the interview window (the window inside the main program window) will say "Untitled Trust." Once you name and save this file (see Chapter 3, Section B, below), the filename you chose will appear in the title bar of the interview window.

The next time you use the program, it will automatically open the trust data file you most recently worked on.

D. Exiting the Program

You can quit *Living Trust Maker* at any time by:

- Double-clicking the System button at the top left corner of the *Living Trust Maker* window,

- Choosing **Exit** from the **File** menu, or
- Pressing ALT+F4.

If you've made any changes since the last time the trust data file was saved, these changes will be automatically saved if the Automatic Save feature is on. (See Chapter 3, Section B.) If the Automatic Save feature is not on, the program will ask whether you want to save your changes before you exit.

If you have printed your trust document the program may remind you that you should not sign the document if you have made any further changes to the trust file since the last time you printed. (See Chapter 7 for more on this.)

Working With Your Trust Data File

A ll of the information you enter into *Living Trust Maker* is stored on your hard disk in a trust data file. This chapter explains how to create, save and open a trust data file.

A. Creating a New Trust Data File

Living Trust Maker automatically creates a new trust data file for you when you start the program for the first time. The words "Untitled Trust" appear in the title bar until you save and name the file. (Saving files is explained in Section B, below.)

Although you *can* create an unlimited number of trust data files with *Living Trust Maker*, under normal usage, you will need only one.

If for some reason you want to create another trust data file (for example, if your first file was just a practice file, and now you want to start over with a new file), choose **New** from the **File** menu. If there is no other trust data file currently open, a new, untitled trust file will immediately be created. If a trust data file is already open, the program will ask if you want to close the that file before the new file is created. (You can only have one trust data file open at a time.) To close the currently open trust data file, click **CLOSE FILE** in the pop-up box. If you click **CANCEL**, the existing file will remain open, and no new file will be created.

Each time you create a new trust data file, the program takes you through several orientation screens that explain the features of the software, and gives you an overview of the law of living trusts. (See Chapter 5, Section B.) Take your time and use these orientation screens to learn about the program and the law of living trusts.

B. Saving Your Trust Data File

There are two ways to save your trust data file. The preferred way is to let the program automatically do it for you whenever it needs to. This is done by the Automatic Save function. You can turn this function off or on by choosing **Automatically Save Changes** from the **File** menu. **Automatically Save Changes** has a check mark next to it when the function is on. We suggest you leave it on.

The other way to save your trust data file is to choose **Save** from the **File** menu. The **Save** command is active (not dimmed) only when you have entered new information that has not yet been saved. If there are no new savable changes since the last time you saved, **Save** is inactive and dimmed. If you leave the Automatic Save function on, **Save** will rarely, if ever, be active.

Regardless of which method you choose (manual or automatic), *you will not be able to save your file until you have gone through the orientation screens and chosen the type of trust you want to make.* (See Chapter, 5, Section C.) Until you reach that part of the program, there is no data to be saved.

Naming Your Trust Data File

The first time you save your trust data, you will be asked to name it. Use a name of eight characters or less. Do not type a three-letter extension. The program automatically adds a ".TRS" extension when you save your file. All trust data files made with *Living Trust Maker* files must have the ".TRS" extension.

Once you have named and saved your file, the filename will appear in the title bar of the interview window.

C. Why You Should Make a Back-Up Copy (Even if You Never Make Back-Up Copies)

You should always keep two copies of your trust data file on diskettes and store them in a safe place with the signed copies of your trust documents. All changes you make to your trust must be made to the same trust file. If you lose this file, or if it becomes damaged, you will not be able to use *Living Trust Maker* to make Trust Amendments in the years to come. (See Chapter 7.) Keeping a back-up copy protects you against hard disk failures and inadvertent deletion of files.

To make a back-up copy, exit the program and copy your trust data file to a floppy disk, network drive, tape drive or other back-up device. If you saved your trust data in the default directory, it will be in the same directory as the LTM.EXE file. (This will be the \LTM2 directory on your C: drive if you installed to the default directory.) Trust data files are the ones that end with a .TRS extension.

D. Opening a Previously Saved Trust Data File

If you have used *Living Trust Maker* before, and saved a trust data file, the program will automatically reopen that file the next time you start the program. Under normal usage, this is precisely what you want the program to do, because, normally you should be using only one trust data file.

If you have not yet printed your trust document, the file will open to the Checklist screen so you can continue from where you left off. (See Chapter 5, Section D.) If you have printed your trust document, the program will ask if you have signed the printed copy. (See Chapter 7.)

If, for some reason, you have created and saved more than one trust data file, and you want to open a different one, choose **Open** from the **File** menu.

If a trust data file is already open, the program will ask if you want to close the currently opened file before it opens another file. (*Living Trust Maker* can only have one trust data file open at a time.) If you click **Cancel**, the existing file will remain open, and you will not be able to open a different file. If you click **Close File**, the currently open trust data file will be saved and closed, then the program will let you open another file.

The program will display a standard Windows Open File dialog, listing all files with a .TRS extension that are in the current directory. Select the file you want to open and click **OK**.

TECHNICAL NOTE:

How *Living Trust Maker* Remembers Which File You Were Using

When you first run *Living Trust Maker*, a file called LTM.INI is saved on your hard disk in the same directory as the LTM.EXE file. (If you used the default installation, this will be the \LTM2 directory.) LTM.INI retains information about what file you were last using. It also records your preferences for printers, fonts, page margins, etc. (See Chapter 6 for more on printing.)

If the LTM.INI file is deleted or removed from this directory, this information will be lost, the program will reset to its default settings, and a new LTM.INI file will be created the next time you run the program.

Also, if the trust data file you were most recently using has been moved or deleted, the program will ask you to select a trust data file the next time you start the program.

Using Online Help

L iving Trust Maker provides several kinds of online assistance:

- **Legal Help** provides assistance in making decisions involving the creation, amendment and revocation of a living trust.
- **Program Help** provides step-by-step instructions on the mechanical aspects of running Living Trust Maker.
- the **Tutorial** provides a basic overview of how to use the program.
- the **Legal Glossary** defines legal terms used in the program.

GETTING HELP FROM THIS MANUAL

Most of the information in the online help is also available in this manual. Legal Help information is contained in the Legal Manual—the second half of this book. Program Help information can be found in the Users' Guide portion—the portion you are reading now.

A. The Windows Help System

Living Trust Maker help works like help for most other Windows programs. If you are experienced in using the Windows Help system, feel free to skip ahead to Chapter 5, Creating a Living Trust, Step-By-Step.

The illustrations on the next several pages show how to use the various buttons and menus on the Help window for both Legal Help and Program Help.

IF YOU NEED HELP USING HELP

For online guidance on how to use the Windows Help system, choose **How to Use Help** from the **Help** menu.

B. Using the Help Window

System buttons
Double-click here
to close the help
window.

Minimize & Maximize buttons
Shrink the help windows down
to an icon or zoom it to fill the
screen.

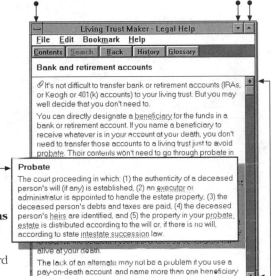

Scroll bar
Lets you see any
help text that
extends past the
buttom edge of
the help
window.

Pop-up definitions
Pop-up definitions
are available by
clicking on any word
that has a dotted
underline. Click
again to hide a pop-
up window.

Windows Help Functions

Windows Help has many functions that you may find useful. You can:

- print any help topic
- copy and paste help text into other Windows applications
- make "bookmarks" so that you can return quickly to specific topics in Help, and
- annotate topics with your own notes.

    See the illustration below for more about these features.

Edit menu •——————
Lets you add your own annotations
to this help topic or copy the text
of the help into a work-processing
document.

File menu •——
Lets you print the current help
topic, exit Windows help or open
a different Windows Help file.

Bookmark button
Lets you add the current help
topic to the Bookmark menu
for easy later reference.

Help menu
• Gives you information on how
to the Windows help system.

```
┌─────────────────────────────────────────┐
│ ─    Living Trust Maker - Legal Help  ▼ ▲ │
│ File  Edit  Bookmark  Help                │
│ Contents  Search  Back  History  Glossary │
│ Bank and retirement accounts              │
│ ⌗ It's not difficult to transfer bank or retirement accounts (IRAs, ▲ │
│   or Keogh or 401(k) accounts) to your living trust. But you may   │
│   well decide that you don't need to                                │
└─────────────────────────────────────────┘
```

Paper clip
Indicates that you have attached an
annotation to this help topic, using the
Edit menu. Click on the paper clip to
see your annotation.

Windows Help menus

Windows Help Buttons

Buttons in the Help window let you

- view a table of contents of Help topics in *Living Trust Maker*
- search help topics by keyword, and
- go back to topics you've previously read.

In Legal Help, you can also view a glossary of legal terms used in *Living Trust Maker*.

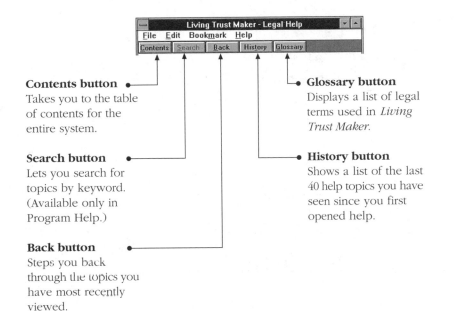

Contents button
Takes you to the table
of contents for the
entire system.

Search button
Lets you search for
topics by keyword.
(Available only in
Program Help.)

Back button
Steps you back
through the topics you
have most recently
viewed.

Glossary button
Displays a list of legal
terms used in *Living
Trust Maker*.

History button
Shows a list of the last
40 help topics you have
seen since you first
opened help.

Windows Help buttons

   If you have a large-screen monitor, you can drag the window to one side
and leave it open while you use the program. If you don't have a large monitor,
you can click on the *Living Trust Maker* program window to bring it to the front,
then press ALT+TAB to switch between the help window and the *Living Trust Maker*
window.

   If you close the help window and reopen it each time you use help, you
will not be able to use the Back or History features.

   To close the Help window, you can either:

• Double-click the System button at the top left corner of the Help window
• Choose **Exit** from the Help window's **File** menu, or
• Press ALT+F4 while the Help window is active (on top).

Users' Guide

C. Using Legal Help

The information in Legal Help helps you make decisions as you go through the program. Because help is context-sensitive, you'll find information that will help you with the specific task you are performing at that moment, such as entering your beneficiaries' names or deciding how to leave property to minors.

Legal Help is available whenever you see a button in the bottom left corner of the current program screen. This button is often labeled LEGAL HELP TOPICS, although sometimes it's labeled with a specific legal topic, such as WHAT NAME TO USE. To view context-sensitive legal help, click the Legal Help button, select **Legal Help** from the **Help** menu, or press the F2 key.

| Legal Help Topics | | What Name to Use |

Legal Help buttons

Legal Help is also sometimes presented on a screen containing a list of help topics. When you double-click on a listed topic, Legal Help on that topic appears in the Help window.

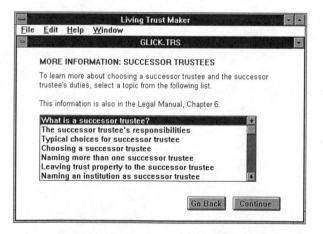

A Legal Help topic list in Living Trust Maker

D. Using the Legal Glossary

An online glossary of legal terms is available from any point in the program by choosing **Legal Glossary** from the **Help** menu. Glossary terms are listed alphabetically. To scroll instantly to a particular part of the alphabetical listing, click on a letter of the alphabet that appears just below the title bar.

All glossary terms are also accessible within Legal Help as well. Whenever you see a word with a dotted underline, you can click on it to view a pop-up glossary definition.

E. Using Program Help

Program Help provides step-by-step instructions on the mechanical aspects of how to use *Living Trust Maker*.

To view Program Help, press the F1 key, or choose **Program Help** from the **Help** menu.

Program Help is context-sensitive. That means it "knows" what part of the program you are using. When you open it, it "guesses" what your problem is and opens to a Program Help topic window (or list of Program Help topics). It may or may not guess correctly.

If it guesses wrong, check the related topics listed at the end of the of help text to see if your question is addressed there. If you find a topic that addresses your problem, click on it.

You can also view a more general Table of Contents for Program Help by clicking the **Contents** button on the button bar at the top of the Help window to. You can also access this list by choosing **Program Help Contents** from the **Help** menu of the *Living Trust Maker* program window.

F. Using the Tutorial

An online tutorial provides a basic overview of how to use the program.

The tutorial is available from any point in the program by choosing **Tutorial** from the **Help** menu. If you have a large-screen monitor, you can drag the window to one side and leave it open while you use the program.

Creating a Living Trust, Step-By-Step

This Chapter shows you, step-by-step, how to create a trust document with *Living Trust Maker*.

STEP-BY-STEP EXAMPLE
As we go through each step, we'll make a sample living trust, using the fictitious family of Olga and Stanley Glick. You may want to make a trust data file of your own and follow along.

A. Before You Begin

Before you start creating your living trust, you should browse the Legal Manual portion of this manual and think about the decisions you'll have to make. What property should be put in the trust? Whom do you want to receive your property after your death. After you've thought about these questions, you're ready to create your trust document.

As you read this Users' Guide portion of the manual, you may also want to follow the step-by-step material in the Legal Manual.

B. Beginning the *Living Trust Maker* Interview

Living Trust Maker is designed to work like an interview. It guides you step-by-step through the process of creating a living trust, explaining each step along the way.

When you create a new trust data file, *Living Trust Maker* begins the interview with a series of screens that introduce the program and the law of living trusts. By the time you're finished, you will have stepped through 20 to 80 screens, depending on how complex your living trust is. You don't have to complete the interview in one sitting. You can stop at any time, and resume later from where you left off.

Here are some basic tips on working with the *Living Trust Maker* interview.

1. Moving From Screen to Screen

You proceed through the interview by moving from one screen to the next, generally by clicking *once* the **OK** or **CONTINUE** button. *Do NOT double-click the* **OK** *or* **CONTINUE** *button. Double-clicking will cause you to skip past screens that you may not even see.*

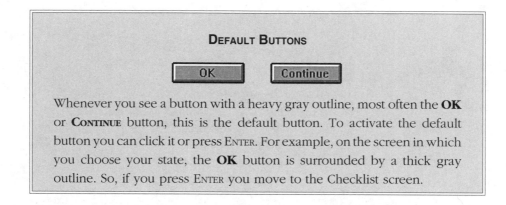

2. Going Back to a Previous Screen

From time to time, you may want to refer to a previous screen to read information or change an answer you entered. To do this, click **GO BACK**. **GO BACK** takes you back one screen at a time. Any previous answers you have entered will be displayed when you get to those screens.

If you enter information on a screen and then click **GO BACK,** information you entered on that screen may not be saved. This is because information is often not saved until you click **OK**. The program will warn you if you are in danger of losing your answers.

The GO BACK button

On some screens the **GO BACK** button is not available. You cannot move backwards from these screens.

3. Using the Program Without a Mouse

There are a few parts of *Living Trust Maker* that can only be used with a mouse. However, if you prefer to use keyboard whenever possible, see the list of keyboard shortcuts in Section A of the Appendix. (You'll find the Appendix at the end of the Users' Guide portion of this manual—not at the back of the book.)

4. If You Can't Decide How to Answer a Question

In some steps of the program you cannot continue with the interview until you enter required information. If you are unable to or don't want to enter the information yet, you can either:

- Click **Go Back** to return to the prior screen, or
- Enter the information as best you can, and later return to the screen to edit your entry.

  Remember, if you're unsure how to answer a question, Legal Help (F2) is usually available to address most questions you might have. If you get can't figure out how to use the software, Program Help (F1) is there to assist you.

C. Selecting the Type of Trust

After you've stepped through the opening series of orientation screens, *Living Trust Maker* asks you to select the type of trust you want to create. Your choices are:

- a trust for an individual, or
- a trust for a married couple.

Trust selection screen

If you need help deciding, click the Legal Help button, labeled **IF YOU'RE NOT SURE**, or consult the Legal Manual, Chapter 4, *What Kind of Living Trust Do You Need?*

Make your selection by clicking on the appropriate button (if it's not already selected), then click **OK**. *Living Trust Maker* will bring up a box in which you must name your trust data file (unless you turned off the Automatic Save function). Remember that the file name must be eight characters or less and cannot contain spaces. (See Chapter 3, Section B, if you need more information on naming and saving your trust data file.)

Once your data has been saved, the file name you chose will be displayed in the title bar of the interview window, with a ".TRS" extension added to the end of it, and you will be at the Checklist, which is described in Section E, below.

STEP-BY-STEP EXAMPLE (continued)

Because Olga and Stanley are married and own property together, they click the **TRUST FOR MARRIED COUPLE** button, then click **OK**.

When the program asks them to name their trust, they follow the DOS file naming rules and name it "Glick." *Living Trust Maker* automatically adds the required .TRS extension. From that point on, GLICK.TRS appears in the title bar of the interview window.

IF YOU CHOOSE THE WRONG KIND OF TRUST

Once you choose the kind of trust and clicked **OK**, you can't later change this trust data file into the other kind of trust. That is, you can't change an individual trust to a shared marital trust or vice versa.

The only way to make a different kind of trust after you leave the trust selection screen is to create a new trust data file. To do so, choose **New** from the **File** menu. (See Chapter 3, Section A, if you need more information on creating a new trust data file.)

D. Using the Checklist

Once you have chosen the kind of trust you want to make, you will come to the Checklist. As shown below, there are, in fact, two different kinds of Checklists used in *Living Trust Maker*. The one you will see depends on the kind of trust document you've decided to make.

Checklist for creating a trust document for individual

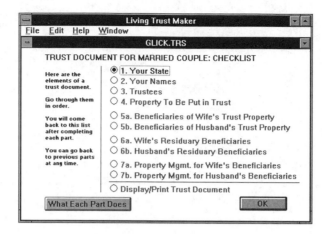

Checklist for creating a trust document for a married couple

The Checklist lists the seven steps or Parts involved in creating a trust document using *Living Trust Maker*. You will go through each Part in the order listed. After completing each part, you return to the Checklist.

REOPENING A FILE THAT YOU'VE ALREADY WORKED ON

As mentioned in Section B, above, you can stop the *Living Trust Maker* interview at any time and resume it later. If you exit *Living Trust Maker* or close your trust data file before you have completed the interview, you will be returned to the Checklist the next time you resume your work.

---

1. Why Some Buttons Are Dimmed

The first time you come to this screen, only **1. YOUR STATE**, will be available to be chosen. All the other Part names are dimmed indicating they are inactive and cannot be chosen.

Additional parts of the program become available one by one, as you complete the previous parts of the program. When you have entered all the information to create your trust, all of the buttons on the Checklist will be active.

2. What the Check Marks Mean

As you complete each part, a check mark appears next to that step to indicate that it has been completed.

If you enter a step but do not enter any information, a check mark will not appear by that step and you will not be able to move on to other steps of the program. To move to the next step, you must enter the required information for the prior step.

> **EXAMPLE:** You enter Part 1, Your State, but don't select a state from the list. When you return to the Checklist screen, Part 1 will not be checked, and you will not be able to continue on to Part 2.

3. Re-Entering a Part of the Program

You can re-enter any step of the program you have already been through (as indicated by a check mark next to its name). As you go through a step you've already worked through, the answers you entered earlier will be visible.

E. Part 1. Selecting Your State

To begin Part 1, click **1. YOUR STATE** on the Checklist (if it isn't already selected), then click **OK**.

You will come to a screen that lists all the states except Louisiana. (You may need to scroll down the list to find your state.)

```
┌─────────────────────────────────────────────────────┐
│ ─           Living Trust Maker              ▼ ▲│
│ File   Edit   Help   Window                         │
│ ┌───────────────── GLICK.TRS ─────────────────── ▼│
│                                                     │
│   YOUR STATE                                        │
│   Select the state that is your legal residence.    │
│                                                     │
│                         ┌─────────────────────┐ ▲ │
│                         │ Florida             │ █ │
│                         │ Georgia             │ █ │
│                         │ Hawaii              │   │
│                         │ Idaho               │   │
│                         │ Illinois            │   │
│                         │ Indiana             │   │
│                         │ Iowa                │   │
│                         │ Kansas              │   │
│                         │ Kentucky            │   │
│                         │ Maine               │ ▼ │
│                         └─────────────────────┘     │
│                                                     │
│  ┌───────────────────────────┐   ┌────────┐ ┌──────┐│
│  │ What Is Your Legal Residence? │   │Go Back │ │  OK  ││
│  └───────────────────────────┘   └────────┘ └──────┘│
└─────────────────────────────────────────────────────┘
```

Your State selection screen

Once you've found your state, select it in one of two ways:

- Double-click the name of your state, or
- Click the name of your state then click **OK.**

    This will return you the Checklist screen.

STEP-BY-STEP EXAMPLE (continued)

After selecting Part 1 and clicking **OK** on the Checklist screen, the Glicks comes to the list of states. The Glick family lives in Illinois, so they scroll down to **Illinois**, click it, and then click **OK**. This takes them back to the Checklist screen.

If You Change Your State Selection

The state you choose determines the sequence of screens you see as you go through the program.

    If you go back and select a different state after completing other Parts of the program, you may get one or two pop-up warnings:

1. If you've completed Part 4 (Property To Be Put in Trust), the program checks to see if the marital property laws in your new state differ substantially from the laws in your old state. If the laws differ, you will be alerted to read the Legal Manual on the marital property laws for your new state.

2. If you've completed Part 7 (Property Management for Young Beneficiaries), you may have to redo this section. Laws regarding property management vary

considerably from state to state. The program will inform you if the laws of your new state do not allow the same kinds of property management as the state you originally selected.

IF YOU CHANGE STATES AFTER YOU'VE SIGNED YOUR TRUST DOCUMENT

Once you print and sign your trust document, you will not be able to change your state within the trust document or any amendments to it. Instead you will need to revoke your living trust and create a new one. See Chapter 9 of the Legal Manual.

F. Part 2. Entering Your Name

To begin Part 2, click button **2** on the Checklist (if it is not already selected), then click **OK**.

GENERAL RULES FOR ENTERING NAMES IN *LIVING TRUST MAKER*

- Use full names, first name first.
- Use only one name; don't enter various versions of a name joined by "aka" (also known as).
- A name cannot exceed 60 characters.

This part varies slightly depending on whether you are making an individual trust or a marital trust.

1. Entering Your Name for an Individual Trust

Type your full name in the box, first name first, and then click the button next to your gender. Gender information is needed for your trust to be grammatically correct. Click **OK** to record your data and return to the Checklist screen.

Your Name screen for an individual trust

2. Entering Your Names for a Marital Trust

Type the full name of each spouse in the appropriate box, first name first. To move from one box to another, click in the box or press TAB. When you are finished, click **OK** or press ENTER to record your answers and return to the Checklist screen.

Your Names screen for a marital trust

STEP-BY-STEP EXAMPLE (continued)

The Glicks type "Stanley Glick" in the *Husband's Name* box, press TAB, and then type "Olga Glick" in the *Wife's Name* box. They then click **OK** to return to the Checklist.

THE NAMES LIST—HOW LIVING TRUST MAKER STORES NAMES

- All names you enter during the course of your interview are stored in a master names list that is part of your trust data file.
- If a name is entered in more than one way, such as "Nicole Gama" and "Nicole H. Gama", the program will treat each as a separate person.
- If you type in the same name, but with different capitalization, the program will stop and ask you which capitalization is correct, and save the one you choose.
- To avoid these problems, use the **Paste From Names List** command (in the **Edit** menu) when you need to enter a name you've entered previously. (Note, this feature is available only when the cursor is flashing in a name box.)

Paste From Names List

Here is a list of names you have used so far.

Select the names you want to paste. The names you choose will be pasted after any names you have already entered.

> Barry Baker
> Gordie Orr
> Laverne Smith
> Louise Finkelstein
> Olga Glick
> Sparky Larussa
> Stanley Glick

[Help]

[Cancel]

[OK]

The Paste From Names List dialog box.

G. Part 3. Naming Your Successor Trustees

To begin Part 3, click button **3** on the Checklist (if it is not already selected), then click **OK**.

This step begins with an introductory screen that explains your role as trustee of your own living trust.

The next screen explains what a successor trustee is and why you need one. Read this information carefully so you understand what the program is about to ask you to do.

The following screen lists numerous Legal Help topics. These answer questions that commonly arise in naming successor trustees. Browse through this list to see if any topics might be relevant to your situation. If you need help using the Legal Help topic list, see Chapter 4, Section C.

After the three introductory screens, you come to a screen in which you name a successor trustee. (The Legal Help topics that were listed in the introduction to this part are also available on this screen, by clicking **LEGAL HELP TOPICS**.)

To enter more than more than one name, press ENTER after each name you type to begin a new line. Make sure to enter only one name per line.

Living Trust Maker

File   Edit   Help   Window

GLICK.TRS

YOUR SUCCESSOR TRUSTEE

Name one or more persons or institutions you want to serve as successor trustee.

If you name more than one successor trustee, they will share responsibility. (On the next screen, you can name an alternate, who will take over if none of your first choices can serve.)

Type only one name per line. Press "Enter" to make a new line.

Barry Baker
Sparky Larussa

[Legal Help Topics]   [Go Back]   [OK]

Your Successor Trustee screen

After you've entered the name(s), click **OK** to move to the next screen.

STEP-BY-STEP EXAMPLE (continued)

The Glicks type in the name of Olga's brother, Barry Baker, press ENTER and then type the name of their friend, Sparky Larussa, to be their successor trustees.

At that point, they are wondering how the two people they've named will share their responsibilities as successor trustees. They click on **LEGAL HELP TOPICS**, then double-click on the topic (**Naming more than one successor trustee**). From this they learn that both trustees must agree on any actions they take.

After reading this, they're satisfied that they understand what will happen, so they click back on the interview window. Then they click **OK** to move to the next screen.

On the next screen, you can enter the name or names of the alternate successor trustee or trustees. This person or persons will serve as trustee if the successor trustee or trustees you named in the previous screen are all unable to serve. (Read the Legal Manual or the online Legal Help for a complete explanation.)

Here again you can type one or more names, pressing ENTER after each name so that each appears on its own line. Click **OK** when you're finished to return to the Checklist screen.

STEP-BY-STEP EXAMPLE (continued)

The Glicks type in the name of a friend, Gordie Orr, to be their alternate successor trustee, and then click **OK.**

By now, if you've been following along and entering information, your Checklist should have three check marks on it. The buttons for Parts 1 through 4 should be active, and the rest of the parts should still be dimmed.

H. Part 4. Listing Your Trust Property

To begin Part 4, click button **4** on the Checklist (if it is not already selected), then click **OK**.

In this part, you list every item of property you plan to transfer to your living trust. If at all possible, list all property items before you name any beneficiaries (in Part 5). You will be able to return to Part 4 and add more property later but, it is more efficient to list all of the property now.

1. Important Legal Considerations

As with Part 3, this part begins with important introductory information. There are important legal considerations regarding property ownership, and the kinds of property you should and should not transfer into a living trust. Take the time to read the introductory information carefully, and read the legal help topics so that you understand what you are about to do. If you don't like reading lots of text on screen, this information is also covered in the Legal Manual (Chapter 5 for individual trusts; Chapter 6 for marital trusts).

2. Adding Property to the List

After a you've read the introductory screens and Legal Help, you will come to the List Trust Property screen. This is where you will type in your items of property that you plan to transfer to your trust.

**The Trust Property list for a marital trust
before any property has been entered**

Every item you include in this list will appear on a document, called a "schedule," that you attach to your trust document. In an individual trust, this document is called Schedule A. In a shared marital trust, there are three schedules, labeled A, B and C—one for co-owned property, and one for each spouse's solely-owned property. *Living Trust Maker* automatically keeps track of all the property you enter and makes sure that every item appears in the appropriate property schedule. (For more information about property schedules, see the Legal Manual, Chapters 5 & 6.)

To see sample property descriptions , click CANCEL to close the property description box, then click the LEGAL HELP TOPICS button on the List Trust Property screen, and click the topic **Sample property descriptions**. When you're finished reading click on the interview window to bring it to the front.

When you're ready to begin listing property, click ADD ITEM TO LIST or press ENTER. A dialog box will pop up in which you type the description of one item of property. The description can be up to 500 characters long. Be sure to follow the three rules for describing property that appear in the dialog box.

Describe Item of Property dialog box for a marital trust

What happens next varies slightly depending on whether you're creating an individual trust or a shared marital trust.

Individual trust

After you describe the property, click **OK** or press ENTER. That property is added to the property list on the List Trust Property screen.

Users' Guide

Marital trust

After you describe the property, identify who owns it by clicking **HUSBAND'S, WIFE'S** or **CO-OWNED**.

PROPERTY OWNERSHIP LAWS FOR MARRIED COUPLES ARE TRICKY

If you haven't read the online Legal Help or the Legal Manual concerning marital property laws, you should do so now. Some items you may think are owned separately by one spouse may be actually owned by both spouses. This is especially true in community property states. See Chapter 6 of the Legal Manual.

After you've clicked an owner button, that property is added to the property list on the List Trust Property screen. A single-letter tag indicates who owns the property: **H** for husband's, **W** for wife's and **C** for co-owned.

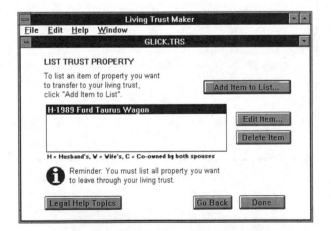

List Trust Property screen after one item of husband's property has been entered

If you mistakenly clicked the wrong owner button, click the item on the property list, then click **EDIT ITEM.** Then click the correct owner button. If you want to edit your description of the property, see Section 3, below.

> **STEP-BY-STEP EXAMPLE (continued):**
>
> Olga and Stanley Glick own some property separately and some together. After reading Legal Help and consulting the Legal Manual (which, among other things, informs them that Illinois is a non-community property state) they decide to put only their two cars and their house into the trust.
>
> The Glicks click **ADD ITEM TO LIST**. They then type in "1989 Ford Taurus Wagon" and click **HUSBAND'S**.
>
> Back at the List Trust Property screen, they again click **ADD ITEM TO LIST**. Now they type in "1994 Honda Accord," and click **WIFE'S**.
>
> They click **ADD ITEM TO LIST** for the last time. They then type "the house at 4553 Elm Street, Normal, Illinois" and click **CO-OWNED**. Back at the List Trust Property screen they click **DONE** to move to the Checklist.

3. Editing Items Already on the Property List

If you need to change a description of property you've entered on the property list, select it from the property list and click **EDIT ITEM,** or simply double-click it.

Your description of the item will appear in a box with the text of the description highlighted. If you want to enter a new description of the property, simply type it—your typing will replace the selected text. If you want to edit the existing description, click the mouse at the point you want to make changes (this will de-select the text and leave the cursor flashing, ready for editing).

What happens next varies slightly depending on whether you're making an individual trust or a shared marital trust:

Individual trust

When you finish editing the description, click **OK** or press ENTER to save your changes and return to the property list.

Shared marital trust

When you finish editing the description, click either **HUSBAND'S**, **WIFE'S** or **CO-OWNED** to save your changes and return to the property list.

Users' Guide

**CHANGING THE PROPERTY OWNERSHIP IN A MARITAL TRUST
AFTER NAMING ITS BENEFICIARY IN PART 5**

If you have already been through Part 5 and named different items for different beneficiaries, and then you return to Part 4 and change property ownership, read Section I.11 below for information on how your beneficiary designations may be affected.

STEP-BY-STEP EXAMPLE (continued)

Note: This particular example is out of sequence. Do not try to follow along on your computer. Just read it.

Olga and Stanley Glick originally listed the 1989 Ford Taurus as "Husband's" property. Then they complete Part 5, where Stanley named beneficiaries for the car.

Suppose they then return to Part 4 to change the owner designation for the Ford Taurus to "Co-owned." Now Olga needs to return to Part 5 and name beneficiaries for her share of the car.

4. Deleting Items From the Property List

To delete an item from the property list, select the item and then click **DELETE ITEM**.

If you have already chosen beneficiaries for the property, this information will be deleted from the trust data file.

5. When You Finish Entering Property Descriptions

When you finish listing or editing the items of property, click **DONE** on the List Trust Property screen to return to the Checklist.

I. Part 5. Naming Beneficiaries of Trust Property

In this step of the program, you name beneficiaries for the trust property you listed in Part 4. This is the longest step of the program, but it's easy if you take it one screen at a time.

To begin Part 5 for an individual trust, click button **5** on the Checklist (if it is not already selected), then click **OK**.

If you're making a shared marital trust, each spouse must go through this part separately. Therefore, Part 5 is divided into Part 5a for the beneficiaries of the wife's trust property and Part 5b for the beneficiaries of the husband's trust property. Either spouse can go first. Click on the appropriate button and click **OK** to begin the step.

Note: If button **5A** or **5B** is inactive (dimmed) it is because no property was listed in Part 4 that is owned or co-owned by that spouse. Before a spouse can name beneficiaries, he or she must own or co-own at least one item of property listed in Part 4. If one spouse does not own any trust property, then you can't make a shared marital trust. (See Legal Manual, Chapter 6.)

STEP-BY-STEP EXAMPLE (continued)

If the Glicks had listed only Stanley's solely-owned property in Step 4, then **5A. BENEFICIARIES OF WIFE'S TRUST PROPERTY** on the Checklist screen would be dimmed and unavailable because Olga has no trust property to give away.

However, since the Glicks listed their house as co-owned, and their cars as separately owned, each of them can name beneficiaries of items of property.

1. Legal Issues to Consider

As in Parts 3 and 4, this Part begins with information and Legal Help about what you are about to do. Be sure to take the time to read this information to be certain you understand what you are about to do and to be aware of any legal rules that may pertain to your situation.

Users' Guide

2. Options for Naming Beneficiaries

Part 5 provides you with two or three options for naming beneficiaries:

❶ OPTION 1: FAST TRACK (shared marital trust only)
Designate your spouse to receive all your trust property.

❷ OPTION 2: FAST TRACK
Name one or more persons to receive all your trust property together.

❸ OPTION 3
Name different persons to receive different items of your trust property.

The first two of these options are the "fast track" options. If you choose a fast track option, all the trust property will go to the beneficiary or beneficiaries you name. You will not be able to leave specific items of trust property to any other person. You will, however, name alternates (who take the trust property if the beneficiary is unable to) for each of the beneficiaries you name to receive all the trust property.

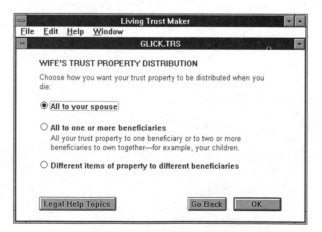

Beneficiary options in a marital trust

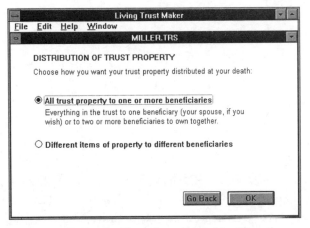

Beneficiary options in an individual trust

1 **If you choose Option 1 (all trust property to your spouse),** your only task in Part 5 is to name alternate beneficiaries who will inherit your trust property if your spouse does not survive you. Skip ahead to Section 6, Naming Alternates for a Beneficiary, and read the subsection If You Named Only One Beneficiary.

2 **If you choose Option 2 (all trust property to one or more beneficiaries),** your tasks in Part 5 are to:
1. Name the beneficiary or beneficiaries who will inherit your trust property.
2. If you named more than one beneficiary, decide whether these "co-beneficiaries" should share the property equally or unequally.
3. Name alternate beneficiaries for each beneficiary you named.

   Skip ahead to Section 4, Entering Beneficiaries' Names.

3 **If you choose Option 3 (different items to different beneficiaries),** you must repeat the following steps for *each gift of property you want to make:*
1. Select the property item or items you want to give away.
2. Name the beneficiary or beneficiaries who will inherit this trust property.
3. If you named more than one beneficiary, decide whether they should share the property equally or unequally.
4. Name alternate beneficiaries for each beneficiary you named.

   Note: In Part 5, you need not name beneficiaries for every item of trust property. Instead, you may name beneficiaries for just a few items and leave

Users' Guide

everything else to the "residuary beneficiary" that you name in Part 6. (See Section J, below.)

STEP-BY-STEP EXAMPLE (continued)

When Stanley goes through Part 5b, he decides to leave all of his trust property to Olga after his death. So he clicks **ALL TO YOUR SPOUSE** (Option 1) and then clicks **OK**. *(This part of the example is continued in Section 6, below).*

When Olga goes through Part 5a, she decides to leave her share of the home to Stanley and her car to her cousins Louise and Laverne. So she clicks **DIFFERENT PROPERTY ITEMS TO DIFFERENT BENEFICIARIES** (Option 3) and then clicks **OK.** *(This part of the example is continued in the next section.)*

3. Selecting Property for Your Beneficiaries

③ This Section Is for Option 3 Users Only.

You start by selecting one or more items of property from the property selection screen.

Wife's property selection screen for a marital trust

In an individual trust, the property selection screen contains the list of property you created in Part 4.

In a marital trust, each spouse is provided with his or her own property selection screen. The list includes items of property owned or co-owned by that spouse but does not include trust property owned separately by the other spouse.

To select items of property, do the following:

- To select only one item, just click on it.
- To select more than one item, hold down the CTRL key as you click on each item.
- To de-select an item that is already selected, hold down the CTRL key and click on the unwanted item.

After you have selected all of the property items you want to give to a beneficiary (or group of beneficiaries) click **OK** to proceed to the next step.

STEP-BY-STEP EXAMPLE (continued)

When Olga moves to the property selection screen, her solely-owned property—her Honda Accord—is listed and preceded by a "W" indicating it is the wife's sole property. Also, the house she co-owns with Stanley is listed. It is preceded by a "C," indicating that its co-owned.

Olga wants Stanley to inherit her share of the house, but she wants her cousins to get the car. To do this, she must make two gifts. She starts with the gift to her cousins by clicking on the car in the property selection screen and then clicking **OK**.

4. Entering Beneficiaries' Names

➋ ➌ This Section Is for Option 2 and Option 3 Users Only.

For Option 2 users, this step is to name one or more beneficiaries to receive all your trust property.

Users' Guide

Naming Beneficiaries screen for Option 2 Users

For Option 3 users, this step is to name one or more beneficiaries to receive the trust property you just selected from the property selection screen (Section 3, above). *Living Trust Maker* lists the description of the property just selected in a box at the bottom left of the screen.

Name Beneficiaries screen for Option 3 Users

REMINDER

Use the **Paste from Names List** command if you want to enter names that you already entered earlier in the program. Remember, the program will treat a name spelled in more than one way as different persons. This could cause confusion and lead to unintended results. (See sidebar in Section F.2, above.)

If you type more than one name, remember to press ENTER after each name so that each name is on a separate line. Don't worry about the order in which you type the names. Each person you name will receive his or her share of the property at the same time. Also, in the next step you will be allowed to specify what fraction of the property each beneficiary will get.

After you enter the names of your beneficiaries, click **OK** to continue.

STEP-BY-STEP EXAMPLE (continued)

Olga is making her first gift (the car to her cousins Louise and Laverne). Since these names have not been entered into the program, Olga cannot use the **Paste from Names List** command. Instead she types their full names: She types Louise Finkelstein and then presses ENTER. She then types Laverne Smith and clicks **OK**.

5. Determining Beneficiaries' Shares of Property

❷ ❸ This Section Is for Option 2 and Option 3 Users Only.

If you name more than one beneficiary to share the trust property, the next screen asks you how you want the beneficiaries to share the property.

**Co-beneficiaries' shares of property
can be equal or unequal**

If you want each beneficiary to receive an equal share, click EQUAL SHARES and then click **OK**.

If you want the beneficiaries to receive unequal shares of the property, click UNEQUAL SHARES and then click **OK**.

Specifying Unequal Shares For Co-Beneficiaries

If you choose to give co-beneficiaries unequal shares of the property, the next screen allows you to specify the fractional share that each beneficiary will receive.

Specifying unequal shares for co-beneficiaries

The beneficiaries' names are presented in a list. *Living Trust Maker* initially gives each beneficiary an equal fractional share of the property. You can change the share of each beneficiary to whatever you wish. Double-click on the beneficiary's name, type in the fraction in the pop-up dialog box, and then click **OK** to close record your change.

```
┌──────────────────────────────────────────────────┐
│ ▬              ENTER PROPERTY SHARE                │
├──────────────────────────────────────────────────┤
│                                                    │
│  Enter the fractional share of the property that the │
│  beneficiary should receive. Use only fractions, such │
│  as 1/3 or 1/4. Do not use percentages.           │
│                                                    │
│      Beneficiary:   Louise Finkelstein             │
│         Share:    ┌──────────┐                     │
│                   │ 1/4      │                     │
│                   └──────────┘                     │
│                   ┌──────────┐   ┌──────────┐      │
│                   │  Cancel  │   │    OK    │      │
│                   └──────────┘   └──────────┘      │
└──────────────────────────────────────────────────┘
```

Enter the beneficiary's share in the pop-up dialog box

- Use only fractions, not percentages.
- Repeat this for each beneficiary whose fractional share you want to change.
- Make sure the fractional shares add up to one; *Living Trust Maker* will not let you continue if they do not.

When you finish, click **DONE**.

STEP-BY-STEP EXAMPLE (continued)

Olga wants to give Louise 1/4 and Laverne 3/4 ownership of the car. So, Olga clicks **UNEQUAL SHARES** on the Co-Beneficiaries' Shares screen and then she clicks **OK**. At the next screen entitled Unequal Shares for Co-Beneficiaries, Louise and Laverne's names are listed preceded by the default fractions of 1/2.

To specify Louise's share, Olga double-clicks on Louise's name in the list and a box pops up. Olga types "1/4" and clicks **OK**. Then she double-clicks on Laverne's name, types "3/4" in the pop-up box, and clicks **OK**.

Louise's and Laverne's fractional shares of 1/4 and 3/4 now appear preceding their names in the list. Olga sees that they add up to one, so she clicks **DONE** to proceed to the next screen.

6. Naming Alternates For a Beneficiary

❶ ❷ ❸ This Section Is for All Users.

The last step in naming beneficiaries for your trust property is to name one or more alternates for each beneficiary. Because Option 1 users only name their spouses as their beneficiary, they should continue with this section.

Option 2 and Option 3 users who named *only one* beneficiary should also continue with this section.

Option 2 and Option 3 users who named *more than one* beneficiary, should skip to Section 7, below.

If You Named Only One Beneficiary

You will move through a few introductory screens and then come to the Name Alternate Beneficiaries screen. Type in the name(s) of the alternates for the beneficiary you named. Type only one name per line and press ENTER to begin each name on a new line.

**Screen for entering alternate beneficiaries for an
"all-to-spouse" fast track gift (Option 1)**

If you don't want to name an alternate for the beneficiary, leave this screen blank. (Make sure you read the online Legal Help or the Legal Manual to understand what happens to the property if you don't name an alternate.)

Click **OK** when you're done to move to the Recap screen and skip to Section 8, below.

> **STEP-BY-STEP EXAMPLE (continued)**
>
> **Note:** This example is out of sequence. Do not try to follow along on your computer. Just read the example for now.
>
> Stanley gives all his trust property to Olga. Here is where he names the person or persons who would receive the property if Olga does not survive him. So Stanley types in the name of his nephew, Alan Fielder.
>
> Stanley then clicks **OK** to move to Recap screen. Satisfied with the wording of the gift, Stanley clicks **DONE**.

7. Naming Alternates for Co-Beneficiaries

❷ ❸ This Section Is for Option 2 and Option 3 Users Only.

If you named more than one beneficiary to share the property, you will move through some introductory screens and then come to the Name Alternate Beneficiaries screen. It offers you three options.

- Choose **THE CO-BENEFICIARIES WHO ARE STILL LIVING** if you want the surviving beneficiary or beneficiaries to be the alternates for each beneficiary.
- Choose **A BENEFICIARY YOU NAME** if you want to name alternates for each co-beneficiary.
- Choose **NO ALTERNATES** if you don't want to name alternates.

Read the Legal Help or the Legal Manual to be sure you understand the legal results of choosing these various options.

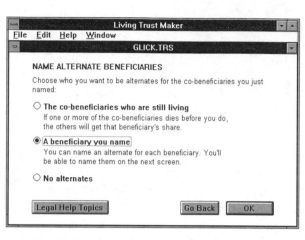

Options for naming alternates for co-beneficiaries

STEP-BY-STEP EXAMPLE (continued)

Olga decides that it would be impractical for her two cousins to share the ownership of the car with anyone except each other. So she clicks THE CO-BENEFICIARIES WHO ARE STILL LIVING. That way, if either cousin dies before Olga does, the other cousin will be given the entire ownership of the car. (If both cousins don't survive Olga, the car will go to the person she names as her residuary beneficiary in Part 6 of the program.)

Olga then clicks **OK** to move to the Recap screen.

If you choose **A BENEFICIARY YOU NAME** you come to a screen with a list of the beneficiaries of this trust property. You can name at least one alternate for each beneficiary listed although you are not required to.

```
┌─────────────────────────────────────────────────┐
│                Living Trust Maker          ▼  ▲  │
│ File  Edit  Help  Window                         │
│ ┌─────────────────────────────────────────────┐ ▼│
│ │              GLICK.TRS                       │  │
│ │                                              │  │
│ │ NAMING ALTERNATE BENEFICIARIES FOR CO-BENEFICIARIES │
│ │ To name an alternate for a beneficiary listed below, double-click the │
│ │ beneficiary's name.                          │  │
│ │                                              │  │
│ │ ┌──────────────────────────────────────────┐│  │
│ │ │Louise Finkelstein                        ││  │
│ │ │Laverne Smith                             ││  │
│ │ │                                          ││  │
│ │ │                                          ││  │
│ │ └──────────────────────────────────────────┘│  │
│ │ * = One or more alternates have been named for this beneficiary. │
│ │                                              │  │
│ │                                              │  │
│ │ ┌──────────────┐        ┌────────┐ ┌──────┐ │  │
│ │ │Legal Help Topics│      │Go Back │ │  OK  │ │  │
│ │ └──────────────┘        └────────┘ └──────┘ │  │
│ └─────────────────────────────────────────────┘  │
└─────────────────────────────────────────────────┘
```

Screen for naming different alternates for co-beneficiaries

Double-click the name of a beneficiary and then type the name(s) of one or more alternates for that beneficiary in the pop-up dialog box.

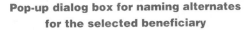

```
┌───────────────────────────────────────────────────────┐
│ ─            NAME ALTERNATE BENEFICIARIES             │
│                                                       │
│ Name alternate beneficiaries for:  Ann Dexheimer      │
│                                                       │
│ Type only one name per line (press "Enter" to make a new line). │
│ You can also use names from the Names List.           │
│ ┌─────────────────────────────────┐ ▲  ┌───────────┐ │
│ │                                 │    │ Names List │ │
│ │                                 │    └───────────┘ │
│ │                                 │    ┌───────────┐ │
│ │                                 │    │  Cancel    │ │
│ │                                 │    └───────────┘ │
│ │                                 │ ▼  ┌───────────┐ │
│ │                                 │    │    OK      │ │
│ └─────────────────────────────────┘    └───────────┘ │
└───────────────────────────────────────────────────────┘
```

**Pop-up dialog box for naming alternates
for the selected beneficiary**

Type one name per line. If you want to enter one or more names that you've previously used in this trust, click **NAMES LIST**, click on the name(s) you want to use as alternates, then click **OK**. Those names will be inserted after any names you have already entered. When you're done naming alternates for the selected beneficiary, click **OK** to close the dialog box.

An asterisk appears to the left of the name of each beneficiary for whom you have named one or more alternates.

If you want to change an alternate, double-click on the beneficiary name again. Make your changes and then click **OK** to record the change.

STEP-BY-STEP EXAMPLE (continued)

If Olga had decided to name her husband as the alternate for both of her cousins, she would have clicked **A BENEFICIARY YOU NAME** on the Name Alternate Beneficiaries for Co-Beneficiaries screen. The next screen would list her cousins as the beneficiaries of the property and Olga would begin to name an alternate beneficiary for each of her cousins.

First she would double-click on Louise's name to pop up the Name Alternate Beneficiaries box. This box asks for the names of the alternate beneficiaries. In this case, Stanley is the only alternate. To make sure his name is spelled the same way it was when she entered it into the program earlier, she might click on the **NAMES LIST** button to call up the Names List box and then click on Stanley's name. After clicking **OK**, Stanley's name would be inserted in the list in the Name Alternate Beneficiaries box. Olga would then click **OK** to confirm her selection and to close the dialog box.

An asterisk would now appear next to Louise's name, indicating that an alternate had been named for her.

Olga would then double-click on Laverne's name and repeat the process.

Finally, Olga would click **OK** on the Name Alternate Beneficiaries to move to the Recap screen.

8. Reviewing Your Work

❶ ❷ ❸ This Section Is for All Users.

After you name the beneficiaries and alternates for trust property, you move to the Recap screen. This screen lets you see how the gift you just entered will be worded in your trust document.

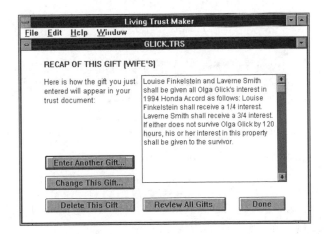

Recap screen for a fast-traok gift (Option 1 or 2)

From the Recap screen, you can easily go back and change aspects of the gift, or delete the gift and start over.

Also, if you are making different gifts to different beneficiaries (Option 3), you can make additional gifts from the Recap screen.

**Recap screen for a user making different gifts
to different beneficiaries (Option 3)**

Changing the gift you just entered

In this part of the program (Part 5) you can change the designation of beneficiaries for the items of property you listed in Part 4. You cannot change the trust property descriptions or add items to the trust property list. Those changes can be made only in Part 4.

To change any aspect of the gift you just entered (other than property descriptions), click **CHANGE THIS GIFT**.

You will return to the same screens you saw when you created the gift the first time. At each screen, your previous answers will be displayed. You can change your answers or leave them as they are. You must step through each screen until you return to Recap screen, even if you only want to change one aspect of the gift.

Deleting the gift you just entered

If you change your mind about a gift while you're looking at it on the Recap screen, you can click **DELETE THIS GIFT**. Deleting a gift does not remove the property from the trust property list. It simply erases the designations of beneficiaries you named for that property.

When you click **DELETE THIS GIFT**, the program will ask you to confirm that you really do want to delete the gift (in case you clicked the button unintentionally). If you confirm that you want to delete the gift, you will:

❶ ❷   return to the multiple-choice screen shown in Section 2, above or,

❸   remain at the Recap screen. The words "No gift made." will appear in the gift preview box. In this case, click **ENTER ANOTHER GIFT** to enter a new gift, or click **DONE** to return to the Checklist screen.

Making additional gifts to different beneficiaries

❸   This Section Is for Option 3 Users Only.

If you are making different gifts to different beneficiaries, you can continue to make additional gifts as long as there are property items for which you have not yet designated beneficiaries. (When there is no more trust property to give away, the **ENTER ANOTHER GIFT** button becomes inactive and dimmed.)

Clicking **ENTER ANOTHER GIFT** returns you to the property selection screen, where you can begin to enter your next gift. When you come to that screen, you will notice that the property you have already given is no longer listed, so that you can't give away the same item more than once or create inconsistencies in your trust document.

Remember, you don't have to name specific beneficiaries for every item of property. Any trust property that hasn't been allocated to a named beneficiary will be given to the person(s) you name as your residuary beneficiary. (See Section J, below.)

STEP-BY-STEP EXAMPLE (continued)

After Olga finishes entering the gift of the car to Louise and Laverne and seeing how the gift will appear in her trust document on the Recap screen, she clicks **ENTER ANOTHER GIFT** to return to the property selection screen. The car is no longer listed on the screen because Olga has already named beneficiaries to inherit it. Only Olga's share of the house is still available for her to give as a gift.

If you want to give away an item of property for which you've already named a beneficiary, you must delete or change this gift so that the property is no longer included in it. Once the gift has been deleted or changed, the item of property will appear on the property selection screen the next time you open it. (For instructions on how to change gifts, see Section 9, below.)

STEP-BY-STEP EXAMPLE (continued):

Olga also wants to leave her half of the house to Stanley. But suppose she accidentally included the house together with the car in the gift to her cousins. In this case she first must delete the house from the gift to her cousins so that the house would reappear on the property selection screen. Then, when Olga returned to make a new gift, the house would be available for her to give to Stanley.

To add new items to the property selection screen, you must return to Part 4.

9. Reviewing and Changing Gifts From the Review All Gifts Screen

❸ This Section Is for Option 3 Users Only. If you are using Options 1 or 2, skip ahead to section 10.

If you make different gifts to different beneficiaries, you can review all your gifts by clicking **REVIEW ALL GIFTS** on the Recap of This Gift screen.

The Recap All Gifts screen

The Recap All Gifts screen displays a numbered list of your gifts in the order in which you entered them. (You can see only a few words of the description of the first item of property in the gift.)

Reviewing a gift

To review a gift, select it from the List of Gifts. (You may need to scroll down the list to find it). The box on the right will show how the selected gift will be worded in the trust document.

Changing an entered gift

To change a gift on the list, select it and then click **CHANGE THIS GIFT**. (This button is dimmed until a gift is selected from the list.) When you elect to change a gift, the program takes you back to the property selection screen. You then proceed through the same steps of the gift entering process you went through before. All your prior answers will be displayed so that you can change any or all of them.

Changing the beneficiary of property

Once you have named a beneficiary of an item of your property, that item will not be available for you to give away in later gifts. To make the item available again you must either:

- delete the gift that includes the item of property, or
- remove the item of property from the gift.

The property will then appear again on the property selection screen for you to give away.

Deleting an entered gift

To delete a gift on the list, select it and click **DELETE THIS GIFT**. Then click **DELETE GIFT** in the pop-up dialog box. Deleting a gift allows you to leave the property to other beneficiaries, but *does not* delete any items from the trust property list. To do that, you must return to Part 4.

Making additional gifts

If you still have trust property for which you have not named a beneficiary, the **ENTER ANOTHER GIFT** button will be active (not dimmed). Click it to return to the property selection screen, where you can select property from the list and start the process of naming beneficiaries to inherit it.

When you finish reviewing your gifts

After you finish entering gifts and reviewing them, click **DONE** to return to the Checklist screen.

10. Re-Entering Part 5 From the Checklist

If you have entered at least one gift, Part 5 will be checked on the Checklist screen. (If you're making a shared marital trust, Part 5 is divided into Parts 5a and 5b.)

If you re-enter Part 5 after it was completed, the re-entry screen will differ depending on which gift option you previously used.

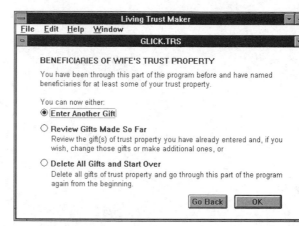

Re-entry screen for Part 5 (Option 3 only).

❶ ❷ This Section Is for Option 1 and Option 2 Users Only.

Choosing **REVIEW GIFTS ALREADY MADE** takes you directly to the Recap screen, which displays the gift you entered. (See Section 8, above.) From there you can review, change or delete the beneficiaries for all your trust property.

Choosing **DELETE ALL GIFTS AND START OVER** deletes the gift you've previously made. You will then be required to name a new beneficiary or beneficaries for the property you entered in Part 4.

❸ This Section Is for Option 3 Users Only.

If there is still trust property for which you haven't named beneficiaries, the **ENTER ANOTHER GIFT** button will be active so that you can make additional gifts. Choosing this button takes you directly to the property selection screen. (See Section 3, above.) From there you begin making an additional gift.

Choosing **REVIEW GIFTS MADE SO FAR** takes you directly to the Recap of All Gifts screen, which lists and displays the gifts you entered. (See Section 9, above.) From there you can review, change or delete gifts.

Choosing **DELETE ALL GIFTS AND START OVER** deletes all of the beneficiary and alternate beneficiary designations you have made. You cannot undo this deletion, so make sure it's what you want before you click **OK**. The list of trust property you entered in Part 4 will remain intact. Just the beneficiary designations for the property are deleted.

11. Changing Property Ownership in a Marital Trust After Naming Its Beneficiary in Part 5

If you have already been through Part 5 and named different beneficiaries for different items, and then you return to Part 4 and change property ownership of an item, the following will occur :

If the property was...	and is now...	then...
Co-owned	Wife's	The property item will be deleted from any gifts entered by Husband.
Co-owned	Husband's	The property item will be deleted from any gifts entered by Wife.
Husband's	Wife's	The property item will be deleted from any gifts entered by Husband. Wife should re-enter Part 5a and designate beneficiaries for the property.
Wife's	Husband's	The property item will be deleted from any gifts entered by Wife. Husband should re-enter Part 5b and designate beneficiaries for the property.
Wife's	Co-owned	Husband should re-enter Part 5b and designate beneficiaries for the property.
Husband's	Co-owned	Wife should re-enter Part 5a and designate beneficiaries for the property.

J. Part 6. Naming Residuary Beneficiaries

In this step, you are asked to enter the name or names of the residuary beneficiary or beneficiaries.

To begin Part 6 for an individual trust, click button **6** on the Checklist (if it is not already selected), then click **OK**.

If you're making a shared marital trust, each spouse must go through this part separately. Therefore, Part 6 is divided into Part 6a for the residuary beneficiaries of the wife's trust property and Part 6b for the residuary beneficiaries of the husband's trust property. Either spouse can go first. Click on the appropriate button and click **OK** to begin the step.

Be sure to read the introductory information and Legal Help in the introductory screens so that you clearly understand what a residuary beneficiary is and what property they will receive.

After the two introductory screens, you come to a screen where you enter the names of your beneficiaries.

```
┌─────────────────────────────────────────────────────────┐
│ ─                   Living Trust Maker              ▼ ▲  │
│  File   Edit   Help   Window                             │
│ ┌─────────────────────────────────────────────────────┐ │
│ │ ▭                     GLICK.TRS                   ▼ │ │
│ │                                                     │ │
│ │  NAME WIFE'S RESIDUARY BENEFICIARY                  │ │
│ │  Name one or more persons or organizations you want │ │
│ │  to be your residuary beneficiary.                  │ │
│ │                                                     │ │
│ │  Type only one name per line. Press "Enter" to make │ │
│ │  a new line.                                        │ │
│ │  ┌──────────────────────────────────────────────┐▲ │ │
│ │  │ Stanley Glick                                │  │ │
│ │  │                                              │  │ │
│ │  │                                              │  │ │
│ │  │                                              │  │ │
│ │  │                                              │▼ │ │
│ │  └──────────────────────────────────────────────┘  │ │
│ │                                                     │ │
│ │  ┌──────────────────┐        ┌─────────┐ ┌──────┐  │ │
│ │  │ Legal Help Topics│        │ Go Back │ │  OK  │  │ │
│ │  └──────────────────┘        └─────────┘ └──────┘  │ │
│ └─────────────────────────────────────────────────────┘ │
└─────────────────────────────────────────────────────────┘
```

Screen for naming residuary beneficiaries

As with beneficiaries, you can name more than one residuary. Just remember to press ENTER after typing each name so that each name is on a separate line. Unlike co-beneficiaries that you may have named in Part 5, you cannot designate unequal shares for co-residuary beneficiaries.

When you are finished, click **OK** to move to the next screen.

The next screen asks you to name one or more persons or organizations to be the alternate residuary beneficiary. Note that, unlike Part 5, if you named more than one residuary beneficiary you can't name different alternates for each one. The persons you name as alternate residuary beneficiaries will take the property only if all of the persons you named in the previous screen cannot.

If you don't want to name any alternates, leave this screen blank. If you name more than one alternate, remember to press ENTER after typing each name so that each name is on a separate line.

Click **OK** when you finish to return to the Checklist screen.

STEP-BY-STEP EXAMPLE (continued)

Olga Glick types in the name of her husband, Stanley Glick, to be the residuary beneficiary of all her trust property. She then clicks **OK**.

On the next screen, she types in the name of her friend Don Overton to be her alternate residuary beneficiary and then clicks **OK**. This returns her to the Checklist screen.

Stanley then goes through this same process, naming his brother, Jeff Glick, as his residuary beneficiary, and naming Don Overton as his alternate residuary beneficiary.

By now, if you've been following along, Parts 1 through 6 on your Checklist screen should have check marks by them, and Parts 7 or 7a and b, Property Management, should now be active.

K. Part 7. Setting Up Property Management for Minors and Young Adult Beneficiaries

In this part, you get a opportunity to set up management for property you are giving to beneficiaries who may be too young to responsibly handle it themselves.

To begin Part 7 for an individual trust, click button **7** on the Checklist (if it is not already selected), then click **OK**.

If you're making a shared marital trust, each spouse must go through this part separately. Therefore, Part 7 is divided into Part 7a for the beneficiaries of the wife's trust property and Part 7b for the beneficiaries of the husband's trust property. Either spouse can go first. Click on the appropriate button and click **OK** to begin the step.

After an introductory screen, the program asks if any of your beneficiaries are under 35. *Living Trust Maker* helps you here by providing a list of all the beneficiaries named. If you click **No**, you are returned to the Checklist screen.

```
┌─────────────────────────────────────────────────────────┐
│ □                    Living Trust Maker              ▼ ▲ │
│ File  Edit  Help  Window                                 │
│ □                       GLICK.TRS                     ▼  │
│                                                          │
│  WIFE'S BENEFICIARIES                                    │
│  Are any of the beneficiaries listed below younger than age 35? │
│                                                          │
│  If so, click "Yes" to find out about property management options. If not, │
│  click "No" to return to the Checklist screen.           │
│                                                          │
│                          Beneficiaries you have named:   │
│                      ┌─────────────────────────────────┐ │
│                      │ Don Overton                     │ │
│                      │ Gloria Sadowski                 │ │
│                      │ Laverne Smith                   │ │
│                      │ Louise Finkelstein              │ │
│                      │ Stanley Glick                   │ │
│                      └─────────────────────────────────┘ │
│                                                          │
│   ┌─────────┐          ┌──────┐ ┌─────────┐ ┌──────┐    │
│   │ Why 35? │          │  No  │ │ Go Back │ │ Yes  │    │
│   └─────────┘          └──────┘ └─────────┘ └──────┘    │
└─────────────────────────────────────────────────────────┘
```

Review your list of beneficaries to see if any are under 35

If you click **YES**, you are presented with information on the importance of setting up property management, how management works, and your options under your state's law. Your property management options differ, depending on whether your state has adopted the Uniform Transfers to Minors Act.

1. States That Have Adopted the Uniform Transfers to Minors Act

If your state allows custodianships under the Uniform Transfers to Minors Act (UTMA), the program will offer you the option of setting up a subtrust or a custodianship under the UTMA for each young beneficiary.

```
┌─────────────────────────────────────────────────┐
│ □              Living Trust Maker            ▼ ▲ │
│  File  Edit  Help  Window                        │
│ ┌─────────────────────────────────────────────┐ │
│ │ □                GLICK.TRS                 ▼ │ │
│ │                                              │ │
│ │  SET UP CHILDREN'S SUBTRUSTS OR CUSTODIANSHIPS│ │
│ │  To set up management for a beneficiary, select the beneficiary's name │
│ │  from the list below. Then click the management method you want to set │
│ │  up.                                         │ │
│ │                                              │ │
│ │  ┌──────────────────────┐                    │ │
│ │  │ Don Overton          │  ┌──────────────────┐ │
│ │  │ Gloria Sadowski      │  │ Set Up/Edit Subtrust... │ │
│ │  │ Laverne Smith        │  └──────────────────┘ │
│ │  │ Louise Finkelstein   │  ┌──────────────────────┐ │
│ │  │ Stanley Glick        │  │ Set Up/Edit Custodianship... │ │
│ │  └──────────────────────┘  └──────────────────────┘ │
│ │  S = Subtrust has been set up.   ┌──────────┐ │ │
│ │  C = Custodianship has been set up. │ Delete │ │ │
│ │                                  └──────────┘ │ │
│ │  ┌──────────────────┐      ┌─────────┐ ┌──────┐ │
│ │  │ Legal Help Topics │      │ Go Back │ │ Done │ │
│ │  └──────────────────┘      └─────────┘ └──────┘ │
│ └─────────────────────────────────────────────┘ │
└─────────────────────────────────────────────────┘
```

Screen for selecting property management in a state that has adopted the UTMA

For each beneficiary, you can choose either kind of property management method, but you cannot choose both.

To set up a property management scheme for a beneficiary, do the following.

1. Click on the beneficiary's name on the list to select the beneficiary.

2. Click either **SET UP/EDIT SUBTRUST** or **SET UP/EDIT CUSTODIANSHIP**. A dialog box will appear, asking for the information required for the kind of management you have selected.

3a. *If you're setting up a subtrust,* the only information required is the age at which the subtrust will end. The age cannot be more than 35 or less than 18. (The trustee of the subtrust is the person you named in Part 3 to be your successor trustee of your living trust. See Legal Help on this subject.)

3b. *If you're setting up a custodianship under the UTMA,* you must name a custodian and an alternate custodian. If you live in a state that allows you to choose the age at which the custodianship will end, you must also specify that age. If the state has a mandatory age at which the custodianship ends, that age is automatically inserted for you by *Living Trust Maker.*

Once you've entered a subtrust or custodianship for a beneficiary, the letters C or S appear next to the beneficiary's name on the beneficiaries list to indicate which kind of management has been chosen.

Deleting a property management arrangement

If you change your mind and want to delete a subtrust or custodianship for a particular beneficiary, select the beneficiary from the list and click **DELETE**.

Switching from one kind of property management to the other

The program will let you change the form of property management you've already set up. If you do this, the program will ask you to confirm that you want to delete the original property management scheme you had set up for that beneficiary.

When you finish

Click **DONE** to return to the Checklist screen when you have finished setting up property managements for your beneficiaries.

STEP-BY-STEP EXAMPLE (continued)

Stanley clicks **7B. PROPERTY MGMT. FOR HUSBAND'S BENEFICIARIES** and then clicks **YES** on the Husband's beneficiaries screen because his nephew Alan Fielder is 15 years old. Stanley next selects Alan Fielder from the beneficiary list. Because Illinois has adopted the Uniform Transfers to Minors Act (UTMA), Stanley has a choice of setting up a custodianship under the UTMA or a subtrust for Alan. Stanley clicks **SET UP/EDIT SUBTRUST** and then types 30 as the age the subtrust ends. He then clicks **OK** to close the pop-up box, and **DONE** to return to the Checklist screen.

2. States That Have Not Adopted the Uniform Transfers to Minors Act

If your state does not allow custodianships under the Uniform Transfers to Minors Act (UTMA), your only choice for property management for a young beneficiary is a child's subtrust.

```
┌──────────────────────────────────────────────────────────────┐
│ −                    Living Trust Maker                   ▼ ▲ │
│ File   Edit   Help   Window                                   │
│ ┌─────────────────────────────────────────────────────────┐▲ │
│ │ −                      GLICK.TRS                        ▼│  │
│ │                                                          │  │
│ │   SET UP CHILDREN'S SUBTRUSTS                            │  │
│ │   From the list below select the name of a beneficiary, │  │
│ │   and then click                                        │  │
│ │   "Set Up/Edit Subtrust..." to set the age at which you │  │
│ │   want the subtrust                                     │  │
│ │   to end.                                               │  │
│ │   ┌─────────────────────────────────┐                   │  │
│ │   │ Don Overton                     │                   │  │
│ │   │ * Gloria Sadowski               │  ┌──────────────┐ │  │
│ │   │ Laverne Smith                   │  │Set Up/Edit   │ │  │
│ │   │ Louise Finkelstein              │  │Subtrust...   │ │  │
│ │   │ Stanley Glick                   │  └──────────────┘ │  │
│ │   │                                 │  ┌──────────────┐ │  │
│ │   └─────────────────────────────────┘  │Delete Subtrust│ │ │
│ │   * = Subtrust has been set up.        └──────────────┘ │  │
│ │                                                          │  │
│ │   ┌──────────────────┐        ┌────────┐ ┌──────┐       │  │
│ │   │ Legal Help Topics│        │Go Back │ │ Done │       │  │
│ │   └──────────────────┘        └────────┘ └──────┘       │  │
│ └─────────────────────────────────────────────────────────┘  │
└──────────────────────────────────────────────────────────────┘
```

Screen for setting up children's subtrusts for beneficiaries in a state that has not adopted the UTMA

To set up a subtrust, click on the name of the beneficiary on the list, and then click **SET UP/EDIT SUBTRUST**. A dialog box will appear, asking for the age at which the subtrust will end. The age cannot be more than 35 or less than 18. (The trustee of the subtrust is the person you named in Part 3 to be your successor trustee of your living trust. See Legal Help on this subject.)

When you set up a subtrust for a beneficiary, an asterisk appears next to the beneficiary's name.

Deleting a subtrust

If you change your mind and want to delete a subtrust for a particular beneficiary, select the beneficiary then click **DELETE SUBTRUST**.

When you finish

Click **DONE** to return to the Checklist screen when you finish setting up subtrusts for your beneficiaries.

Displaying, Printing and Exporting Your Trust Document

Users' Guide

You can display, print or export your trust document only after you've completed Parts 1 through 7 of *Living Trust Maker.*

You'll know when you have entered enough information to display your trust document because the **DISPLAY/PRINT TRUST DOCUMENT** button on the Checklist screen will no longer be dimmed.

Click **DISPLAY/PRINT TRUST DOCUMENT** on the Checklist and then click **OK** to move to the Review and Print Your Declaration of Trust screen.

**When you're done entering your trust information,
you come this screen.**

This screen allows you to display your trust document, or "Declaration of Trust." Once the document is displayed you can format it the way you like, and print it. (See Sections B and C, below)

You can also export your Declaration of Trust as a plain text (ASCII) file from this screen. (See Section D, below.)

Before you sign your trust document, it is important to read it, either on screen, or on a printed draft copy, and check to make sure that it reflects your wishes. If you find anything you want to change, return to the Checklist. From there you can re-enter any part of the program and change your answers.

Note: Once you've signed your trust document, *Living Trust Maker* will not let you reprint it again. You can only change a signed trust document by making a "Trust Amendment." (See Chapter 7.)

A. Displaying Your Declaration of Trust

Click **DISPLAY/PRINT TRUST DOCUMENT** to display your Declaration of Trust.

After a few moments, the Document Preview window opens, and the first page of an instruction sheet is displayed. The page number is indicated on the "button bar" at the top of the Document Preview window.

The actual trust document starts on a separate page after the instructions, generally page 3.

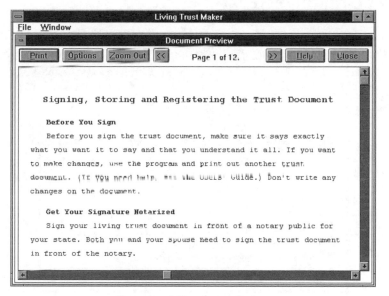

Document Preview window

When a Declaration of Trust is displayed onscreen, you can view each page of it, but you cannot edit any of it. This is to prevent you from inserting language that may later cause legal problems or confusion.

Navigating Within the Document Preview Window

The Document Preview window displays only one page at a time.

- To move from page to page, click the <u><<</u> or <u>>></u> button.
- To move around each page of the instruction sheets and the Declaration of Trust, use the scroll bars, arrow keys and the PAGE UP and PAGE DOWN keys.

- To see an entire page on screen at one time, click **Zoom Out**. To zoom back in on the page, click **Zoom In**.
- To close the Document Preview window and return to the Review and Print Your Declaration of Trust screen, click **Close** or choose **Close** from the **File** menu.

B. Changing the Appearance of Your Declaration of Trust

To change the appearance of your Declaration of Trust, click **Options** on the button bar of the Document Preview window to open the Print Options dialog box. From here, you can change the page margins, line-spacing, footer format, and font of your Declaration of Trust.

Print Options dialog box

To change the page margins

To change the right, left, top or bottom margin, double-click in the margin field you want to change and type the new margin. You can also click in the margin field and edit the current margin.

To change the line spacing

To change the space between lines, click the button next to the line spacing you desire. **Tight Spacing** gives you single spacing, **Standard Spacing** gives you one and one-half spacing, and **Loose Spacing** gives you a double-spaced document. The default line spacing is "Standard."

To change footer and character set information

If you want the footer of each printed page to be in a type size smaller than that used for the Declaration of Trust, select **Footers in smaller type.** If this option is off, then the footers will appear in the same size type as the body of the trust document. If you want the footer to be in boldface, select **Footers in bold type**. If this option is off, the footers will print as plain text.

If you plan to print the Declaration of Trust on a printer that does not support the extended ASCII character set (for example, a daisy-wheel printer), select **Use only standard ASCII characters**. Leave this option off if your printer supports characters such as bullets and long dashes.

To change fonts

To change the font (typeface), its size, or its style (for example, bold or italics) click **Font** to open the Microsoft Windows Font dialog box.

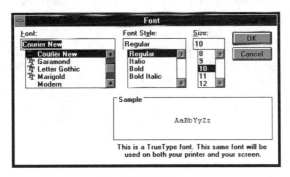

Font dialog box

For more information on the options available in the Font dialog box, see the Microsoft Windows user's guide. When you are finished making any changes, click **OK** in the Font dialog box to return to the Print Options dialog box.

KEEP IT SIMPLE

It is a good idea to keep your Declaration of Trust and any other document you make with *Living Trust Maker* looking fairly plain. Most legal documents these days are printed in plain old Courier font (the typeface commonly used by typewriters). Strange or overly fancy fonts may raise unnecessary questions about the validity of your trust.

To change the printer setup

To change the paper size, click **SETUP** at the bottom of the Print Options dialog to open the Microsoft Windows Print Setup dialog box. (Note: We do not recommend "Specific Printer" from within *Living Trust Maker*. For best results, use the printer that is set up as your "default" printer.)

Print Setup dialog box

For more information on the options available in the Print Setup dialog box, see the Microsoft Windows user's guide. When you are finished making any changes, click **OK** in the Print Setup dialog box to return to the Print Options dialog box.

C. Printing Your Declaration of Trust

To print your Declaration of Trust, you must first display it onscreen. Then, click **PRINT** on the button bar of the Document Preview Window. The Declaration of Trust and accompanying instructions will print to the default printer set up in your Windows installation.

Read the instruction sheets and appropriate Chapter 7 of the Legal Manual for information about how to sign your Declaration of Trust, have it notarized, and register it, if necessary.

Remember that, once you sign your trust document, *Living Trust Maker* will not allow you to print it again. Any further changes you want to make will have to be made by using "Trust Amendments." (See Chapter 7, below, and Chapter 9 of the Legal Manual.)

D. Exporting the Text of Your Declaration of Trust

Living Trust Maker allows you to export your Declaration of Trust and the instruction sheets to a plain text (ASCII) file. All word processors that can read plain text files can load the plain text file produced by *Living Trust Maker*.

Please do not call Nolo Press Technical Support for instructions on how to use your word processing software. We are happy to answer questions on how to format your trust using *Living Trust Maker's* built-in formatting options. However, we are not equipped to offer tech support for other publisher's word-processing software. Call the tech support department of the word-processing software publisher if you need assistance running its software.

There is really no reason to export your trust document to a text file. Most formatting including font, font size and page margins, can be done from within *Living Trust Maker* itself. (See Section C, above.)

Users' Guide

> ### DO NOT CHANGE THE LANGUAGE OF YOUR TRUST DOCUMENT UNDER ANY CIRCUMSTANCES
>
> Even slight changes can seriously affect the usefulness of your documents. Changes in the language can create confusion, contradictions and legal problems. If you have questions about the language in your documents, or if you would like to change the language in them, take the documents to an experienced estate planning attorney and get advice on how to accomplish your goals.
>
> Furthermore, if you or your attorney make any changes to the language of your trust, you will not be able to use *Living Trust Maker* to amend your trust later. (See Chapter 7, below.)

To export the text of the Declaration of Trust to a plain text (ASCII) file, you must be at the Review and Print Your Declaration of Trust screen. Click **EXPORT TRUST DOCUMENT.** After a few moments, a dialog box appears for you to name the text file. The text file will be saved with the name you give it, plus a .TXT extension.

Export trust screen

To view or print the exported document, you will have to open the text file with your word processor. The steps for opening and editing a plain text (ASCII) should be found in the manual that came with your word processor.

This exported file has no formatting (such as bold and italics) and no headers or footers. You will have to put in the headers, footers and formatting manually with your own word processor. Print a copy of your trust directly from *Living Trust Maker* to use as a reference, to make sure that you format the exported version correctly.

Amending or Revoking Your Trust After You've Signed It

Users' Guide

If you have printed your trust document, the next time you open your trust data file *Living Trust Maker* will ask whether you have signed the printed document.

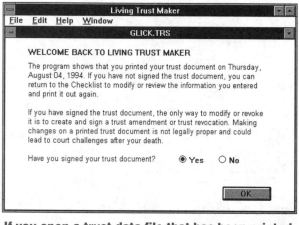

If you open a trust data file that has been printed, you'll see this screen.

As explained in Chapter 7 of the Legal Manual, your Declaration of Trust has no legal effect until you print it and sign it. If you have not signed your Declaration of Trust, you can tear it up and print out a new copy at any time, with no legal consequences. Think of the unsigned copies as rough drafts.

On the other hand, if you *have* signed your Declaration of Trust, from that point on, changes to your trust can be made only by printing and signing a separate document called a Trust Amendment. (See Chapter 9, Section E of the Legal Manual for complete instructions on when you should create a Trust Amendment.) You can also revoke your trust by printing and signing a document called a Trust Revocation. (See Chapter 9, Section H of the Legal Manual for an explanation of when and how to revoke your trust.)

In keeping with the legal rules just described, if you click **No** (that you have not signed the document) *Living Trust Maker* assumes that you have printed only a draft copy, and returns you to the Checklist so you can make further modifications.

On the other hand, if you click **YES** (that you have signed the document) the program asks you to enter the date on which you signed your trust.

```
┌─────────────────────────────────────────────────────┐
│ ─            Living Trust Maker              ▼ ▲ │
│ File  Edit  Help  Window                              │
│ ─                  GLICK.TRS                       ▼ │
│                                                       │
│   DATE YOU SIGNED                                     │
│   Please look at your original signed trust document, │
│   and enter the date you signed it. Make sure you     │
│   enter the correct date; you won't be able to change │
│   it later.                                           │
│   ┌───────────────────────────────────────────┐     │
│   │ August 10, 1994                            │     │
│   └───────────────────────────────────────────┘     │
│   If you click "OK", Living Trust Maker will freeze   │
│   the data you have entered up to this point. To make │
│   any future changes to the trust document, you will  │
│   have to print and sign trust amendments.            │
│                                                       │
│                         ┌─────────┐  ┌─────────┐     │
│                         │ Go Back │  │   OK    │     │
│                         └─────────┘  └─────────┘     │
└─────────────────────────────────────────────────────┘
```

If you answer "Yes" you've signed your trust document, you must enter the date you signed it.

This date is used to identify and name the amendment or revocation you are currently creating. For example, if the Glicks signed their Declaration of Trust on June 29, 1994, the title of the first amendment to the trust would be "Amendment to The Glick Revocable Living Trust dated June 29, 1994."

PERMISSIBLE DATE FORMATS

Living Trust Maker accepts a wide variety of common date formats on this screen. For example, 7/4/94 or July 4, 1994 are both permissible. Regardless of how you enter the date, the date will appear in the long date format in all printed documents. For example, even if you type in 7/4/94, it will appear in documents as July 4, 1994.

Once you enter the date you signed the document and click **OK**, the program saves that information in your trust file, and "freezes" the trust data. This is the data that makes up your final, signed, legally-binding copy of your Declaration of Trust.

From this point on, you can still make additional changes to your trust data, but these changes will generate Trust Amendments. You cannot reprint or modify

Users' Guide

your original Declaration of Trust document once you indicate that you have signed it.

IF YOU EXPORTED YOUR ORIGINAL TRUST DOCUMENT

If, despite our advice, you exported your original trust document, changed some of its language and signed the modified copy, then *you cannot use* Living Trust Maker *to make amendments to your living trust.* Trust amendments must be precisely worded to exactly match the text of the original document. If you modified the original document, the amendments will not be coordinated with the original document and may well cause legal problems for you and your heirs.

A. Choosing to Amend or Revoke Your Living Trust

Once you've entered the date you signed your trust document, *Living Trust Maker* asks whether you want to Amend or Revoke your trust.

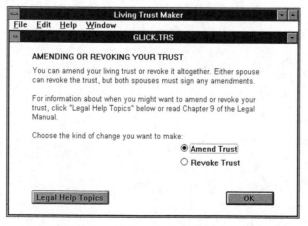

Screen for amending or revoking your trust

As explained in Chapter 9 of the Legal Guide, in most circumstances, you will want to amend your living trust, not revoke it. Read the Legal Manual and the Legal Help for this screen to help you make the right choice.

If you want to amend your living trust, click **AMEND TRUST** and then **OK**. If you want to revoke your living trust, click **REVOKE TRUST** and then **OK**.

If you are revoking your trust, skip to Section D, below.

> **STEP-BY-STEP EXAMPLE (continued)**
>
> A couple of years after creating their living trust, Olga and Stanley Glick reread their Declaration of Trust and decide that it needs to be amended. The Glicks start *Living Trust Maker* and open their trust data file GLICK.TRS.
>
> The Glicks then confirm that their Declaration of Trust was signed. After checking their original Declaration of Trust, they determine that they signed it on July 7, 1994 so they type in that date and click **OK**. After reading the Legal Help topics on Amending or Revoking Your Trust, they're sure that, in their situation, they need to amend their living trust (rather than revoke it) so they click **AMEND TRUST** and **OK** to reach the Amendment Menu screen.

B. Amending Your Living Trust

Making trust amendments involves the same basic steps as entering your trust data for the first time. The Amendment Menu screen lists the kinds of changes you can make in your living trust. As in the main program, in a marital trust, each spouse can independently make changes to their beneficiaries, residuary beneficiaries, and property management selections. See Chapter 9, Section E of the Legal Manual to learn about when you might want to make each kind of change.

The Amendment Menu for a marital trust

You can make as few or as many changes as you want in any order you wish. Unlike the Checklist in the main program, there are no check marks to tell you which parts you have changed. When you display your Trust Amendment document, all of the changes you have made will be combined into one document.

THINGS YOU CANNOT AMEND

Read Chapter 9 of the Legal Manual for a situations in which you should use a trust revocation, rather than an amendment. Certain things cannot be changed by an amendment to your *Living Trust Maker* trust.

When creating amendments you may notice that *Living Trust Maker* bypasses many of the informational screens that you encountered in when making your original trust document. However, you can still gain access to the all of the legal help topics that were available when you made your original trust document, plus a few additional topics relevant only to making amendments, by clicking the **LEGAL HELP TOPICS** button whenever it appears.

1. Changing Successor Trustees

Changing your successor trustee in an amendment involves the same basic steps as when you first named your successor trustee in Part 3 of the main program. (See Chapter 5, Section G.)

STEP-BY-STEP EXAMPLE (continued)

The Glicks decide they want to change their successor trustee. So they choose **CHANGE SUCCESSOR TRUSTEE** on the Amendment Menu, and click **OK**. When they get to the correct screen, they highlight the name of their former friend, Sparky Larussa, and press the DELETE key to remove him as a successor trustee. Then they type Rose Liebman to add her as a successor trustee and click **OK** to move to the next screen.

The Glicks decide to keep Gordie Orr as their alternate successor trustee so they press **OK** to return to the Amendment Menu.

2. Adding, Removing and Editing Property Items

Adding or Removing Property

The program allows you to add or remove property in the same manner as you did in the main program (see Chapter 5, Section H) with a few notable differences:

- An asterisk is placed next to items of property being currently added to the trust to help you identify them.
- If you remove all your trust property the program will not let you display or print an amendment. Your trust must contain at least one item of trust property. (See Chapter 5 of the Legal Manual.) Likewise, a marital trust must contain at least one item of property that was co-owned or owned by each spouse. (See Chapter 6 of the Legal Manual.)

> ### REMEMBER TO TRANSFER THE PROPERTY TO YOUR TRUST
>
> If you add property to your living trust, you must transfer ownership of it to your living trust. If you remove property from the list, remember to transfer it out of the living trust. (See Chapter 7 of the Legal Manual.)

Naming beneficiaries for property added by amendment

If your living trust is set up so that you can give different property to different beneficiaries, you will most likely want to name beneficiaries for the items of property that you are adding to the trust. See Section 3, below, for instructions on how to name beneficiaries for newly added property.

Editing property

You cannot edit the description of property items that were already in the list before you started making the current amendment. You can only delete these items if you wish, and then add them again with a new description.

You can, however, edit a description of any property item you have added to the trust in the current amendment. You can edit these items in the same way you edited items when you created your original trust document. (See Chapter 5, Section H3.)

If you are amending a marital trust, you also can use the **EDIT ITEM** button to change the ownership designation of any item, including those that were already in the list before you started making the current amendment. For example, you can change the ownership designation from Husband to Co-owned or from Co-owned to Wife.

STEP-BY-STEP EXAMPLE (continued)

Stanley clicks **ADD OR REMOVE TRUST PROPERTY** on the Amendment Menu and then clicks **OK**. After moving through several introductory screens, he reaches the List Trust Property screen.

Stanley clicks **ADD ITEM TO LIST** and then types in "the set of China I received as an inheritance from my uncle Joe." He then clicks **HUSBAND'S**. The set of china is added to the property list accompanied by an asterisk (indicating it is an item of property being added by this amendment) and an H (indicating that it is his solely-owned property).

Stanley then clicks **DONE** to return to the Amendment Menu. Because all of Stanley's property goes to Olga at his death, Stanley does not need to choose beneficiaries for the property being added to the trust.

Olga wants to add a piece of real estate she purchased recently to the living trust and give it to her cousins Louise and Laverne in equal shares.

First, Olga clicks **ADD ITEM TO LIST** and then types "the parcel of land at the intersection of County Road 345 and Bushnell Road in Corn County, Illinois." She clicks **WIFE'S** and the parcel of land is added to the property list accompanied by an asterisk and a "W."

Olga then clicks **DONE** to close the property list and return to the Amendment Menu.

3. Changing Beneficiaries

Changing beneficiaries in a trust amendment involves the same steps as you followed in Part 5 of the main program when you originally named your beneficiaries. (See Chapter 5, Section I.)

If you are adding trust property in this amendment and your trust is set up to give different property items to different beneficiaries, you should designate beneficiaries for this property. You can do this by making another gift or changing an existing gift to include the new property item. (See Chapter 5, Section I, above on how to change gifts and make additional ones.)

STEP-BY-STEP EXAMPLE (continued)

Olga wants name beneficiaries for the piece of real estate that she added to the trust in the previous example. She clicks CHANGE WIFE'S BENEFICIARIES and moves to the Recap screen. Here she clicks ENTER ANOTHER GIFT, and selects the real estate from the list of available items. She then proceeds through the screens to name her cousins Laverne and Louise as beneficiaries who will receive equal shares and who will each be the alternate beneficiary of the other.

Remember, if you add any young beneficiaries, you should set up property management for them. (See Section 5, below.)

4. Changing Residuary Beneficiaries

Changing beneficiaries in a trust amendment involves the same steps as you followed in Part 6 of the main program when you originally named your residuary beneficiaries. (See Chapter 5, Section J.)

STEP-BY-STEP EXAMPLE (continued)

Olga wants to add her young niece Abigail Wong as another alternate Residuary Beneficiary.

Olga clicks CHANGE WIFE'S RESIDUARY BENEFICIARIES then clicks **OK**. She then goes through the information screens. She is satisfied with Stanley as her residuary beneficiary so she continues until she reaches the Change Alternate Residuary Beneficary screen.

Olga clicks on the space after Don Overton, her alternate residuary beneficiary, and then presses ENTER to start a new line. Here she types "Abigail Wong" and then clicks **OK** to return to the Amendment Menu. Stanley is satisfied with his residuary beneficiary arrangements, so he does not enter this part.

5. Changing Property Management for Beneficiaries

Use this part of the program to:

- change the property management arrangements you set up for young beneficiaries in your living trust, or
- set up management for a new beneficiary you have added in this amendment.

To do either one, or both, click **CHANGE PROPERTY MANAGEMENT FOR BENEFICIARIES** and then follow the same steps that you followed in Part 7 of the main program when you first set up property management for your beneficiaries. (See Chapter 5, Section K, above.)

STEP-BY-STEP EXAMPLE (continued)

Olga wants to set up property management for Abigail Wong, who she added as a beneficiary in the previous example.

Olga clicks **CHANGE PROPERTY MGMT. FOR WIFE'S BENEFICIARIES** and then clicks **OK**. After reading the next introductory screen and clicking **CONTINUE**, she reaches the screen that allows her to set up property management for young beneficiaries.

Because the Glicks reside in Illinois, a state that has adopted the UTMA, Olga is given the choice of setting up a subtrust or custodianship. Olga selects Abigail's name from the list of beneficiaries and clicks **SET UP/EDIT SUBTRUST**. In the pop up dialog box she types 35 (the age Abigail's subtrust will end). She then clicks **OK** to close the dialog up box, and then clicks **DONE** to return to the Amendment Menu.

C. Displaying, Exporting and Printing a Trust Amendment

If you have made any changes to your trust data, the **DISPLAY/PRINT TRUST AMENDMENT** button on the Amendment Menu becomes active. To view and/or print your Trust Amendment, click **DISPLAY/PRINT TRUST AMENDMENT** and then **OK** on the Amendment Menu .

This brings you to a screen that allows you to display or export your Trust Amendment. This screen works the same way as the screen that displayed and printed your original trust document. (See Chapter 6 if you need to refresh your memory.)

**The screen from which you can display and
export your Trust Amendment**

Read Chapter 9 of the Legal Manual for a discussion of how to read your trust amendment. The Legal Manual also contains important information on keeping your trust amendment with your original trust document.

Note: If the only change you made was to add to property to your trust, the only document that prints out will be the revised property schedules. Read Chapter 9 of the Legal Manual for a discussion of what to do with these property schedules.

When you're finished working on your trust amendment, click **CONTINUE**, to view an information screen from which you can exit *Living Trust Maker* by clicking **QUIT**.

THE NEXT TIME YOU REOPEN YOUR TRUST DATA FILE

The next time you open your trust data file, *Living Trust Maker* will ask if you have signed your Trust Amendment that you printed.

If you answer "No" you will be able to modify this amendment further, and print it out again.

If you answer "Yes" *Living Trust Maker* will ask you to enter the date you signed the amendment. At that point, the trust data file will again be "frozen," incorporating the changes in your signed Trust Amendment. Any further changes to your trust data file will be printed in a new Trust Amendment.

Be sure to read Chapter 9 of the Legal Manual for information on signing and storing Trust Amendments.

D. Displaying, Exporting and Printing a Trust Revocation

If you've chosen to revoke your trust (see Sections A and B, above) you move to an introductory screen and then the Review and Print Your Trust Revocation screen. This screen works the same way as the screen that displayed and printed your original trust document. See Chapter 6 if you need to refresh your memory.

Users' Guide

| Living Trust Maker |
| File Edit Help Window |

GLICK.TRS

REVIEW AND PRINT YOUR TRUST REVOCATION

Now you are ready to display and print out your trust revocation.

[Display/Print Trust Revocation]

[Export Trust Revocation...]

[Go Back] [Quit]

**Screen from which you can display and
export your Trust Revocation**

Be sure to read Chapter 9 of the Legal Manual for important instructions on how to revoke your trust.

When you're finished printing your Trust Revocation, click **Quit** to exit *Living Trust Maker* or choose **New** from the **File** menu to begin creating a new trust document.

Troubleshooting

A. Problems That May Arise

This section of the manual briefly discusses some common technical difficulties you might encounter in running *Living Trust Maker* on Windows.

On-screen help is also available by pulling down the **Help** menu.

1. Problems Reading the Installation Disk

If you try to run "A:SETUP" from the Program Manager's Run command, and receive a message:

"Application Execution Error", cannot find A:SETUP, or one of its components"

this means that your disk drive cannot read the setup disk—your disk drive is on the blink or the disk is defective.

Remove the disk from the drive.

Check the disk drive by using another disk that you have used before. If the disk drive operates properly, then the disk you have received may be defective. Contact Nolo Press Technical Support (see Section B, below).

2. Additional Error Messages

Error	What It Means	What To Do
An error occurred: couldn't find the requested DOS path name.	DOS couldn't find the path for a file it wants to open.	Call Nolo Technical Support.
An error occurred while assembling the document.	The resource files of the program might be damaged.	Reinstall all program files. Try again. If that doesn't work, call Nolo Technical Support.
An error occurred: couldn't find the requested file.	You may have too many files open.	Either quit other applications and TSR's or modify the FILES setting in your CONFIG.SYS file to a higher value.
Disk access denied.	The disk is locked.	Unlock it by sliding back the write-protect tab so that the hole in the top corner of the disk is closed.
Internal error: *Living Trust Maker* attempted to access nonexistent memory.	This shouldn't happen in *Living Trust Maker* and it is probably a sign of a bug.	Try to remember the steps you did before the error appeared, then call Nolo Technical Support.

Error	What It Means	What To Do
Internal error: attempt to overwrite existing file.	*Living Trust Maker* is attempting to overwrite an existing file without permission. This shouldn't happen in *Living Trust Maker*.	Try to remember the steps you did before the error appeared, then call Nolo Technical Support.
Internal error: bad file number requested.	This is a DOS error meaning that a bad file number was passed to one of its routines.	Try to remember the steps you did before the error appeared, then call Nolo Technical Support.
Internal error: memory blocks have been destroyed. (ECONTR)	Don't worry. Your computer is not damaged. Memory that was allocated to *Living Trust Maker* has been improperly used by some other application.	Quit *Living Trust Maker* without saving your changes, as the whole system is probably unstable. Restart your machine.
Sorry, an internal error occurred.	Something very serious is wrong with the program, either because of a disk error, memory error, or (gasp!) a bug.	Quit, restart the program and attempt to repeat what you did. The problem may clear up on its own. If not, try reinstalling the application. If that doesn't work, contact Nolo Technical Support.
Sorry, an internal data-module error occurred.	Something very serious is wrong with the internal data structures stored by the program.	Quit and restart the program and attempt to repeat what you did. The problem may clear up on its own. If not, contact Nolo Technical Support.
Sorry, the trust data has reached an internal limit.	The trust data file has reached an internal limit and cannot be used further.	Contact Nolo Technical Support.
Sorry, a needed resource cannot be found.	The resource files of the program might be damaged.	Reinstall all program files and try again. If that doesn't work, call Nolo Technical support.
Sorry, the file has been corrupted and cannot be read.	Your trust data file has been corrupted (the program detected a checksum error).	Use a backup file. There is a possibility that your disk drive may be faulty.
Sorry, the file has been severely corrupted and cannot be read.	Your trust data file has been seriously corrupted, and *Living Trust Maker* is unable to read it.	Use a backup file.
Sorry, *Living Trust Maker* can open only one file at a time.	You attempted to open more than one *Living Trust Maker* trust data file.	Open only one trust data file at a time.

Error	What It Means	What To Do
Sorry, this file cannot be read by *Living Trust Maker*.	You are trying to open a file that is not recognized by *Living Trust Maker*.	If you are sure the file you are attempting to use is a *Living Trust Maker* data file, try a backup copy. If that doesn't work, contact Nolo Technical Support.
Sorry, *Living Trust Maker* ran out of memory	The program ran out of memory.	Try quitting any other program running under Windows. Turn on virtual memory (if you are running Windows in Enhanced mode). Or, buy more RAM.
System Error; Internal XVT Error: XXXXX-XXXXX	Something very serious is wrong with the program, either because of a disk error, memory error, or (gasp!) a bug.	Jot down the numbers that appear in the dialog. Quit and restart the program, then repeat what you did. If that doesn't work, contact Nolo Technical Support.
Sorry, *Living Trust Maker* was unable to open the resource file	*Living Trust Maker* couldn't find the file named "LTMRES.DLL"	Make sure "LTMRES.DLL" is in the same directory as *Living Trust Maker*. Try reinstalling all program files.
Living Trust Maker cannot open any more files	Your computer has too many files open.	Either quit other applications and TSR's or modify the FILES setting in your CONFIG.SYS to a higher value.
Living Trust Maker cannot open that file (it may be locked).	*Living Trust Maker* was not allowed to open a file because it didn't have permission to open it, either because it is in use, or it is locked.	Check to make sure you don't have two instances of *Living Trust Maker* running. Also check that the file (or the disk) is not locked.

3. Other Problems that Might Arise

Displayed and printed document shows line after line of "/////"

These hash marks are there as a precaution. *Living Trust Maker* has built-in formatting that forces certain blocks of text to stay together on the same page.

For example, it is a requirement for making a legally valid living trust that a few lines setting out something of substance in your living trust appear on the same page as your signature and the signatures on your witnesses. Often this results in a page break which leaves less than a full page of text on the previous page. When space is left at the bottom of the page, but there is more text of the document on the next page, it is customary to fill in remaining the "blank" lines with hash marks—the "/////" you see on the page.

This prevents someone from later tampering with your living trust and filling in the blank space with additional clauses after you have signed it.

Printing problems running under Windows

Most Windows printing problems are caused by the Print Setup being set incorrectly. Select **Print Setup** from the **File** menu. Check to make sure the settings for your printer are correct. For example, if your printer uses a sheet feeder, make sure the print setup for your printer is set for sheet feeding.

Don't double-click CONTINUE or OK buttons

To move through the *Living Trust Maker* interview, you only have to click once on the **CONTINUE** or **OK** button. If you double-click, you may skip a screen that contains contain important information.
   If it seems that you missed a screen, or that the sequence of screens is incorrect, make sure that you haven't inadvertently double-clicked. If you do skip a screen, you can generally go back to the one you missed by clicking the **GO BACK** button.

Using SVGA and XGA video drivers

Living Trust Maker screens may not display properly with some Super-VGA and XGA video drivers. If you experience display problems, try using the SVGA or XGA driver that offers a "small fonts" option. Using a "larger fonts" option will cause the button text and screen text to wrap improperly.
   You can change your display driver by running Windows Setup.
   Note: You may need your original Windows installation disks to change to a different display driver.
   If this does not fix the problem, use a VGA display driver such as VGA or VGA 3.0 in a standard 640x480 or 800x600 mode.

You must select specific printer to have print options take effect

If you need to change any of these settings, select your printer as the "specific printer"—rather than the default printer—and then change the other settings. Otherwise any changes you make will not take effect.

Do not use the "Generic Text Only" print driver

Living Trust Maker is not designed to work with the "Generic Text Only" print driver that comes with Windows. If you use it, you will likely experience problems printing and/or using the program. Use a print driver that is designed to work with the printer you are using. If no other print driver is available to you, see page 6/7 of the *Users' Guide,* Section D, "Exporting to a Text File."

B. Calling Nolo Press Technical Support

If you have problems that are not cleared up in the Troubleshooting section, call Nolo Press Technical Support: (510) 549-4660 between 9 am and 5 pm Pacific Time, Monday through Friday.

When you call, try to be in front of the computer with which you are having the problem. And please have the following information ready:
- version of *Living Trust Maker*
- the point in the program where the problem occurred
- whether you can duplicate the problem
- version of DOS you are running (which you can get by typing "VER" at the DOS command prompt)
- version of Windows you are running (which you can get by choosing the **About the Program Manager** command from the **Help** menu)
- the brand and model of computer you are using, and
- the brand and model of printer—if you are having trouble printing.

The following information may also be helpful, which you can get by typing MSD at the DOS command prompt.
- type of BIOS (Brand)
- amount of RAM
- description of any special printer or monitor interface hardware, and
- any TSRs or screen savers you are running.

Appendix

A. Keyboard Shortcuts

USING KEYBOARD SHORTCUT COMMANDS IN *LIVING TRUST MAKER*

Press...	To...
ENTER	Trigger default button (if one exists).
ESC	Trigger CANCEL, CLOSE or No button in pop-up dialogs.
F1	Open Program Help window.
F2	Open Legal Help window.
CTRL+O	Open a dialog box from which you can select and open an existing trust data file.
CTRL+S	Save the current trust data file when the Automatic Save function is turned off.
CTRL+Z	Undo the most recent text editing you have done on the current screen if the change has not been seaved yet. (Note: Undo will not revert a button selection).
CTRL+X	Cut selected text.
CTRL+C	Copy selected text.
CTRL+V	Paste contents of clipboard.
DEL	Delete selected text.
CTRL+A	Select all text.
ALT+F4	Exit the program (or closes help if the help window is on top).

B. Navigating and Selecting From the Keyboard

USING THE "DROP DOWN" MENUS AT THE TOP OF THE SCREEN

To...	Press...
Open a drop down menu	ALT+ the underlined key in the menu name; for example to drop down the Edit menu, press ALT+E
Select a menu item or command from an menu that is already opened	The underlined key in the menu item or command; for example to select Paste from Names List from the dropped-down Edit menu, press N.

NAVIGATING WITHIN AN INTERVIEW SCREEN

To...	Press...
Move to the next text box, list, button or group of radio buttons.	TAB
Move to the previous text box, list, button or group of radio buttons	SHIFT+TAB
Highlight the next radio button in a group when one radio button is selected, or next item in a selected list	Down Arrow
Highlight the previous radio button in a group when one radio button is selected, or previous item in a selected list	Up Arrow
Activate the default button (as indicated by a thicker outline), or the selected button if there is no default.	ENTER

IF CURSOR IS IN A TEXT ENTRY FIELD

To...	Press...
Start a new line	ENTER
Move one character to left	Left Arrow
Move one character to right	Right Arrow
Move one line up	Up Arrow
Move one line down	Down Arrow
Move to beginning of line	HOME
Move to end of line	END
Move one word to left	CTRL+Left Arrow
Move one word to right	CTRL+Right Arrow

NAVIGATING WITHIN THE DOCUMENT PREVIEW WINDOW

To...	Press...
Move to the next page in a document	ALT+>
Move to the previous page in a document	ALT+<
Scroll to the top of the currently displayed page	PAGE UP
Scroll to the bottom of the currently displayed page	PAGE DOWN

C. Ten Essential Tips

1. Don't turn off the Automatic Save function.

Although you can turn off **Automatically Save Changes** from the **File** menu, we recommend that you leave it on. You never know when the electricity will go down or your computer is accidentally turned off. For more information about the Automatic Save function, see Chapter 3, Section B.

2. Don't lose your trust data file; store it in a safe place because you will need it whenever you want to amend your trust.

When you finish your work each session, copy your trust data file to a floppy diskette and store it in a safe place. You will need this file to make any amendments to your living trust in the future. You may want to store this diskette with your signed trust document, or in some other safe place where you will have access to it for many years to come.

3. Take the time to read the context-sensitive Legal Help.

Not all of the information you need to know is on the interview screens. Instead, *Living Trust Maker* puts lots of important information into the Legal Help topics that appear throughout the program. The information in these Legal Help topics is crucial to your understanding of how a living trust works, and alerts you to legal issues that you should be aware of. You can get Legal Help whenever you see a Legal Help button or a list of Legal Help topics displayed on screen.

4. Take advantage of the Legal Glossary, the Tutorial and Program Help.

An online tutorial provides a basic overview of how to use the program. It is available from any point in the program by choosing **Tutorial** from the **Help** menu.

The online Glossary of legal terms is available from any point in the program by choosing **Legal Glossary** from the **Help** menu.

Press F1 or choose **Program Help** from the **Help** menu to get Program Help dealing with the mechanical aspects of running the *Living Trust Maker* program.

Program Help is context-sensitive. In other words, it is written expressly for the interview screen you're working with.

Use these tools liberally.

5. Type only one name per line.

When you enter names in the program remember that each name must be on a separate line. To start a new line just press ENTER.

6. Use the Paste From Names List feature.

Living Trust Maker treats names spelled differently as different persons. To be sure you are spelling a name the same way each time, use the **Paste From Names List** feature in the **Edit** menu.

7. Follow these simple rules when describing property.

When describing the property you intend to transfer to your living trust, follow these simple rules so that your trust documents read correctly:

- Don't use the word "my." For example, don't enter the property as "my coin collection." You can use the word "the."
- Don't begin with a capital letter unless you're entering a proper name. For example, "Porsche 911" is fine but "Station wagon" is incorrect.
- Don't add a period to the end of the description.

8. Stick to standard fonts in your trust documents.

Your trust documents are no place to try out a new font like Futura Extra Black Condensed Italic. Although *Living Trust Maker* provides access to all the fonts you've installed in Windows, it's best to stick with a font that's easy to read, for example Times Roman, Courier or Helvetica in 10 or 12 point.

9. Don't export your trust document.

There is really no reason to export your trust document, and many good reasons not to. *Living Trust Maker's* built-in formatting options should be sufficient to make an attractive, professional-looking document. If you're having trouble printing directly from *Living Trust Maker*, call Nolo Technical Support.

If you export your trust, you run the risk of inadvertently changing language that could create confusion, contradictions and legal problems.

10. If you do export your trust document, don't change the language of the trust.

As mentioned above, changing the language of your trust document could create confusion, contradictions and legal problems. In addition, you will not be able to use *Living Trust Maker* to make trust amendments, because the language of the amendments will not correspond to the language of your original trust.

LEGAL

MANUAL

Before You Begin

L *iving Trust Maker* is a straightforward, easy-to-use piece of software. You will go through the program step by step, answering a series of questions about your property and who you want to inherit it. Your answers will be incorporated into a Declaration of Trust. When signed and notarized, this trust document creates your living trust.

Along the way, the program offers on-screen legal help. A list of Legal Help topics will appear before you're asked to enter each new kind of information. You can look at as many of the help topics as you wish, or skip them altogether.

You'll have an easier time of it, however, if you don't rely solely on the on-screen legal help. We suggest that you take time now to read this manual, to get familiar with living trusts and think about how you want to use yours.

Keep in mind that creating a living trust has important, long-term consequences for your family and their finances. It's worth doing right, which means educating yourself about your options so you can make well-informed decisions.

Before you begin, you should read at least two chapters in this manual:

- Chapter 2, About Living Trusts, and
- Chapter 4, What Kind of Living Trust Do You Need?

Here are the key decisions to think about before you ever sit down at the computer:

- what kind of living trust (individual or shared) to make
- what property you want to put into the trust
- whom you want to receive it after your death

- who you want to distribute the property after your death, and
- what you want to do about property inherited by young beneficiaries.

If you're really prepared, you can probably breeze through the program and be ready to print your trust document in less than an hour. (You don't have to finish the program all at one sitting; you can quit and save whatever you've done.) As you use the program, consult either Chapter 5, Creating an Individual Trust, or Chapter 6, Creating a Shared Marital Trust. Each follows the program step by step.

CHECKLIST FOR CREATING A VALID LIVING TRUST

√ Prepare the trust document with *Living Trust Maker*.
√ Print out the trust document and sign it in front of a notary public.
√ Transfer ownership of the property listed in the trust document into the trust.
√ Update your trust document when needed.

Icons Used in This Manual

Look for these icons to alert you to certain kinds of information.

WARNING
This icon alerts you to pitfalls you may encounter when preparing and presenting your case.

RESOURCES
This icon highlights lists of books and other resources you may want to consult.

CONTACT AN EXPERT
This icon gives practial suggestions for gettin g technical or legal advice on a particular topic.

About Living Trusts

A revocable living trust lets your family inherit your property without going through the probate court process, which is notoriously slow, expensive and, for most people, unnecessary. In the probate process, a deceased person's will is proved valid in court, the person's debts are paid and the remaining property is distributed to its inheritors. In most instances, where there is no dispute about the validity of a will, no fears of huge creditors' lawsuits and no fights among relatives, formal probate court proceedings are a waste of time and money.

If you set up a living trust while you are alive, the people who inherit your property don't have to bother with a probate court proceeding. And that means they won't have to spend any of your hard-earned money to pay for court and lawyer fees.

A. What Is a Trust?

A trust can seem like a mysterious creature, dreamed up by lawyers, wrapped in legal jargon and used for mysterious purposes. But in practice, a trust isn't complicated. Here are the basics.

1. The Concept of a Trust

A trust, like a corporation, is an entity that exists only on paper but is legally capable of owning property. You can create a trust simply by preparing and signing a document called a Declaration of Trust.

Once the trust has been created, you can transfer property to it. The trust becomes the legal owner. There must, however, be a flesh-and-blood person actually in charge of the property; that person is called the trustee. The trustee manages the property on the behalf of someone else, called the beneficiary.

Those, then, are the essential elements of every trust: the trust, the property, the trustee and the beneficiary.

There are many kinds of trusts. Some are designed to save on taxes, others to manage property. The kind of trust you create with *Living Trust Maker* is a "probate-avoidance revocable living trust."

2. Probate-Avoiding Revocable Living Trusts

A revocable living trust is primarily designed to reduce or eliminate the need for probate court proceedings.

First, an explanation of the name. It's called "revocable" because you can revoke it at any time. And it's called a "living" trust because it's created when you're alive, not at your death like some other kinds of trusts. (Sometimes living trusts are known by their Latin name: *inter vivos* (among the living) trusts.)

When you create a revocable living trust, you transfer ownership of some or all of your property to the living trust. You also appoint yourself trustee of your living trust, with full power to manage trust property. So you keep absolute control over the property in your living trust, even though technically it's owned by the living trust.

> **EXAMPLE:** Ashley, an unmarried woman, creates a revocable living trust and transfers her valuable property—a house and some stocks—into the trust's name. She names herself as trustee of the trust. As trustee, she can sell, mortgage or give away the trust property, or take it out of the trust and put it back into her name.

After you die, the person you named in your trust document to be "successor trustee" takes over. He or she is in charge of transferring the trust property to the family, friends or charities you named as the trust beneficiaries. No probate is necessary for property that was transferred to the living trust. In most cases, the whole thing can be handled within a few weeks. When the property has all been transferred to the beneficiaries, the living trust ceases to exist.

Because a probate-avoidance living trust lets your property go, after your death, to the relatives, friends or charities you choose, it performs the same function as a will. The crucial difference is that property left through a will must go through probate, while property in a living trust can go directly to your inheritors.

⚠ "BACK-UP" WILLS

Every living trust should be backed up by a will, to handle property not transferred to the living trust and for several other reasons. See Chapter 3, A Living Trust as Part of Your Estate Plan.

A Mini-Glossary of Living Trust Terms

Unfortunately, you can't escape legal lingo entirely when you deal with living trusts. A complete on-screen glossary is always available when you're running the program. (See the Users' Guide.) But keeping it to a minimum, here's what you need to know:

The person who sets up the living trust (that's you, or you and your spouse) is called a **grantor, trustor** or **settlor**. These terms mean the same thing and are used interchangeably.

The property you transfer to the trust is called, collectively, the **trust property, trust principal** or **trust estate**. (And, of course, there's a Latin version: the trust *corpus*.)

The person who has complete power over the trust property is called the **trustee**. The person who sets up the trust (the grantor) is the original trustee of a living trust, thus keeping total control over property in the trust. If a married couple creates one shared marital trust, both are trustees.

The person the grantor names to take over as trustee after the grantor's death (or, with a shared marital trust, after the death of both spouses) is called the **successor trustee.** The successor trustee's job is to transfer the trust property to the beneficiaries, following the instructions in the Declaration of Trust. The successor trustee may also manage trust property inherited by young beneficiaries (that's explained in Section B, below). Often, the successor trustee is a grown child of the grantor or another trusted relative or friend who inherits a large share of the trust property.

The people or organizations who get the trust property when the grantor dies are called the **beneficiaries** of the trust. (While the grantors are alive, they are technically the only beneficiaries of the trust.)

B. Important Features of a Living Trust

The main reason for setting up a revocable living trust is to save your family time and money by avoiding probate. But there are other advantages as well. Here is a brief rundown of the major features of a living trust.

1. Property in a Living Trust Doesn't Go Through Probate

As mentioned, property left by a will must go through probate before it can be transferred to the beneficiaries. And if you don't make a will or some other arrangement to designate who gets your property (living trust or joint tenancy, for example), the property also goes through probate. It is distributed to close relatives according to state "intestate succession" law.

During the probate process, a court oversees the distribution of a deceased person's property. The cost of probate varies widely from state to state, but probate attorney, court and other fees often eat up about 5% of your estate (the property you leave at death), leaving that much less to go to the people or charities you want to get it. If the estate is complicated, the fees can be even larger. Lawyer fees, set by statute or local custom, often bear no relation to the actual work done by the attorney.

	Estate #1	Estate #2
Value of property in estate:	$200,000	$400,000
Approximate cost of probate:	$10,000	$20,000

At least as bad as the expense of probate is the delay it causes. Often, probate takes a year or two, during which time the beneficiaries generally get nothing unless the judge allows the decedent's immediate family a "family allowance." In some states, this allowance is a pittance—only a few hundred dollars. In others, it can amount to thousands.

From the family's point of view, probate's headaches are rarely justified. If the estate contains standard kinds of property—a house, stocks, bank accounts, a small business, cars—and no relatives are fighting about it, the property merely needs to be handed over to the new owners. In the vast majority of cases, the probate process entails nothing more than tedious paperwork, and the attorney is nothing more than a very highly paid clerk.

Even England—the source of our antiquated probate laws—abolished its elaborate probate system years ago. It survives in this country because it is so lucrative for lawyers; they can charge a hefty fee for what is, for the most part, just routine paperwork.

Given the needless drawbacks of probate, it's not surprising that people have sought ways around it. The living trust, which functions like a will but avoids the probate process, is the most popular.

2. Out-of-State Real Estate Doesn't Have to Be Probated in That State

The only thing worse than regular probate is out-of-state probate. Usually, an estate is probated in the probate court of the county where the decedent was living before he or she died. But if the decedent owned real estate in more than one state, it's usually necessary to have a whole separate probate proceeding in each. That means the surviving relatives must probably find and hire a lawyer in each state, and pay for multiple probate proceedings.

With a living trust, out-of-state property can be transferred to the beneficiaries without probate in that state.

3. You Can Avoid the Need for a Conservatorship

A living trust can be useful if the person who created it (the grantor) becomes incapable, because of physical or mental illness, of taking care of his or her financial affairs. The person named in the living trust document—a relative, friend or anyone else—to take over as trustee at the grantor's death can also take over management of the trust if the grantor becomes incapacitated, as certified in writing by a physician. When a couple sets up a trust, if one person becomes incapacitated, the other takes sole responsibility. The person who takes over has authority to manage all property in the trust, and to use it for the grantor.

> **EXAMPLE:** Margaret creates a living trust, appointing herself as trustee. The trust states that if she becomes incapacitated, and a physician signs a statement saying she no longer can manage her own affairs, her daughter Elizabeth will replace her as trustee.

If there is no living trust and no other arrangements have been made for someone to take over property management if you become incapacitated, someone else must get legal authority, from a court, to take over. Typically, the spouse or adult child of the person seeks this authority and is called a conservator or guardian.

⚠ You should also give your successor trustee (or spouse) the authority to manage property that has not been transferred into the trust if you become incapacitated. The best way to do that is to prepare and sign a document called a Durable Power of Attorney for Financial Management.

In addition, if you are concerned about dying a natural death without the unauthorized use of life support systems, you'll want to prepare and sign some other documents. Planning for incapacity is discussed in more detail in Chapter 3, A Living Trust as Part of Your Estate Plan.

4. Your Estate Plan Remains Confidential

When your will is filed with the probate court after you die, it becomes a matter of public record. A living trust, on the other hand, is a private document in most states. Because the living trust document is never filed with a court or other government entity, what you leave to whom remains private. (There is one exception: Records of real estate transfers are always public.)

Some states require that you register your living trust with the local court. But there are no legal consequences or penalties if you don't. (Registration is explained in Chapter 7, Signing, Storing and Registering Your Trust Document.)

The only way the terms of a living trust might become public is if—and this is unlikely—someone files a lawsuit to challenge the trust or collect a court judgment owed by the grantor. (See Section D, below.)

5. You Can Change Your Mind at Any Time

You have complete control over your revocable living trust and all the property you transfer to it. You can:

- sell, mortgage or give away property in the trust
- put ownership of trust property back in your own name
- add property to the trust
- change the beneficiaries
- name a different successor trustee (the person who distributes trust property after your death)
- revoke the trust completely.

If you and your spouse create the trust together, both spouses must consent to changes, although either of you can revoke the trust entirely. (See Chapter 9, Living With Your Living Trust.)

6. You Can Name Someone to Manage Trust Property for Young Beneficiaries

If there's a possibility that any of your beneficiaries will inherit trust property while still young (not yet 35), you may want to arrange to have someone manage that property for them until they're older. If they might inherit before they're legally adults (18, in most states), you should definitely arrange for management. Minors are not allowed to control significant amounts of property, and if you haven't provided someone to do it, a court will have to appoint a property guardian.

When you create a living trust with *Living Trust Maker*, you can arrange for someone to manage property for a young beneficiary. In most states, you have two options:

- Have your successor trustee (or your spouse, if you created a shared marital trust) manage the property in a "child's subtrust" until the child reaches an age you designate.
- Appoint someone as a "custodian" to manage the property until the child reaches an age specified by your state's Uniform Transfers to Minors Act (21 in most states, but up to 25 in California, Nevada and Alaska).

Both methods are explained in Chapters 5 and 6.

C. Drawbacks of a Living Trust

A living trust does have unique problems and complications. The drawbacks aren't significant to most people, but you should be aware of them before you create a living trust.

1. Recordkeeping and Paperwork

Setting up a living trust isn't difficult or expensive, but it requires some paperwork. The first step is to use *Living Trust Maker* to create and print out a trust document, which you should sign in front of a notary public. So far, the amount of work required is no more than writing a will.

There is, however, one more essential step to making a living trust effective. You must make sure that ownership of all the property you listed in the trust document is legally transferred to you as trustee of the trust.

If an item of property doesn't have a title (ownership) document, listing it in the trust document is enough to transfer it. So, for example, no additional paperwork is required for most books, furniture, electronics, jewelry, appliances, musical instruments and many other kinds of property.

But if an item has a title document—real estate, stocks, mutual funds, bonds, money market accounts or vehicles, for example—you must change the title document to show that the property is owned by your living trust. For example, if you want to put your house into your living trust, you must prepare and sign a new deed, transferring ownership from you to you as trustee of the trust.

After a revocable living trust is created, little day-to-day recordkeeping is required. No separate income tax records or returns are necessary as long as you are both the grantor and the trustee. (IRS Reg. § 1.671-4.) Income from property in the living trust should be reported on your personal income tax return.

You must keep written records whenever you transfer property to or from the trust, which isn't difficult unless you transfer a lot of property in and out of the trust. (Chapter 9, Living With Your Living Trust, discusses transferring property in and out of your living trust.)

> **EXAMPLE:** Monica and David Fielding put their house in a living trust to avoid probate, but later decide to sell it. In the real estate contract and deed transferring ownership to the new owners, Monica and David sign their names "as trustees of the Monica and David Fielding Revocable Living Trust."

2. Transfer Taxes

In most states, transfers of real estate to revocable living trusts are exempt from transfer taxes that are usually imposed on real estate transfers. But in a few states, transferring real estate to your living trust could trigger a tax. (See Chapter 8, Transferring Property to the Trust.)

3. Difficulty Refinancing Trust Property

Because legal title to trust real estate is held in the name of the trustee, a few banks and title companies may balk if you want to refinance it. They should be sufficiently reassured if you show them a copy of your trust document, which specifically gives you, as trustee, the power to borrow against trust property.

In the unlikely event you can't convince an uncooperative lender to deal with you in your capacity as trustee, you'll have to find another lender (which shouldn't be hard) or transfer the property out of the trust and back into your name. Later, after you refinance, you can transfer it back into the living trust.

4. No Cutoff of Creditors' Claims

Most people don't worry that after their death, creditors will try to collect large debts from property in the estate. In most situations, the surviving relatives simply pay the valid debts, such as outstanding bills, taxes and last illness and funeral expenses. But if you are concerned about the possibility of large claims, you may want to let your property go through probate instead of a living trust.

If your property goes through probate, creditors have only a certain amount of time to file claims against your estate. A creditor who was properly notified of the probate court proceeding cannot file a claim after the period—about six months, in most states—expires.

On the other hand, when property isn't probated, creditors still have the right to be paid (if the debt is valid) from the property. There is no formal claim procedure, however. The creditor may not know who inherited the deceased debtor's property, and once the property is found, the creditor may have to file a lawsuit, which may not be worth the time and expense.

> **EXAMPLE:** Elaine is a real estate investor with a good-sized portfolio of property. She has many creditors and is sometimes named in lawsuits. It might be to her advantage to have assets transferred by a probate court procedure, which cuts off the claims of creditors who are properly notified of the probate proceeding.

If you want to take advantage of probate's creditor cutoff, you must let *all* your property pass through probate. If not, there's a good chance the creditor could still sue (even after the probate claim cutoff) and try to collect from the property that didn't go through probate and passed instead through your living trust.

D. When Living Trusts Can Fail

Living trusts usually work easily and smoothly to transfer property at death.

When living trusts fail, it is usually because the property listed in the trust document was not actually transferred to the trust. If property that has a title document (such as real estate, stocks or vehicles) isn't owned in the trustee's name, the terms of the Declaration of Trust have no effect on it. At the owner's death, it passes under the terms of his or her will or, if there is no will, under the state's "intestate succession" law. (How to transfer property to a living trust is explained in Chapter 8, Transferring Property to the Trust.)

Court challenges to living trusts, like challenges to wills, are rare. You don't need to concern yourself with them unless you think a close relative might have an axe to grind after your death.

1. Challenges to the Validity of the Trust

Someone who wanted to challenge the validity of a living trust would have to bring a lawsuit and prove that:

- when the grantor made the trust, he or she was mentally incompetent or unduly influenced by someone, or
- the trust document itself is flawed—for example, because the signature was forged.

It's generally considered more difficult to successfully challenge a living trust than a will. That's because your continuing involvement with a living trust after its creation (transferring property in and out of the trust, or making amendments) shows that you were competent to manage your affairs.

2. Lawsuits From Spouses

Most married people leave much, if not all, of their property to their spouses. But if you don't plan to leave your spouse at least half of your property, your spouse may have the right to go to court and claim some of your property after your death. Such a challenge wouldn't wipe out your whole living trust, but might take some of the property you had earmarked for other beneficiaries and give it to your spouse.

The rights of spouses vary from state to state. The most important differences are between community property states and non-community property states.

Wherever you live, if you don't plan to leave at least half of the property in your estate to your spouse, you should consult a lawyer experienced in estate planning.

a. Community property states

Arizona	Louisiana	New Mexico	Washington
California	Nevada	Texas	Wisconsin
Idaho			

In these states, the general rule is that spouses together own all property that either acquires during the marriage, except property one spouse acquires by gift or inheritance. Each spouse owns a half-interest in this "community property."

You are free to leave your separate property and your half of the community property to anyone you choose at death. Your spouse—who already owns half of all the community property—has no right to inherit any of it. But if you don't want to leave anything to your spouse, you should make a will and include in it a specific statement to that effect. If you don't, in certain situations your spouse may be able to claim at least some—possibly all—of your half of the community property after your death.

b. Non-community property states

Alabama	Indiana	Montana	Pennsylvania
Alaska	Iowa	Nebraska	Rhode Island
Arkansas	Kansas	New Hampshire	South Carolina
Colorado	Kentucky	New Jersey	South Dakota
Connecticut	Maine	New York	Tennessee
Delaware	Maryland	North Carolina	Utah
District of Columbia	Massachusetts	North Dakota	Vermont
Florida	Michigan	Ohio	Virginia
Georgia	Minnesota	Oklahoma	West Virginia
Hawaii	Mississippi	Oregon	Wyoming
Illinois	Missouri		

In these states, you cannot disinherit your spouse. A surviving spouse who doesn't receive one-third to one-half of the deceased spouse's property (through a will, living trust or other method) is entitled to insist upon that much. The exact share

Legal Manual

depends on state law. In short, a spouse who doesn't receive the minimum he or she is entitled to under state law (the "statutory share") may be entitled to some of the property in your living trust.

Even property given away *before* death may legally belong to the surviving spouse under these laws. For example, take the case of a man who set up joint bank accounts with his children from a previous marriage. After his death, his widow sued to recover her interest in the accounts. She won; the Kentucky Supreme Court ruled that under Kentucky's "dower" law, a spouse is entitled to a half-interest in the other spouse's personal property (everything but real estate). Her husband had not had the legal right to give away her interest in the money in the accounts. *(Harris v. Rock*, 799 S.W.2d 10 (Ky. 1990). Most non-community property states have similar dower or "curtesy" laws.)

State law may also give your spouse the right to inherit the family residence, or at least use it for his or her life. The Florida constitution, for example, gives a surviving spouse the deceased spouse's residence. (Fla. Const. Art. 10, § 4.)

 Plan Your Estate, by Denis Clifford and Cora Jordan (Nolo Press) contains a state-by-state list of surviving spouses' rights.

3. Lawsuits by a Child

Children usually have no right to inherit anything from their parents. There are two exceptions: laws that give minor children certain rights and laws that are designed to protect children who are unintentionally overlooked in a will.

a. Minor Children

State law may give your minor children (less than 18 years old) the right to inherit the family residence. The Florida constitution, for example, prohibits the head of a family from leaving his residence in his will (except to his spouse) if he is survived by a spouse or minor child. (Fla. Const. Art. 10, § 4.)

b. Overlooked Children

State laws protect offspring who appear to have been unintentionally overlooked in a parent's will (the legal term is a "pretermitted heir"). Although these laws mention only wills, not living trusts, it's possible that a court could apply them to a living trust, reasoning that the living trust is serving the function of a will. And as living trusts become more widespread, state legislatures may expand their laws to include children not mentioned in living trusts.

Typically, these laws protect a child who is born after the parent's will is signed, and who of course is not mentioned in the will. The law presumes that the parent didn't mean to cut that child out, but simply hadn't yet gotten around to writing a new will. The child will be entitled to a share (the size is determined by state law) of the deceased parent's estate, which may include property in a living trust.

It's also possible that a disinherited—and angry—child could challenge a will, even though he or she was alive when the will was signed.

If you don't want to leave any property to one or more of your children— perhaps they already have plenty of money, or you've already given them their inheritances—the easy way to avoid any later misunderstandings, hurt feelings or legal claims is to make a will and mention each child in it. You can simply mention the child, leave a token amount ($1 is common) or include a brief explanation of why you're not leaving him or her any property. (See Chapter 3, A Living Trust as Part of Your Estate Plan.)

Overlooked grandchildren. Children have no right to inherit from their grandparents unless their parent has died. In that case, the grandchildren essentially take the place of the deceased child and are entitled to whatever he or she would have been legally entitled to.

E. Creditors

A living trust does not provide any protection from creditors, at least while you're alive. Technically, the trust owns the trust property. But because you keep the power to transfer the property back to yourself or revoke the trust entirely, the law doesn't allow you to shield trust property from creditors. So if a creditor sues you and wins, and a court issues a judgment against you, the creditor can seize trust property to pay off the judgment.

As a practical matter, a living trust can, however, provide some protection after your death. When property in your living trust is distributed to the trust beneficiaries after your death, creditors are not notified. They may never find out where the property went, and it may not be worth their while to file lawsuits to try to collect from the property. When property goes through probate, on the other hand, creditors must receive written notice of the court proceeding, which gives them a chance to file claims.

F. Estate Taxes

Living Trust Maker cannot help you reduce federal or state estate taxes. Neither can other probate-avoidance techniques such as joint tenancy or pay-on-death bank accounts. The taxing authorities don't care whether or not your property goes through probate; all they care about is what you owned at your death. Property you hold in joint tenancy or leave in a revocable living trust is still considered part of your estate for federal estate tax purposes.

Another kind of living trust, the "marital life estate trust" or "A-B trust," however, is designed to save on estate taxes. *Living Trust Maker* does not create this kind of trust.

If your estate is worth more than $600,000 when you die, it will be subject to federal estate tax unless the property is left to a spouse or charity. (For information on marital life estate trusts and other ways to reduce federal estate taxes, see Chapter 3, A Living Trust as Part of Your Estate Plan.)

 For instructions on how to create a marital life sestate trust, see *Make Your Own Living Trust,* by Denis Clifford (Nolo Press).

A Living Trust as Part of Your Estate Plan

Legal Manual

A revocable living trust can accomplish most people's main estate planning goal: leaving their property to their loved ones while avoiding probate. But it is not, by itself, a complete estate plan. For example, a living trust such as the one produced by *Living Trust Maker* doesn't provide any estate tax savings. And parents of young children can't use a living trust to appoint a personal guardian to care for their minor children.

This chapter outlines estate planning methods that you may want to explore in addition to the living trust. If you want more information, consult one of the books or software packages listed below, or see a lawyer who has experience in estate planning.

Basically, estate planning includes:

- deciding who will get your property when you die
- deciding who will take care of your children and their finances if you die while they are young
- setting up procedures and devices to minimize probate fees at your death
- if your estate is large, planning to reduce estate taxes
- arranging for someone to make financial and healthcare decisions for you if at some time you can no longer do so yourself.

NOLO PRESS ESTATE PLANNING RESOURCES

Nolo Press publishes several books and software packages that give detailed estate planning information and hands-on help. We think they are the best available. All of them are good in every state but Louisiana.

WillMaker 5, by Nolo Press.
This software for Macintosh, Windows and DOS computers can create a legally valid back-up will to complement your living trust. *WillMaker* allows you to name personal guardians for your minor children and direct your executor to use certain of your property to pay your last debts and taxes, things you can't do with *Living Trust Maker*.

WillMaker 5 also lets you create a living will or healthcare directive to direct doctors to give you the kind of care you want if you become unable to communicate your wishes. You can also make a document setting out your desires for funeral arrangements.

Plan Your Estate, by Denis Clifford and Cora Jordan.

This book covers all the estate planning methods briefly discussed in this chapter, and many more. It explains everything from simple probate-avoidance techniques such as joint tenancy to sophisticated ways to minimize estate taxes.

Nolo's Simple Will Book, by Denis Clifford.

If you don't want to use a computer to prepare your will, this book includes all the instructions and forms you need to do it on paper.

Make Your Own Living Trust, by Denis Clifford.

This book provides tear-out forms and instructions for making a simple probate-avoidance living trust or a marital life estate trust, which can reduce estate taxes.

Beat the Nursing Home Trap: A Consumer's Guide to Choosing & Financing Long-Term Care, by Joseph Matthews.

This book is a compendium of alternatives for evaluating and paying for long-term healthcare. It will help everyone involved—the older person in need of care, as well as the spouse, family and friends—deal with difficult decisions. It's especially valuable for older couples who want to be able to care for one spouse without bankrupting the other.

Who Will Handle Your Finances If You Can't?,
by Denis Clifford and Mary Randolph.

With this book you can arrange for someone to manage, if you become incapacitated, any property that you have not transferred to your living trust. (Remember that if your successor trustee takes over for you because you are incapacitated, he or she has authority only over property owned by your living trust.) The key is a document called a "Durable Power of Attorney for Finances," which is discussed in Section F, below

Nolo's Personal RecordKeeper, by Carol Pladsen and Ralph Warner.

This software (Macintosh and DOS) lets you make a thorough record of what you own and what estate planning steps you've taken. It's organized into 27 categories, including real estate, pensions, bank accounts and emergency information. It will be invaluable to the people who will be in charge of winding up your affairs after your death.

A. What a Revocable Living Trust Can't Do

The revocable living trust you create with *Living Trust Maker* is designed to avoid probate.

- This trust is *not* designed to save on federal estate taxes. It is not an "A-B" or "marital life estate" trust, designed to make the most of each spouse's $600,000 estate tax exemption. (This sort of trust is useful primarily for elderly couples who own more than $600,000 worth of property; see Section D, below.)
- This trust is *not* designed to let you express your wishes about dying a natural death free of life-prolonging medical technology—for that, you need a "living will" or a Durable Power of Attorney. (See Section F, below.)

B. Using a Back-Up Will

Even though you create a living trust, you will almost certainly need a simple back-up will, too. Like a living trust, a will is a document in which you specify what is to be done with your property when you die.

1. Why Make a Back-Up Will

Having a will is important for several reasons.

First, a will is an essential back-up device for property that you don't get around to transferring to your living trust. For example, if you acquire property shortly before you die, you may not think to transfer ownership of it to your trust— which means that it won't pass under the terms of the trust document. But in your back-up will, you can include a clause that says who should get any property that you don't specifically transfer to your living trust or leave to someone in some other way.

If you don't have a will, any property that isn't transferred by your living trust or other probate-avoidance device (such as joint tenancy) will go to your closest relatives, in an order determined by state law. These laws are called "intestate succession" laws, and they may not distribute property in the way you would have chosen. For example, if you die leaving a spouse and children, all the property that isn't subject to a living trust or will may be divided among your spouse and children. If your children are minors, that means there must be a court proceeding to get a guardian appointed to manage the property for them.

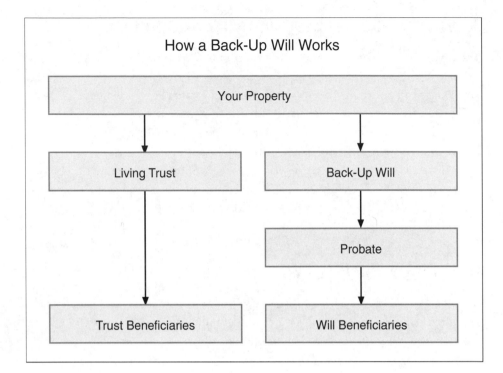

How a Back-Up Will Works

Your Property

Living Trust

Back-Up Will

Probate

Trust Beneficiaries

Will Beneficiaries

Second, in a will you can name someone to be the personal guardian of your minor child, in case you and the child's other parent die while the child is still under 18. You can't do that in a living trust.

Finally, if you want to disinherit your spouse or a child, you must make your wishes clear in a will. (State law may restrict your freedom to disinherit a spouse or minor child; see Chapter 5 or 6.)

How to Make a Back-Up Will

Making a will is a fairly simple process. *Nolo's Simple Will Book* and *WillMaker* both contain complete instructions.

Unless your needs are unusually complicated, you probably don't need a lawyer. Just be sure to follow the instructions carefully.

How to Use *WillMaker* to Make a Back-Up Will

If you have already made a will with *WillMaker:*

- Review your previous entries about name, state, county, marital status and children.
- Review your specific bequest entries and eliminate any that involve property you have transferred to your living trust.
- Review your choice for residuary beneficiary to make sure this is the person you want to get all property not transferred to the living trust or left to a specific beneficiary.
- If you have minor children, review your choice for a personal guardian.
- If any beneficiary is a minor, review your previous choice for management. If the minor is also a beneficiary under your living trust, select the UTMA option if it is available in your state. If it isn't, use the children's trust option. If you use the UTMA option both in your living trust and in your back-up will, make your choices consistent.
- Review your choices for paying of debts and taxes. If most of your property has been placed in the living trust, it's probably best to leave no instructions for paying debts or taxes in your will. If you identify assets to be sold, select non-trust assets.
- Review your choice for personal representative. If possible, choose the same person as your successor trustee, or your spouse if you're making a shared living trust.
- Carefully follow the instructions that print out with your will to make it valid in your state.

If you have never used *WillMaker:*

After providing some introductory information, *WillMaker* uses a question-and-answer format.

To make a back-up will, focus on a few parts of the program. Your main job is to make sure that the terms of your will are consistent with your living trust. After the introductory material (name, state, marital status, children), focus on:

- your residuary beneficiary
- your choice for personal guardian of your minor children (if any)
- property management for minor children (if any). If you provide management for these same children in your living trust, use the UTMA option if it's available for your state. If you haven't, use either the UTMA or children's trust option (on-screen help is available)
- your personal representative. If possible, choose the same person as your successor trustee or your spouse, if you're making a shared living trust.

You may bypass the specific bequest part of the program as well as the selection on paying debts and taxes.

Carefully follow the instructions in the manual for making your will valid.

2. Avoiding Conflicts Between Your Will and Living Trust

When you make both a living trust and a back-up will, pay attention to how the two work together. If your will and your trust document contain conflicting provisions, at the least you will create confusion among your inheritors, and at the worst, bitter disputes—maybe even a lawsuit—among friends and family.

Here are some no-no's:

- Don't leave the same property in your living trust and will, even if it's to the same beneficiary. If you transfer the property to your living trust and name a beneficiary in the trust document, that's all you need to do. Mentioning the property in the will raises the possibility of probate.
- Don't leave the same property to different beneficiaries in your will and your living trust.
- Don't name different people to be executor of your will and successor trustee of your living trust, especially if you think they might quarrel about how your affairs should be handled. There's one important exception: If you make a

shared marital trust, you may name your spouse as executor of your will, but not as successor trustee—the successor trustee takes over only after both spouses have died. (See Chapter 5 or 6, Part 3.)

3. Pour-Over Wills

Some lawyers urge people who make living trusts to make "pour-over wills" as well. A pour-over will takes all the property you haven't gotten around to transferring to your living trust and, at your death, leaves it to the trust.

Pour-over wills (named because everything is "poured over" from the will to your living trust) do *not* avoid probate. All property that is left through a will—any kind of will—must go through probate. It makes no difference that the beneficiary of the will is a living trust. If the value of the property left through a pour-over will is small, some states exempt it from probate or offer streamlined probate procedures. But the same is true whether or not the will is a pour-over one.

Pour-over wills are not usually a good idea. It's better to simply use a standard back-up will to take care of this property. In the back-up will, you can name the people you want to get the property, and skip the unnecessary extra step of pouring the property through the living trust after your death.

When used as a back up will, a pour over will actually has a disadvantage that standard wills don't: It forces the living trust to go on for months after your death, because the property left through the will must go through probate before it can be transferred to the trust. Usually, the property left in a living trust can be distributed to the beneficiaries, and the trust ended, within a few weeks after the person's death.

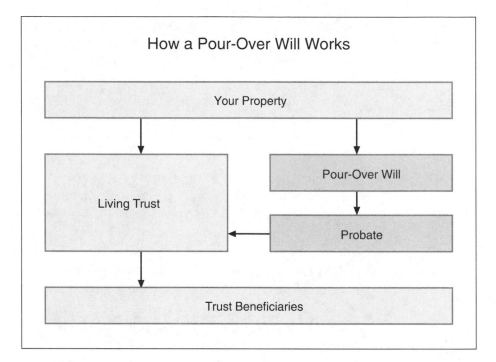

How a Pour-Over Will Works

EXAMPLE: Joy transfers her valuable property to her living trust. She also makes a pour-over will, which states that any property she owns at death not specifically left to someone in the will goes to the living trust. When Joy dies, the property left through her will goes to the trust and is distributed to the residuary beneficiary of her living trust, her son Louis. The living trust must be kept going until probate of the will is finished, when property left by the will is poured over into the living trust.

If Joy had simply named Louis as the residuary beneficiary of a plain back-up will, the result would have been the same, but the process would have been simpler. The living trust would have been ended a few weeks after Joy's death. And after probate was finished, Louis would have received whatever property passed through Joy's will.

There is, however, one situation in which you might want to use a pour-over will. If you set up a child's subtrust for a young beneficiary in your living trust, you may want any property that child inherits through your will to go into the subtrust. Otherwise, you would create two trusts for the beneficiary; one in the will and one in your living trust.

EXAMPLE: Jessica makes a living trust and leaves the bulk of her property to her 12-year-old son. She arranges, in the trust document, for any trust property her son inherits before the age of 30 to be kept in a subtrust, managed by Jessica's mother.

Jessica also makes a back-up will, in which she also leaves everything to her son and again arranges for a subtrust to be set up if she should die before her son reaches age 30. So if Jessica dies before her son reaches 30, two subtrusts will be set up to manage property for him.

If Jessica used a pour-over will, any property her son inherited through the will would go into the subtrust created by her living trust. Only half the paperwork of maintaing the subtrust would be necessary.

C. Other Probate-Avoidance Methods

A living trust is not the only way to transfer some kinds of assets without probate, and it's not always the best. For example, it would probably be cumbersome to have your personal checking account held in the name of your living trust.

Fortunately, you can mix and match probate-avoidance techniques. Just put whatever property you want in your living trust, and choose other transfer methods—which also avoid probate   for the rest of your property.

You might, for example, want to put your checking account into joint tenancy with your spouse; at your death, your spouse would automatically take sole ownership of the account. Some helpful probate-avoidance methods are discussed below.

1. Pay-on-Death Accounts (Banks and Government Securities)

Setting up a pay-on-death account, also called an informal bank account trust or revocable trust account, is an easy way to transfer cash at your death, quickly and without probate. All you do is designate one or more persons you want to receive the money in the account when you die.

You can use any kind of bank account, including savings, checking or certificate of deposit accounts. You can also register ownership of certain kinds of government securities, including bonds, Treasury Bills and Treasury Notes, in a way that lets you name a beneficiary to receive them at your death.

PROBATE-AVOIDANCE METHODS

METHOD	ADVANTAGES	DISADVANTAGES
Revocable living trust	Flexible, private. Easy to create. You keep control over property during your life.	Some paperwork involved. May need attorney if yours is a complicated estate.
Pay-on-death accounts (revocable trust accounts)	Easy to create, using a form provided by the institution or agency.	Limited to bank accounts and some government securities.
Naming beneficiary of pension plan or retirement account	Easy to do. Beneficiary inherits all funds in the account at your death.	None, unless particular program imposes limits.
Life insurance	Good way to provide quick cash for beneficiaries or to pay estate taxes. Proceeds don't go through probate.	Family members may not need much immediate cash if they don't rely on you to support them, so expense of policy may not be justified.
Joint tenancy with right of survivorship	Easy to create.	Not available in a few states. If you don't already own property in joint tenancy, you may not want to add another owner, who could sell his share. (For larger estates, there are negative gift tax consequences, too.) Can be a problem if a co-owner becomes incapacitated. No probate avoidance if all joint owners die at once.
Gifts of property made while you're alive	Reduces amount of property in your estate, which avoids both probate and estate taxes.	You lose control over property given away. Large gifts use up part of your federal gift/estate tax exemption. Insurance policies must be given away at least three years before death, or proceeds are included in your taxable estate.
State laws that allow simplified probate proceedings	Exempts certain property from formal probate.	Applies only to small estates; you may still need an attorney to explain the technicalities of your state's laws.
Transfer-on-death designation for motor vehicles	Easy to do. All you do is name, on your registration form, someone to inherit your vehicle.	Currently available only in a few states (including California and Missouri), but other states are considering similar programs.
Transfer-on-death registration for securities	Easy to do. All you do is name, on the registration form, someone to inherit the securities at your death.	Currently available only in Arkansas, Colorado, Kansas, Minnesota, Missouri, Montana, Nebraska, New Mexico, North Dakota, Ohio, Oregon, Virginia, Washington, West Virginia, Wisconsin and Wyoming.

EXAMPLE: Terry opens a savings account in the name of "Terry Kelinkoff, trustee for Lynn Harris." When Terry dies, whatever money is in the account will go to Lynn.

During your life, the beneficiary has no right to the money in the account. You can withdraw some or all of the money, close the account or change the beneficiary, at any time. When you die, the beneficiary can claim the money by showing the bank the death certificate.

Like other bank accounts, a pay-on-death account may be temporarily frozen at your death, if your state levies death taxes. The state will release the money to your beneficiaries when shown that your estate has ample funds to pay the taxes.

Most banks have forms for setting up this kind of account, and they don't charge more for keeping your money this way. Before you open a pay-on-death account, ask your bank if there are any special state law requirements about notifying the beneficiary. In a few states, a pay-on-death provision isn't effective unless you have notified the beneficiary that you've set up the account. Your bank should be able to fill you in on your state's rules.

2. Pension Plans and Retirement Accounts

Retirement accounts such as IRAs and Keogh accounts weren't designed to be probate-avoidance devices, but they can easily be used that way. All you have to do is name a beneficiary to receive the funds still in your pension plan or retirement account at your death, and the funds will not go through probate.

After age 70, however, federal law requires you to withdraw at least a certain amount every year or face a monetary penalty. The amount is refigured every year, based on your current life expectancy.

3. Life Insurance

Life insurance is a good way to provide surviving family members with quick cash for debts, living expenses and, in larger estates, estate taxes. And because you name the beneficiary in the policy itself, not in your will, life insurance proceeds don't go through probate.

The only circumstance in which life insurance proceeds are subject to probate is if the beneficiary named in the policy is your estate. That's done occasionally if the estate will need immediate cash to pay debts and taxes, but it's usually counterproductive. It's almost always a better idea to name your spouse, children or other beneficiary who can take the money free of probate and use it to pay debts and taxes.

Although the proceeds of a life insurance policy don't go through probate, they are included in your estate for federal estate tax purposes. If you think your estate will be liable for federal estate taxes (which usually means that it must be worth more than $600,000 at your death), you can reduce the tax bill by giving ownership of the policy to the beneficiary at least three years before your death. When ownership of the policy itself is transferred, gift tax may be assessed based on the present value of the policy. But at your death, the proceeds will not be counted as part of your taxable estate.

For help with choosing a life insurance policy from the bewildering array now available, see *How to Buy the Right Life Insurance Policy at the Right Price* (Consumer Reports Books).

LIFE INSURANCE TO PROVIDE FOR YOUR CHILDREN

If you have young children but not much money, consider buying a moderate amount of term life insurance, which would provide cash to support your children if you died while they were still young. Because term life insurance pays benefits only if you die during the covered period (often five or ten years), it's far cheaper than other types of life insurance. You can stop renewing the insurance when by the end of the term, the children will be on their own or your estate will be large enough to support them until they are.

---

4. Joint Tenancy

Joint tenancy is one of the most popular probate-avoidance devices around. It's an efficient and practical way to transfer some kinds of property, but for other kinds of property, a living trust is a better choice.

a. How Joint Tenancy Works

Joint tenancy is a way two or more people can hold title to property they own together. It is available in almost all states (see list below).

STATE LAW RESTRICTIONS ON JOINT TENANCY	
Alaska	No joint tenancy in real estate, except for husband and wife
Pennsylvania	No joint tenancy in real estate (but this rule has been questioned in court decisions)
Tennessee	No joint tenancy except for husband and wife
Texas	No joint tenancy in any kind of property unless there's a written joint tenancy agreement signed by the owners

For estate planning purposes, the most important characteristic of joint tenancy is that when one joint owner (called a joint tenant) dies, the surviving joint owners automatically get complete ownership of the property. This is called the "right of survivorship." The property doesn't go through probate court—there is only some simple paperwork to fill out to transfer the property into the name of the surviving owner.

EXAMPLE: Evelyn and her daughter own a car in joint tenancy. When Evelyn dies, her half-interest in the car will go to her daughter without probate. Her daughter will need only to fill out a simple form to transfer ownership of the car into her own name.

Joint tenancy certainly has the virtue of simplicity. To create a joint tenancy, all the co-owners need to do is pay attention to the way they are listed on the document that shows ownership of property, such as a deed to real estate, a car's title slip or a card establishing a bank account. In the great majority of states, by calling themselves "joint tenants with the right of survivorship," the owners create a joint tenancy. (In a few states, additional specific words are necessary. If you aren't sure how to word a title document, ask a real estate lawyer or someone at a land title company.) All joint tenants must own equal shares of the property.

A joint tenant cannot leave his or her share to anyone other than the surviving joint tenants. So even if Evelyn, in the preceding example, left a will giving her half-interest in the car to her son instead of her daughter, the daughter would still get the car.

This rule isn't as ironclad as it may sound. A joint tenant can, while still alive, break the joint tenancy by transferring his or her interest in the property to someone else (or, in some states, to himself, but not as a "joint tenant"). The new owner isn't a joint tenant with the other original owners.

> **EXAMPLE:** David, Jan and Loren own property together in joint tenancy. David sells his one-third interest to Paul. Paul is not a joint tenant with Jan and Loren; he is a "tenant in common," free to leave his property to whomever he wants. Jan and Loren, however, are still joint tenants with respect to their two-thirds of the property; when one of them dies, the other will own the two-thirds.

Joint bank accounts. If you and someone else want to set up a joint tenancy account together, so that the survivor will get all the funds, normally you can do it in a few minutes at the bank. But in a few states, you may need to comply with certain formalities. Texas state law, for example, requires a written agreement—not just a signature card—to set up such an account. Your bank should be able to tell you about any requirements.

b. When to Consider Joint Tenancy

Joint tenancy often works well when couples (married or not) acquire real estate or other valuable property together. If they take title in joint tenancy, probate is avoided when the first owner dies.

But there are advantages to transferring the property to your living trust, even if you already own it in joint tenancy.

First, a living trust, unlike joint tenancy, allows you to name an alternate beneficiary—someone who will inherit the property if the first beneficiary (your spouse) doesn't survive you. If you own property in joint tenancy, and you and your spouse die at the same time, the property will go to the residuary beneficiary named in your will—but it will have to go through probate first.

Second, if you transfer joint tenancy property to a living trust, you will avoid probate both when the first spouse dies and when the second spouse dies. With joint tenancy, probate is avoided only when the first spouse dies. The second spouse, who owns the property alone after the first spouse's death, must take some other measure—such as transferring it to a living trust—to avoid probate.

c. When to Think Twice About Joint Tenancy

Joint tenancy is usually a poor estate planning device when an older person, seeking only to avoid probate, puts solely-owned property into joint tenancy with someone else. Doing this creates several potential problems that don't occur with a living trust:

You can't change your mind. If you make someone else a co-owner, in joint tenancy, of property that you now own yourself, you give up half ownership of the property. The new owner has rights that you can't take back. For example, the new owner can sell or mortgage his or her share. And even if the other joint tenant's half isn't mortgaged, it could still be lost to creditors.

> **EXAMPLE:** Maureen, a widow, signs a deed that puts her house into joint tenancy with her son to avoid probate at her death. Later, the son's business fails, and he is sued by creditors. His half interest in the house may be taken by the creditors to pay the court judgment, which means that the house might be sold. Maureen would get the value of her half in cash; her son's half of the proceeds would go to pay the creditors.

By contrast, if you put property in a revocable living trust, you don't give up any ownership now. You are always free to change your mind about who you want to get the property at your death.

There's no way to handle the incapacity of one joint tenant. There can be serious problems if one joint tenant becomes incapacitated and cannot make decisions. The other owners must get legal authority to sell or mortgage the property. That may mean going to court to get someone (called a conservator, in most states) appointed to manage the incapacitated person's affairs. (This problem can be partially dealt with if the joint tenant has signed a document called a "Durable Power of Attorney," giving someone authority to manage her affairs if she cannot. See Section F, below.)

With a living trust, if you (the grantor) becomes incapacitated, the successor trustee (or the other spouse, if it's a shared marital spouse) takes over and has full authority to manage the property. No court proceedings are necessary.

Gift taxes may be assessed. If you create a joint tenancy by making another person a co-owner, federal gift tax may be assessed on the transfer. This probably isn't a reason not to transfer property; making a gift can be a sound estate planning strategy. But be aware that if gifts to one person (except your spouse) exceed $10,000 per year, you must file a gift tax return with the IRS. (There's one other exception: If two or more people open a bank account in joint tenancy, but one person puts all or most of the money in, no gift tax is assessed against that person. A taxable gift may be made, however, when a joint tenant who has contributed little or nothing to the account withdraws money from it.) (See Section D, below.)

Surviving spouse misses an income tax break. If you make your spouse a joint tenant with you on property you own separately, the surviving spouse could miss out on a potentially big income tax break later, when the property is sold.

When it comes to property owned in joint tenancy, the Internal Revenue Service rule is that a surviving spouse gets a stepped-up tax basis only for the half of the property owned by the deceased spouse. The tax basis is the amount from which taxable profit is figured when property is sold. When the property is later sold, this means higher tax if the property went up in value between the time the joint tenancy was created and when the first spouse died.

You may not face this problem if you live in a community property state. If property held in joint tenancy is actually community property, the entire property will qualify for a stepped-up tax basis if the surviving spouse can show the IRS that it was in fact community property. But it's up to you to prove it; when one spouse dies, the IRS presumes that property held in joint tenancy is not community property.

5. Tenancy by the Entirety

"Tenancy by the entirety" is a form of property ownership that is similar to joint tenancy, but is limited to married couples. It is available only in the states listed below.

STATES THAT ALLOW TENANCY BY THE ENTIRETY

Alaska*	Indiana*	Missouri	Oregon*
Arkansas	Kentucky*	New Jersey*	Pennsylvania
Delaware	Maryland	New York*	Tennessee
District of Columbia	Massachusetts	North Carolina*	Vermont
Florida	Michigan*	Ohio	Virginia*
Hawaii	Mississippi	Oklahoma	Wyoming*

*allowed for real estate only

Tenancy by the entirety has almost the same advantages and disadvantages of joint tenancy and is most useful in the same kind of situation: when a couple acquires property together. When one owner (spouse) dies, the surviving co-owner (the other spouse) inherits the property. The property doesn't go through probate.

If property is held in tenancy by the entirety, neither spouse can transfer his or her half of the property alone, either while alive or by will or trust. It must go to the surviving spouse. (This is different from joint tenancy; a joint tenant is free to transfer his or her share to someone else during his life.)

> **EXAMPLE:** Fred and Ethel hold title to their house in tenancy by the entirety. If Fred wanted to sell or give away his half-interest in the house, he could not do so without Ethel's signature on the deed.

6. Gifts

If you make gifts while you're alive, there will be less property in your estate to go through probate when you die. But if probate avoidance is your goal, usually it's better to use one of the other methods discussed above, which let you keep control over your property while you're alive, than to give away everything before you die.

Making sizeable gifts may be a good strategy if you and your spouse expect to have a combined estate worth more than $600,000 at your death, and you want to reduce the eventual federal estate tax bite. (See Section D, below.)

7. Simplified Probate Proceedings

Many states have begun, albeit slowly, to dismantle some of the more onerous parts of probate. They have created categories of property and beneficiaries that don't have to go through a full-blown probate court proceeding. If your family can take advantage of these procedures after your death, you may not need to worry too much about avoiding probate.

Almost every state has some kind of simplified (summary) probate or out-of-court transfer process for one or more of these categories:

Small estates. For "small estates," many states have created an out-of-court procedure that lets people collect the property they've inherited by filling out a sworn statement (affidavit) and giving it to the person who has the property.

Typically, the beneficiary must also provide some kind of proof of his or her right to inherit, such as a death certificate and copy of the will. What qualifies as a small estate varies from state to state; the maximum goes from $5,000 to $60,000.

Personal property. In some states, the only property that qualifies for simplified transfer procedures is personal property—that is, anything except real estate.

Property left to the surviving spouse. In some states, if a surviving spouse inherits less than a certain amount of property, no probate is necessary.

Most people leave property that is worth more than can be passed without probate under state probate simplification laws. In many states, if the value of your entire estate exceeds the maximum set by law for simplified probate, you cannot use simplified probate procedures—even if most of your property is being passed through probate-avoidance devices such as a living trust.

> **EXAMPLE:** At her death, Jane has an estate worth $300,000. Her major asset is her home, worth $200,000, which she passes to her daughter through a living trust. She also passes $80,000 worth of other property through other probate-avoidance devices. That leaves $20,000 of property. In Jane's state, the maximum estate size for streamlined probate procedures is $25,000. But Jane's heirs can't use the simplified procedures for the last $20,000 of property, because Jane's total estate exceeds the limit.

In some states, however, even if your total estate is too large, you can still make use of the simplified procedures if the amount that actually goes through probate is under the limit. So, to continue with the example, in some states, the $20,000 of Jane's estate that isn't taken care of by other probate-avoidance devices could go through the simplified probate procedure.

 Every state's approach is listed in *Plan Your Estate,* by Denis Clifford and Cora Jordan (Nolo Press).

D. Federal Gift and Estate Tax

The revocable living trust you make with *Living Trust Maker* won't help you save on estate taxes. If you and your spouse expect to have a combined estate worth more than $600,000, or you have already given away large amounts of property (more than $10,000 in one year to one beneficiary), consult a lawyer or tax planner about ways to reduce your federal estate taxes.

This section briefly discusses the basics of the federal estate and gift tax.

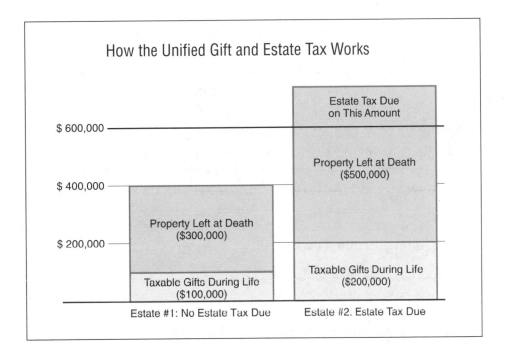

1. How the Federal Gift and Estate Tax Works

The federal government taxes both gifts made during life and at death. That's why the proper name of the federal estate tax is the "unified gift and estate tax." Congress reasoned that if only gifts made at death were taxed, everyone would give away as much property as they could during their lives. No tax is paid until your death (unless you give away an enormous amount of property while you're alive), when your combined gift and estate tax liability is calculated.

The tax won't affect you unless you give away or leave a substantial amount of property. First, many gifts are exempt from tax (see Section 2, below). In addition, you can transfer up to another $600,000 of property, either by gifts while you are alive or at your death (by living trust, will or other method), without incurring federal gift and estate tax.

EXAMPLE: Susan doesn't make any taxable gifts during her life and leaves $500,000 worth of property at her death, using a living trust and back-up will. Her estate owes no federal gift and estate tax.

Property you leave to your spouse (as long as he or she is a U.S. citizen) is not taxed, regardless of amount. (Property left to a non-citizen spouse does not qualify for the unlimited marital deduction.) This is called the marital deduction. There is no comparable estate tax exemption for unmarried couples.

⚠ THE MARITAL DEDUCTION TRAP

Older couples who have a combined estate of more than $600,000 and rely on the marital deduction will probably be in for big estate tax bills on the death of the second spouse, who gets no marital deduction. (See Section 2.b, below.)

2. Reducing Estate Tax Liability

A living trust, or any other probate-avoidance technique, has no effect on estate tax liability. Property you leave in joint tenancy or in a living trust is still considered part of your estate for federal estate tax purposes. There are, however, a few strategies to reduce the tax bill. We discuss them briefly here.

If you want to take steps to reduce eventual estate taxes, consult *Plan Your Estate*, by Denis Clifford and Cora Jordan (Nolo Press), or see a knowledgeable attorney.

a. Gifts

If you don't need all your income and property to live on, making sizeable gifts while you're alive can be a good way to reduce eventual federal estate taxes.

Tax-exempt gifts. Only gifts larger than $10,000 made to one person or organization in one calendar year count toward the $600,000 exemption. You can give smaller gifts tax-free.

EXAMPLE: Allen and Julia give their two daughters each $20,000 every year for four years. They have transferred $160,000 without becoming liable for gift tax.

Other gifts are exempt regardless of amount, including:

- gifts between spouses who are U.S. citizens (gifts to spouses who are not United States citizens are exempt only up to $100,000 per year)
- gifts paid directly for medical bills or school tuition, and
- gifts to tax-exempt charitable organizations.

If you make gifts subject to tax during your life, they are counted toward the $600,000. But though you will have to file a gift tax return, you don't pay any tax when you make a gift unless you give away more than $600,000 worth of property during your life. Otherwise, your combined gift and estate tax liability is paid after your death, out of the property in your estate.

EXAMPLE: Harry gives his daughter $25,000 one year. Although he must file a federal gift tax return, he does not pay tax on the $15,000 that is not tax-exempt. At his death, if his taxable gifts and the property he leaves exceed $600,000, his estate will have to pay tax.

Gifts made within three years of death. A few types of gifts made in the last three years of someone's life are considered part of that person's taxable estate—that is, they don't qualify as gifts for tax purposes. The most important, for most people, are gifts of life insurance policies and gifts made directly from a revocable trust—that is, from the trustee to the recipient. (IRS Technical Advice Memorandum 8609005.)

For that reason, it's important not to give away property directly from your living trust if you are concerned about estate tax. If you give away trust property within three years before your death, the IRS considers the property part of your estate at your death—which means estate taxes may be due on it. (IRS Letter Ruling 9049002 (1990).) To get around this rule, simply transfer the property from the living trust to yourself, and then give it away. That way, the property you give away won't be considered part of your taxable estate when you die.

b.   Marital Life Estate Trusts

Despite the marital deduction, which eliminates estate tax on property left to a surviving spouse who is a U.S. citizen, most elderly couples who have a combined estate of more than $600,000 should avoid leaving large sums to one another. The marital deduction really just postpones estate tax until the second spouse dies.

Say, for example, a husband leaves all his property to his wife. At the husband's death, no estate tax is due. But when the widow dies, the marital deduction won't apply. Her estate will have to pay a much larger tax than if the husband had left his property directly to children or other beneficiaries.

If the surviving spouse is not elderly, this isn't a problem. She has plenty of time to enjoy or give away the property. But for older couples, piling lots of money into the survivor's estate can be a real tax trap.

One way around this trap is for each spouse to put their property in a "marital life estate trust," sometimes called an "A-B trust." When one spouse dies, his or her half of the property is held in trust for the children. The surviving spouse gets certain rights to the deceased spouse's half of the property for life; for example, the right to live in the family home or to receive any income the property generates. When the second spouse dies, the property goes to the children outright. Using this kind of trust keeps the second spouse's estate half as small as it would be if the property were left to the spouse—which means that estate taxes may be avoided altogether.

These examples show how a marital life estate trust can cut back drastically on estate taxes.

EXAMPLE 1: No life estate trust. Thomas and Maria, husband and wife, are in their mid-70s, and each has an estate worth $550,000. Thomas dies in 1993. He leaves all his property to Maria, so no estate tax is assessed because of the marital deduction. But the size of Maria's estate rises to $1,100,000 (plus any appreciation). At Maria's death, all property worth more than $600,000 that is not exempt (because it was given to a tax-exempt charity or for some other reason) is heavily taxed. The tax bill: $194,000.

EXAMPLE 2: With life estate trust. Thomas and Maria each establish a marital life estate trust, with the income to go to the survivor for life and the principal to the children at the survivor's death. When Thomas dies, Maria's estate remains at $550,000, plus any income she receives from the trust property.

Maria dies in 1994. Because $600,000 can be left to anyone free of estate tax, there is no estate tax liability either from Maria's $550,000, which now goes to the children, or from Thomas's $550,000, which now goes to the children under the terms of the trust.

Unlike a probate-avoidance revocable living trust, a marital life estate trust controls what happens to property for years after the first spouse's death. A couple that makes one must be sure that the surviving spouse will be financially and emotionally comfortable receiving only the income from the money or property placed in trust, with the children (or other persons) as the actual owner of the property.

Marital life estate trusts have other uses besides saving on estate taxes; see Section G, below.

Living Trust Maker does not create a marital life estate trust. If you want such a trust, you can find forms and instructions in *Make Your Own Living Trust*, by Denis Clifford (Nolo Press), or see an experienced estate planning lawyer.

c. Generation-Skipping Trusts for Grandchildren

A "generation-skipping" trust won't reduce your own estate tax liability; it can, however, exempt up to $1 million from tax in the next generation.

With this kind of trust, your children are entitled to receive income from trust property but can't touch the principal. The principal goes to your grandchildren at the death of your children. The property you leave in such a trust is included in your taxable estate when you die. But it's not included in your children's taxable estate when they die.

E. State Death Taxes

Twenty-four states and the District of Columbia have effectively abolished state death taxes. Nevada is the only state with no death taxes, period. All the other states listed below impose only a "pickup tax," which means the state is entitled to part of any federal estate tax you pay. You don't pay any extra state tax.

STATES WITHOUT DEATH TAXES

Alabama	Florida	Missouri	Utah
Alaska	Georgia	Nevada	Vermont
Arizona	Hawaii	New Mexico	Virginia
Arkansas	Illinois	North Dakota	West Virginia
California	Maine	Oregon	Washington
Colorado	Minnesota	Texas	Wyoming
District of Columbia			

The rest impose death taxes on:

- all real estate owned in the state, no matter where the deceased lived, and
- all other property of residents of the state, no matter where it's located.

1. Your Residence for State Death Tax Purposes

State death taxes apply to all persons who live permanently in that state. If you divide your time between a state that doesn't impose inheritance tax (or has very low ones) and one with high death taxes, you'll want to establish your permanent residence in the lower tax state.

> **EXAMPLE:** A couple divides the year between Florida and New York. Florida effectively has no death taxes. New York imposes comparatively stiff estate taxes, with rates ranging from 2% for $50,000 or less, to 21% for $10,100,000 or more. Other things being equal, it makes sense for the couple to make Florida their legal residence.

To establish your legal residence in a particular state, you should should register all vehicles there, keep bank and other financial accounts there and vote there.

Establishing residence in a no-tax state can be tricky if you also live in a high-tax one, because the high-tax state has a financial incentive to conclude that you really reside there. If you have a large estate, and a complicated two-or-more-state living situation, consult a knowledgeable tax lawyer or accountant.

2. Estate Planning for State Death Taxes

If you live or own real estate in a state that has death taxes, consider the impact of those taxes on your estate. In many instances, the bite taken from estates by state death taxes is annoying but relatively minor.

In some states, however, tax liability is significant, especially for property given to non-relatives. For example, Nebraska imposes a 15% death tax rate if $25,000 is left to a friend, but only 1% if it's given to a spouse.

Death tax rules for all states are summarized in *Plan Your Estate*, by Denis Clifford and Cora Jordan (Nolo Press). More detailed information is available from state tax officials.

F. Planning for Incapacity

A living trust can be a big help if you become unable to manage your own affairs, because your successor trustee (or your spouse, if you make a shared marital trust) can take over management of trust property. That person, however, has no power over any of your other financial or health affairs. For that reason, you should prepare some other documents as well and coordinate them with your living trust.

1. Durable Powers of Attorney

The best way to plan for the management of your financial affairs not covered by your living trust is to use a document called a "Durable Power of Attorney for Finances." This document gives a trusted person you choose, called your "attorney-in-fact," the legal authority to manage your finances (except for property owned by your living trust) on your behalf.

You may also want to appoint a trusted person (not necessarily the same person) to make healthcare decisions for you. You can do this with a document called a "Durable Power of Attorney for Healthcare."

Both documents can be worded so that they only take effect if you become incapacitated.

Instructions and forms for preparing durable powers of attorney for finances are in *Who Will Handle Your Finances If You Can't?,* by Denis Clifford and Mary Randolph (Nolo Press).

2. Living Wills

If you're concerned about being hooked up to life support systems, and other issues surrounding dying a natural death, you may also want a "living will." (Despite the confusingly similar names, living wills and living trusts are completely different animals.)

A living will is a document addressed to your doctors. In it you state your preferences about treatment, including life support systems. You may also, depending on state law, be able to name a "proxy"—a trusted relative or friend who can make certain healthcare decisions for you. The extent to which doctors must follow your instructions depends on your state's law and what you specify in the living will. Some states, for example, do not require a doctor to stop artificial feeding even if a patient's living will requested it. And in some states, living wills are effective only after you have been diagnosed with a terminal illness.

But even if not legally binding, your living will can serve as valuable evidence of your wishes if family, friends or doctors disagree about the treatment you should receive.

You can make a living will tailored to your state's laws with *WillMaker 5.0,* software from Nolo Press.

Reminder. Whatever arrangements you make concerning your wishes in case of incapacity, be sure to let your family know what your wishes are, what documents you have signed and where you keep them.

G. Long-Term Property Distribution Methods

In certain circumstances, you may want to dictate how your property is to be distributed over many years. You may want to leave property to people who, for one reason or another, may not be able to manage it for themselves. Or you may want to leave property to your spouse for his or her life, but be sure it eventually goes to your children. This is especially true if you marry later in life and have children from a former marriage.

Here, we briefly discuss a few methods to accomplish these goals, but you'll need a lawyer's help.

For instructions on how to leave property to a minor or young adult, and have someone manage it until the beneficiary is older, see Chapter 5 or 6, Part 7.

1. Marital Life Estate Trusts

If you have children from a previous marriage, you may want your current spouse to have some of your property during his or her life, but ensure that the property eventually goes to your children. That way, children receive a fair share of your property, and your spouse receives income for the rest of his or her life.

The technique is for each spouse to leave his or her property in a "marital life estate trust," discussed as a tax-saving device in Section D, above. The survivor receives interest income from trust property, and often the use of real estate in the trust. The property itself goes to the first spouse's children when the surviving spouse dies.

Whether or not this arrangement is a good one depends on your situation. If relations could become strained between your children and your current spouse, you may very well not want to set things up so that they essentially share ownership of property for many years.

2. Spendthrift Trusts

If you want to leave property to an adult who just can't handle money, a "spendthrift trust," which doles the money out little by little, is a good idea. A spendthrift trust keeps the money from being squandered by the beneficiary or seized by the beneficiary's creditors.

3. Trusts for Disabled Persons

A person with a physical or mental disability may not be able to handle property, no matter what his or her age. Often, the solution is to establish a trust with a competent adult as trustee to manage the trust property.

The trust should be carefully prepared by an expert familiar with the state law, so that the trust won't jeopardize the beneficiary's eligibility for government benefits.

4. Flexible Trusts

You may want the determination of how your property is spent after your death to be decided in the future, not before you die. The usual way to do this is to create a "sprinkling trust," authorizing the trustee to decide how to spend trust money for several beneficiaries.

What Kind of Living Trust Do You Need?

L*iving Trust Maker* makes two kinds of revocable living trusts: one for an individual and one for a married couple. Your first decision—probably an easy one—is to decide which is right for you.

A. If You Are Single

If you are single, you must use the individual trust. You can use it to transfer any of your property—both property you own in your name alone and your share of co-owned property, including partnership property.

If you and someone else own valuable items of property together—a house, for example—you can each transfer your half-interest to a separate living trust. An alternative, if you both want the survivor to inherit the property, is to use another probate-avoidance method, such as holding title to the property in joint tenancy. (But this may have adverse tax consequences; see Chapter 3, A Living Trust as Part of Your Estate Plan.)

B. If You Are Married

If you are married, you and your spouse have a choice: You can create a shared living trust or separate individual ones. Or you could make a shared trust and individual trusts.

Most couples prefer to make one shared trust, because that way they don't have to divide property they own together. But you may want to make separate trusts if you and your spouse own most of your property separately. Another reason to make separate trusts is if both spouses want to keep complete control over their own trust property. With a shared trust, either spouse has authority over all trust property while both spouses are alive. (See Chapter 6, Creating a Shared Marital Trust.)

Before you make this decision, make sure you understand the marital property laws of your state. This section briefly explains the two systems of marital property laws: community property and non-community property.

IF YOU'RE UNSURE OF YOUR MARITAL STATUS

Most people are quite certain of their marital status. If you're not, here's what you need to know.

The divorce decree. Don't assume you're divorced until you have a final decree of divorce (or dissolution, as it's called in some states) issued by a state court in the United States.

If you think you're divorced but never saw the final decree, contact the court clerk in the county where you think the divorce was granted. Give the clerk your name, your ex-spouse's name and the date, as close as you know it, of the divorce.

Legal separation. Even if a court has declared you and your spouse legally separated, and you plan to divorce, you are still married. It's not over until you get the divorce decree.

Foreign divorces. Divorces issued to U.S. citizens by courts in Mexico, the Dominican Republic or another country may not be valid if challenged, especially if all the paperwork was handled by mail. In other words, if you or your spouse got a quickie foreign divorce, you may well be still married under the laws of your state. If you think that someone might make a claim to some of your property after your death based on the invalidity of a foreign divorce, see a lawyer.

Common law marriages. In some states, a couple can become legally married by living together, intending to be married and presenting themselves to the world as a married couple. Even in states that allow such common law marriages, most couples who live together don't have common law marriages. If you really do have a valid common law marriage, you must go to court and get a divorce to end it—there's no such thing as a common law divorce.

Common law marriages can be created in Alabama, Colorado, District of Columbia, Georgia, Idaho, Iowa, Kansas, Montana, New Hampshire (for inheritance purposes only), Ohio, Oklahoma, Pennsylvania, Rhode Island, South Carolina and Texas. If a common law marriage is created in one of these states, and the couple moves to another state, they are still legally married.

Gay or lesbian couples. No state allows marriage between two people of the same sex, even if a religious ceremony has been performed.

Legal Manual

1. Community Property States

Arizona	Louisiana	New Mexico	Washington
California	Nevada	Texas	Wisconsin
Idaho			

In these states, the general rule is that spouses share everything 50-50. All property earned or otherwise acquired by either spouse during the marriage, regardless of whose name is on the title slip, is community property. Each spouse owns a one-half interest in it. Property acquired by one spouse by gift or inheritance, however, or before marriage, is not community property; it is the separate property of that spouse.

For example, if while married you bought real estate with money you earned during marriage, your spouse legally owns a half interest in it, unless you both signed an agreement keeping it separate.

Typically, most property owned by spouses is community property, especially if they have been married for a number of years. So it usually makes sense to make one shared marital trust.

> **EXAMPLE:** Rob and Cecile live in Nevada, a community property state. They have been married for 20 years. Except for some bonds that Cecile inherited from her parents, virtually all their valuable property—house, stocks, car—is owned together. The money they brought to the marriage in separate bank accounts has long since been mixed with community property, making it community property too. Rob and Cecile decide to make a shared living trust.

Making two individual living trusts would require splitting ownership of the co-owned assets, which can be a clumsy process. For example, to transfer a co-owned house into two separate trusts would require the spouses to sign and record a deed transferring half-interests in the house to separate trusts. And to transfer household furnishings to separate trusts, spouses would have to allocate each item to a trust or each risk transferring a half-interest in a couch to separate trusts.

There is another advantage to making a shared trust if the spouses want to leave significant trust property to each other. With a shared trust, property left by one spouse to the survivor stays in the living trust when the first spouse dies; no transfer is necessary when the first spouse dies. With separate trusts, property left to the surviving spouse must usually be transferred first from the trust to the surviving spouse, and then (to avoid probate) to the surviving spouse's living trust.

If you and your spouse own most of your property together but each have some separate property, a shared marital trust is fine. You can transfer all of it to the trust, and each spouse can name beneficiaries (including each other) to receive his or her separate property.

If, however, you and your spouse own most of your property separately, you may want to make individual trusts. Most couples in this situation fit one of these profiles:

- You and your spouse signed an agreement stating that each spouse's earnings and other income are separate, not community property, and you have kept your property separate.
- You are recently married and have little or no community property.
- You each own mostly separate property acquired before your marriage (or by gift or inheritance), which you conscientiously keep from being mixed with community property. Couples who marry later in life and no longer work often fit into this category. Not only is the property they owned before the marriage separate, but federal Social Security benefits and certain retirement plan benefits are also separate, not community, property.

If you and your spouse decide on separate living trusts, each of you will transfer your separately owned property to your individual trust. If you own some property—a house, for example—together, you can each transfer your portion to your trust.

2. Non-Community Property States

Alabama	Indiana	Montana	Pennsylvania
Alaska	Iowa	Nebraska	Rhode Island
Arkansas	Kansas	New Hampshire	South Carolina
Colorado	Kentucky	New Jersey	South Dakota
Connecticut	Maine	New York	Tennessee
Delaware	Maryland	North Carolina	Utah
District of Columbia	Massachusetts	North Dakota	Vermont
Florida	Michigan	Ohio	Virginia
Georgia	Minnesota	Oklahoma	West Virginia
Hawaii	Mississippi	Oregon	Wyoming
Illinois	Missouri		

It's increasingly common for couples, especially if they are older and have children from a prior marriage, to sign an agreement (before or during the marriage) to own property separately. Or they may not make a formal agreement, but carefully avoid mixing their property together. If you and your spouse each own substantial amounts of separate property and want to make sure it is kept that way, you may prefer to make individual living trusts.

In a non-community property state, it's usually fairly easy for spouses to keep track of who owns what. The spouse whose name is on the title document (deed, brokerage account paper or title slip, for example) owns it.

EXAMPLE: Howard and Louisa live in Indiana, a non-community property state. Both have grown children from prior marriages. When they married, they moved into Howard's house. They both have their own bank accounts and investments, and one joint checking account which they own as joint tenants with right of survivorship.

Each makes an individual living trust. Howard, who dies first, leaves his house to Louisa, but most of his other property is left to his children. The funds in the checking account are not included in his living trust, but pass to Louisa, also without probate, because the account was held in joint tenancy. Howard's other accounts go to his children, under the pay-on-death arrangement he has with the bank. (Joint tenancy, pay-on-death accounts and other probate-avoidance methods are discussed in Chapter 3, A Living Trust as Part of Your Estate Plan.)

SPOUSE'S OR MINOR CHILD'S RIGHT TO INHERIT

Your spouse or minor child may have the right, under state law, to inherit some of your property after your death. A living trust does not let you evade those laws. (See Chapter 2, About Living Trusts.)

Creating an Individual Trust

Legal Manual

Whena you create your living trust document with *Living Trust Maker*, you have only a few choices to make. Basically, you must decide five things:

- Whether to make an individual living trust or a shared trust with your spouse.
- What property you want to put in your living trust.
- Who you want to receive the trust property at your death. These people or organizations are the beneficiaries of your living trust.
- Who is to be the successor trustee—the person you want to distribute trust property at your death.
- How you should arrange for someone to manage trust property inherited by beneficiaries who are too young to handle it without supervision.

You may already have a good idea of how you want to decide these issues. This chapter discusses the factors you should think about as you make each decision. It is organized the same way as the program is (Parts 1 through 7), so that you can easily refer to it while you're actually running *Living Trust Maker*. It's a good idea, though, to read through this chapter before you sit down at the computer—it will make the whole process clearer and easier.

CHECKLIST FOR CREATING A VALID LIVING TRUST

√ Prepare the trust document with *Living Trust Maker*.

√ Print out the trust document and sign it in front of a notary public.

√ Transfer ownership of the property listed in the trust document into the trust.

√ Update your trust document when needed.

An Overview:
How an Individual Trust Works

Here, in brief, are the important points about how an individual trust works:

Control of trust property. You will be the trustee of your living trust, so you'll have control over the property in the trust.

Amendments or revocation. At any time, you can revoke the trust, add property to it, remove property from it, or modify any term of the trust document.

After your death. After you die, the person named in the trust document as successor trustee takes over. He or she is responsible for distributing trust property to the beneficiaries and managing any trust property left to a young beneficiary in a child's subtrust (explained later).

Here's an example to show you how the trust works.

EXAMPLE: Lenora sets up a revocable living trust to avoid probate. In the trust document, she makes herself the trustee, and appoints her son Ben as successor trustee, to take over as trustee after her death. She transfers her valuable property—her house, savings accounts and stocks—to the living trust.

The trust document states that Lenora's grandson, Max, is to receive the stocks when she dies. She provides that if Max is not yet 21 when she dies, the stocks will stay in a "child's subtrust," managed by the successor trustee Ben. Everything else goes to her son, Ben.

When Lenora dies, Ben follows the terms of the trust document and in his capacity as trustee, distributes all the trust property except the stocks to himself, without probate.

He also manages the stocks inherited by Max, who is 16 at Lenora's death, until his 21st birthday. When all the property in the subtrust is given to Max or spent on his behalf, the subtrust ends.

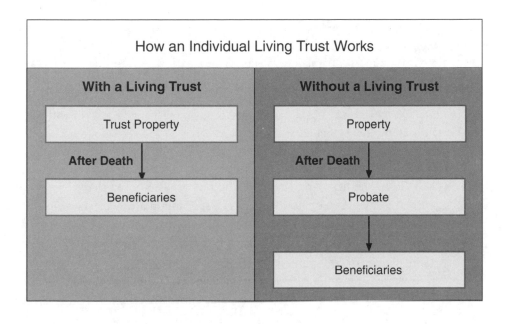

Part 1: Your State

In this part of the program, you choose the state that is your legal residence, also called your "domicile." That's the state where you live now and intend to keep living.

Your choice affects many aspects of your living trust, including the ways you can set up management for any trust property young beneficiaries may inherit and, if you are married, what property belongs to each spouse.

(You may notice that the list of states on the screen doesn't include Louisiana. We didn't forget it—but because Louisiana law is different from all other states, you can't use this program if you live there.)

A. If You Live in More Than One State

If during the course of a year you live in more than one state, your residence is the state with which you have the most significant contacts—where you vote, register vehicles, own valuable property, have bank accounts or run a business.

If you might be justified in claiming more than one state as your legal residence, you may want to arrange your affairs so that your legal residence is in the state with the most advantageous state estate tax laws. Some states (such as New York) impose stiff inheritance taxes; others (California and Florida, for example) have essentially no inheritance tax. If you have significant contacts with more than one state and a substantial estate, it may pay to have a lawyer with tax and estate planning experience advise you.

> **EXAMPLE:** Geraldine spends about half the year in Florida and the other half in New York. She has bank accounts and real estate in both states.
>
> To take advantage of Florida's lack of a state inheritance tax, she registers her car in Florida, votes there and moves her bank accounts there. This leaves her owning nothing in New York but a condominium near where her son lives. She decides to sell him the condo and lease it back six months of every year, severing her last important property ownership contact with New York.

B. If You Live Outside the United States

If you are living outside the U.S., your residence is the state you still have contacts with and expect to return to. If you don't maintain ties with a particular state and have a large estate, see a lawyer to discuss what state you should declare as your residence.

If you are in the Armed Forces and living out of the country temporarily, your legal residence is the state you declared as your Home of Record—the state you lived in before going overseas, or where your spouse or parents live.

Part 2: Your Name

The information the program next asks you for is easy: your name. The name you enter in this part of the program will form part of the name of your trust. For example, if you enter "William S. Jorgensen," your trust will be named "The William S. Jorgensen Revocable Living Trust." Your name will also automatically appear as the original trustee of your living trust (see Part 3, below).

Enter your name the way it appears on other formal business documents, such as your driver's license or bank accounts. This may or may not be the name on your birth certificate.

EXAMPLE: Your birth certificate lists your name as Rose Mary Green. But you've always gone by Mary, and always sign documents as Mary McNee, your married name. You would use Mary McNee on your living trust.

Use only one name; don't enter various versions of your name joined by "aka" (also known as).

If you go by more than one name, be sure that the name you use for your living trust is the one that appears on the ownership documents for property you plan to transfer to the trust. If it isn't, it could cause confusion later, and you should change the name on your ownership documents before you transfer the property to the trust.

EXAMPLE: You use the name William Dix for your trust, but own real estate in your former name of William Geicherwitz. You should prepare and sign a new deed, changing the name of the owner to William Dix, before you prepare another deed to transfer the property to your living trust.

Part 3: Trustees

To be legally valid, every trust must have a trustee—a person or institution to manage the property owned by the trust. When you create a living trust with this program, you are the trustee now. Someone else, who you named in the trust document to be the successor trustee, takes over after you have died.

A. The Original Trustee

You will be the original trustee of your living trust. As trustee, you will have complete control over the property that will technically be owned by the trust.

As a day-to-day, practical matter, it makes little difference that your property is now owned by your living trust. You won't have any special duties as trustee of your trust. You do not even need to file a separate income tax return for the living trust. Any income the property generates must be reported on your personal income tax return, as if the trust did not exist.

You have the same freedom to sell, give away or mortgage trust property as you did before you put the property into the living trust. The only difference is that you must now sign documents in your capacity as trustee. It's that easy.

> **EXAMPLE:** Celeste wants to sell a piece of land that is owned in the name of her living trust. She prepares a deed transferring ownership of the land from the trust to the new owner, and signs the deed as "Celeste Tornetti, trustee of the Celeste Tornetti Revocable Living Trust dated February 4, 1994."

NAMING SOMEONE ELSE AS TRUSTEE

In the unlikely event you don't want to be the original trustee of your living trust, you cannot use the trust created by *Living Trust Maker;* you need to see an estate planning lawyer to draw up a more specialized living trust. Naming someone else as trustee has important tax consequences and means you give up control over trust property.

B. The Successor Trustee

You must choose a successor trustee—someone to act as trustee after your death or incapacity. (Incapacity is the inability to manage your affairs. The trust document created by *Living Trust Maker* defines incapacity and requires that incapacity must be documented in writing by a physician before the successor trustee can take over management of the trust property.) The successor trustee has no power or responsibility while you are alive and capable of managing your affairs.

1. The Successor Trustee's Duties if You Are Incapacitated

If you become physically or mentally incapacitated, as certified in writing by a physician, and unable to manage your affairs, the successor trustee takes over management of the property in your living trust.

In this situation, the successor trustee has authority to use trust property for your healthcare, support and welfare. The law requires him or her to act honestly and prudently in managing the property. And because you are no longer the trustee, the new trustee must file an income tax return for the trust. At your death, any remaining trust property is distributed to your beneficiaries.

The successor trustee has no power over property not in your living trust, and no authority to make healthcare decisions for you. For this reason, it's also wise to create documents called Durable Powers of Attorney, giving the successor trustee authority to manage property not owned in the name of the trust and to make healthcare decisions. (See Chapter 3, A Living Trust as Part of Your Estate Plan, Section F.)

2. The Successor Trustee's Duties After Your Death

After your death, the successor trustee takes over as trustee. His or her primary responsibility is to distribute trust property to the beneficiaries named in your Declaration of Trust. That is usually a straightforward process that can be completed in a few weeks. An outline of the steps the successor trustee needs to take to transfer certain common kinds of property is in Chapter 10, After a Grantor Dies.

The successor trustee may, however, have long-term duties if the trust document creates a child's subtrust for trust property inherited by a young beneficiary (this is explained in Part 7, below).

3. Choosing a Successor Trustee

The person or institution you choose as successor trustee will have a crucial role: to manage your trust property (if you become incapacitated) or distribute it to your beneficiaries (after your death).

If the successor trustee is in charge of managing property over the long term, the trust document produced by *Living Trust Maker* gives him or her very broad authority, so that the trustee will be able to do whatever is necessary to respond to the demands of the circumstances. For example, the trustee has the power to invest trust funds in accounts, such as money market accounts, that are not federally insured. The trustee is also free to spend trust income or property for the health and welfare of the incapacitated spouse or the beneficiary of a child's subtrust.

Obviously, when you are giving someone this much power and discretion, you should choose someone with good common sense whom you trust completely, such as an adult son or daughter, other relative or close friend. If you don't know anyone who fits this description, think twice about establishing a living trust.

In most situations, the successor trustee will not need extensive experience in financial management; common sense, dependability and complete honesty are usually enough. A successor trustee who may have long-term responsibility over a young beneficiary's trust property needs more management and financial skills than a successor trustee whose only job is to distribute trust property. The successor trustee does have authority, under the terms of the trust document, to get any reasonably necessary professional help—from an accountant, lawyer or tax preparer, perhaps—and pay for it out of trust assets.

Usually, it makes sense to name just one person as successor trustee, to avoid any possibility of conflicts. But it's legal and may be desirable to name more than one person. For example, you might name two or more of your children, if you don't expect any disagreements between them and you think one of them might feel hurt and left out if not named.

Carefully consider the issue of conflicts, however. If you name more than one person as successor trustee, all of them must agree before they can act on behalf of the trust. If they can't agree, it could hold up the distribution of trust property to your beneficiaries. In extreme situations, the other trustees might even have to go to court to get the recalcitrant trustee removed, so that your instructions can be carried out. The result might be more bad feeling than if you had just picked one person to be trustee in the first place.

Having more than one successor trustee is especially likely to cause serious problems if the successor trustees are in charge of the property you have left to a young beneficiary in a child's subtrust. The trustees may have to manage a young beneficiary's property for many years, and will have many decisions to make about how to spend the money—greatly increasing the potential for conflict. (Children's subtrusts are discussed in Part 7, below.)

If you name more than one successor trustee, and one of them can't serve, the others will serve. If none of them can serve, the alternate you name (later in this section of the program) will take over.

It's perfectly legal to name a beneficiary of the trust (someone who will receive trust property after your death) as successor trustee. In fact, it's common.

EXAMPLE: Mildred names her only child, Allison, as both sole beneficiary of her living trust and successor trustee of the living trust. When Mildred dies, Allison uses her authority as trustee to transfer the trust property to herself.

The successor trustee does not have to live in the same state as you do. But if you are choosing between someone local and someone far away, think about how convenient it will be for the person you choose to distribute the living trust property after your death. Someone close by will probably have an easier job, especially with real estate transfers. But for transfers of property such as securities and bank accounts, it usually won't make much difference where the successor trustee lives.

INSTITUTIONS AS SUCCESSOR TRUSTEES

Normally, your first choice as successor trustee should be a flesh-and-blood person, not the trust department of a bank or other institution. Institutional trustees charge hefty fees, which come out of the trust property and leave less for your family and friends. And they probably won't even be interested in "small" living trusts—ones that contain less than several hundred thousand dollars worth of property.

But if there's no close relative or friend you think is capable of serving as your successor trustee, probably your best bet is to consider naming a private trust services company as successor trustee. Typically, their fees are pricey, but as a rule they charge less than a bank, and your affairs will probably receive more personal attention.

For a very large living trust, another possibility is to name a person and an institution as co-successor trustees. The bank or trust services company can do most of the paperwork, and the person can keep an eye on things and approve all transactions.

Obviously, before you finalize your living trust, you must check with the person or institution you've chosen to be your successor trustee. You want to be sure your choice is willing to serve.

If you don't, you may well create problems down the line. The person you've chosen may not want to serve, for a variety of reasons. And even if the person would be willing, if he or she doesn't know of his or her responsibilities, transfer of trust property after your death could be delayed.

If you choose an institution, you must check out the minimum size of trust it will accept and the fees it charges for management, and make arrangements for how the institution will take over as trustee at your death.

AVOIDING CONFLICTS WITH YOUR WILL AND OTHER DOCUMENTS

Your living trust gives your successor trustee the authority to manage trust property if you become incapacitated. To avoid conflicts, it's a good idea to name the person you choose as successor trustee in your will and Durable Power of Attorney for Finances, too.

- In your will, appoint your successor trustee to be executor, to be responsible for distributing your property (except living trust property) after your death.
- In your Durable Power of Attorney for Finances, appoint your successor trustee to be your attorney-in-fact, to have authority to make financial and property management decisions for property (except property owned in the name of the living trust) if you become incapacitated.

---

4. Payment of the Successor Trustee

Typically, the successor trustee of a simple probate-avoidance living trust isn't paid. This is because in most cases, the successor trustee's only job is to distribute the trust property to beneficiaries soon after the grantor's death. Often, the successor trustee inherits most of the trust property.

An exception is a successor trustee who manages the property in a child's subtrust. In that case, the successor trustee is entitled, under the terms of the trust document, to "reasonable compensation." The successor trustee decides what is reasonable and takes it from the trust property left to the young beneficiary.

Allowing the successor trustee to set the amount of the payment can work well, as long as your successor trustee is completely trustworthy. If the young beneficiary feels the trustee's fees are much too high, he or she will have to go to court to challenge them. If you want to restrict the successor trustee's freedom to decide on payment, see a lawyer.

The trust document created by *Living Trust Maker* does not require the successor trustee to post a bond (a kind of insurance policy) to guarantee conscientious fulfillment of his or her duties.

5. Naming an Alternate Successor Trustee

Living Trust Maker asks you to name an alternate, in case your first choice as successor trustee is unable to serve.

If you named more than one successor trustee, the alternate won't become trustee unless none of your original choices can serve.

EXAMPLE: Caroline names her two children, Eugene and Vanessa, as successor trustees. She names a close friend, Nicole, as alternate successor trustee. Because Vanessa is ill and can't serve as trustee, Eugene acts as sole successor trustee. If he becomes unable to serve, Nicole would take over.

If no one you named in the trust document can serve, the last trustee to serve has the power to appoint, in writing, another successor trustee. (See Chapter 10, After a Grantor Dies.)

EXAMPLE: To continue the previous example, if Nicole were ill and didn't have the energy to serve as successor trustee, she could appoint someone else to serve as trustee.

Part 4: Property to Be Put in Trust

Now you're getting to the heart of the program. In this part, you must list each item of property you want to transfer to your living trust. It will take some thought to decide what property to include and how to list it in the trust document. (Later in the program, you will name beneficiaries to receive each item of trust property at your death.)

This is a crucial step: Any property you don't list will not go into your living trust and will not pass under the terms of the trust. It may instead have to go through probate.

Adding property to the trust later. If you mistakenly leave something out or acquire more valuable property after you create your trust, you will be able to add it to your living trust. Chapter 9, Living With Your Living Trust, explains how.

A. Inventory Your Valuable Property

The first step is to take inventory—write down the valuable items of property you own. The categories listed below should jog your memory.

Even if you plan to leave everything to your spouse or children, you must make a list. That's because every item (or group of items, in some circumstances) must be specifically described and listed in the trust document.

When you list your property in the program, you can group items, if you're leaving them all to one beneficiary. For example, if you want to leave all your books to your best friend, there's no need to describe each one individually—unless your collection includes some particularly valuable or important books that you want to make extra sure get to the beneficiary.

After you've made an inventory, the next section will help you decide which items you want to transfer to your living trust so they don't have to go through probate after your death.

GETTING ORGANIZED

While you're taking stock of all your valuable property, it might be a good time to go a step further and gather the information your family will need at your death.

You can use your computer to get organized by using *Nolo's Personal RecordKeeper* database program. It can keep track of all the important information in your family's life, including securities data, investments, real estate records, medical information, insurance records, credit card information and more.

(Ordering information is in the back of the manual.)

VALUABLE PROPERTY

Animals

Antiques

Appliances

Art

Books

Business interests

 –Sole proprietorship

 –Partnership

 –Corporation

Business property (if you

 own a sole proprietorship)

Cameras & photographic

 equipment

Cash accounts

 –Certificates of deposit

 –Checking

 –Money market funds

 –Savings

China, crystal, silver

Coins, stamps

Collectibles

Computers

Copyrights, patents, trademarks

Electronic equipment

Furniture

Furs

Jewelry

Limited partnership

Precious metals

Real estate

 –Agricultural land

 –Boat/Marina dock space

 –Co-op

 –Condo

 –Duplex

 –House

 –Mobile home

 –Rental property

 –Time-share

 –Undeveloped land

 –Vacation house

Retirement accounts

 –401(k) plans

 –IRAs

 –Keogh plans

Royalties

Securities

 –Bonds

 –Commodities

 –Mutual funds

 –Stocks

 –U.S. bills, notes and bonds

Tools

Vehicles

 –Cars

 –Motorcycles

 –Bicycles

 –Boats

 –Motor homes/RVs

 –Planes

⚠ IF YOU'RE MARRIED

If you are married but are making an individual trust, remember that you can transfer to the trust only the property you own. To be sure you understand what you own and what your spouse owns, see Chapter 6, Creating a Shared Marital Trust, Part 4.

VALUABLE PROPERTY INVENTORY

_____

_____

_____

_____

_____

_____

_____

_____

_____

_____

_____

B. Decide What Property to Put in Your Living Trust

Now that you've got a list of what you own, you're ready to decide what items you want to transfer to your living trust. You're creating a revocable living trust primarily to avoid probate fees. As a general rule, the more an item is worth, the more it will cost to probate it. That means you should transfer at least your most valuable property items to your living trust (or use some other probate-avoidance device to leave them at your death). Think about including:

- houses and other real estate
- jewelry, antiques, furs and valuable furniture
- stock in a closely-held corporation
- stock, bond and other security accounts held by brokerages
- small business interests
- money market and bank accounts
- other financial accounts
- patents and copyrights
- precious metals
- valuable works of art
- valuable collections of stamps, coins or other objects.

> ### ADDING PROPERTY TO YOUR LIVING TRUST
>
> You will be able to add property to your living trust at any time. As trustee, you can always sell or give away property in the trust. You can also take it out of the living trust and put it back in your name as an individual. Chapter 9, Living With Your Living Trust, explains how to make these changes.

You don't need to put everything you own into a living trust to save money on probate. For some assets, you may decide to use other probate-avoidance devices instead of a living trust. Property that is of relatively low value (the amount depends on state law) may be exempt from probate or qualify for a streamlined probate procedure that's relatively fast and cheap. (See Chapter 3, A Living Trust as Part of Your Estate Plan.)

Even if the non-trust property does have to go through regular probate, attorney and appraisal fees are generally based on the value of the probated property, so they'll be relatively low.

This section discusses how to decide whether or not to transfer various kinds of property to your living trust.

1. Real Estate

The most valuable thing most people own is their real estate: their house, condominium or land. Many people create a living trust just to make sure a house doesn't go through probate. You can probably save your family substantial probate costs by transferring your real estate through a living trust.

If you own the property with someone else, however, you may not want to transfer your real estate to an individual living trust. (See Section 8, Co-Owned Property, below.)

Co-op apartments. If you own shares in a co-op corporation that owns your apartment, you'll have to transfer your shares to your living trust. You may run into difficulties with the corporation; some are reluctant to let a trust, even a revocable trust completely controlled by the grantor, own shares. Check the co-op corporation's rules to see if the transfer is allowed.

2. Small Business Interests

The delay, expense and court intrusion of probate can be especially detrimental to an ongoing small business. Using your living trust to transfer business interests to beneficiaries quickly after your death is almost essential if you want the beneficiaries to be able to keep the business running.

If you want to control the long-term management of your business, however, a revocable living trust is not the right vehicle. See an estate planning lawyer to draft a different kind of trust, with provisions tailored to your situation.

Different kinds of business organizations present different issues when you want to transfer your interest to your living trust:

Sole proprietorships. If you operate your business as a sole proprietorship, with all business assets held in your own name, you can simply transfer your business property to your living trust like you would any other property. You should also transfer the business's name itself: that transfers the customer goodwill associated with the name.

Partnership interests. If you operate your business as a partnership with other people, you can probably transfer your partnership share to your living trust. If there is a partnership certificate, it must be changed to include the trust as owner of your share.

Some partnership agreements require the people who inherit a deceased partner's share of the business to offer that share to the other partners before taking it. But that happens after death, so it shouldn't affect your ability to transfer the property through a living trust.

It's not common, but a partnership agreement may limit or forbid transfers to a living trust. If yours does, you and your partners may want to see a lawyer before you make any changes.

Solely-owned corporations. If you own all the stock of a corporation, you should have no difficulty transferring it to your living trust.

Closely-held corporations. A closely-held corporation is a corporation that doesn't sell shares to the public. All its shares are owned by a few people who are usually actively involved in running the business. Normally, you can use a living trust to transfer shares in a closely-held corporation by listing the stock in the trust document and then having the stock certificates reissued in the trust's name.

You'll want to check the corporation's bylaws and articles of incorporation to be sure that if you transfer the shares to a living trust, you will still have voting rights in your capacity as trustee of the living trust; usually, this is not a problem.

If it is, you and the other shareholders should be able to amend the corporation's bylaws to allow it.

There may, however, be legal restrictions on your freedom to transfer your shares to a living trust. Check the corporation's bylaws and articles of incorporation, as well as any separate shareholders' agreements.

One fairly common rule is that surviving shareholders (or the corporation itself) have the right to buy the shares of a deceased shareholder. In that case, you can still use a living trust to transfer the shares, but the people who inherit them may have to sell them to the other shareholders.

3. Bank and Retirement Accounts

It's not difficult to transfer bank or retirement accounts (IRAs, or Keogh or 401k accounts) to your living trust. But you may well decide that you don't need to.

You can directly designate a beneficiary for the funds in a bank or retirement account. If you name a beneficiary to receive whatever is in your account at your death, you don't need to transfer those accounts to a living trust just to avoid probate. Their contents won't need to go through probate in the first place.

This option can be especially useful for personal checking accounts, which you may not want to transfer to your living trust—it can be difficult to cash checks that say the account is owned by a revocable living trust.

A living trust, however, offers one advantage that most pay on-death arrangements do not: If you transfer an account to a living trust, you can always name an alternate beneficiary to receive the account if your first choice as beneficiary isn't alive at the time of your death. The lack of an alternate may not be a problem if you use a pay-on-death account and name more than one beneficiary to inherit the funds, however; if one of the beneficiaries isn't alive, the other(s) will inherit the money.

Pay-on-death accounts are discussed in Chapter 3, A Living Trust as Part of Your Estate Plan.

4. Vehicles and Property That Is Often Sold

Some kinds of property are cumbersome to keep in a living trust. It's not a legal problem, just a practical one. Two common examples are:

- **Cars or other vehicles you use.** Having registration and insurance in the trust's name could be confusing, and some insurance companies balk at insuring cars that technically are owned by living trusts. If you have valuable antique autos, or a mobile home that is permanently attached to land and considered real estate under your state's law, however, you may want to go ahead and transfer ownership to your living trust. You should be able to find an insurance company that will cooperate.

- **Property you buy or sell frequently.** If you don't expect to own the property at your death, there's no compelling reason to transfer it to your living trust. (Remember, the probate process you want to avoid doesn't happen until after your death.) On the other hand, if you're buying property, it's no more trouble to acquire it in the name of the trust.

> ⚠ **OTHER ARRANGEMENTS FOR PROPERTY NOT IN YOUR LIVING TRUST**
> If you choose not to put valuable items in your living trust, you may want to make arrangements to have them avoid probate in some other way. If you don't, they will pass to the residuary beneficiary of your back-up will. (See Chapter 3, A Living Trust as Part of Your Estate Plan.)

5. Life Insurance

If you own a life insurance policy at your death, the proceeds given to the named beneficiary do not go through probate. (They are, however, considered part of your estate for federal estate tax purposes.)

If you have named a minor or young adult as the beneficiary of an insurance policy, however, you may want to name your living trust as the beneficiary of the policy. Then, in the trust document, you name the child as beneficiary of any insurance proceeds paid to the trust and arrange for an adult to manage the policy proceeds if the beneficiary is still young when you die. If you don't arrange for management of the money, and the beneficiary is still a minor (under 18) when you die, a court will have to appoint a financial guardian after your death. (Young beneficiaries are discussed in Part 7, below.)

Passing the proceeds of a life insurance policy through your living trust is a bit more complicated than leaving other property this way. You must take two steps:

1. Name the living trust as the beneficiary of your life insurance policy. (Your insurance agent will have a form that lets you change the beneficiary of the policy.)

2. When you list property items in the living trust document, list the proceeds of the policy, not the policy itself. (Section C, below, contains sample descriptions.)

6. Securities

If you buy and sell stocks regularly, you may not want to go to the trouble of acquiring them in the living trust's name and selling them using your authority as trustee of the trust.

Fortunately, there's an easier way to do it: hold your stocks in a brokerage account that is owned in the living trust's name. All securities in the account are then owned by your living trust, which means that you can use your living trust to leave all the contents of the account to a specific beneficiary. If you want to leave stock to different beneficiaries, you can either establish more than one brokerage account or leave one account to more than one beneficiary to own together.

Stock in closely-held corporations. See Section 2, Small Business Interests, above.

AN ALTERNATIVE: PAY-ON-DEATH REGISTRATION

Some states allow ownership of securities to be registered in a "transfer-on-death" form. (These states have adopted the Uniform Transfer-on-Death Security Registration Act.) In those states, you can designate someone to receive the securities, including mutual funds and brokerage accounts, after your death. No probate will be necessary. Ask your broker about the forms you need to fill out to name a beneficiary for your securities.

States that allow transfer-on-death securities registration are Arkansas, Colorado, Kansas, Minnesota, Missouri, Montana, Nebraska, New Mexico, North Dakota, Ohio, Oregon, Virginia, Washington, West Virginia, Wisconsin and Wyoming.

Legal Manual

7. Cash

It's common for people to want to leave cash to beneficiaries—for example, to leave $5,000 to a relative, friend or charity. Don't, however, just type in "$5,000 cash" when you list the property you want to transfer to the living trust. There's no way to transfer cash to a living trust.

You can, however, easily accomplish the same goal by transferring ownership of a cash account—savings account, money market account or certificate of deposit, for example—to your living trust. You can then name a beneficiary to receive the contents of the account. So if you want to leave $5,000 to cousin Fred, all you have to do is put the money in a bank or money market account, transfer it to your living trust and name Fred, in the trust document, as the beneficiary.

If you don't want to set up a separate account to leave a modest amount of cash to a beneficiary, think about buying a savings bond and leaving it to the beneficiary, or leaving one larger account to several beneficiaries.

> **EXAMPLE:** Michael would like to leave some modest cash gifts to his two grown nephews, Warren and Brian, whom he's always been fond of. He puts $5,000 into a money market account and then transfers the account into his living trust. In his trust document, he names Warren and Brian as beneficiaries of the account. After Michael's death, the two nephews will inherit the account together, and each will be entitled to half of the funds.

8. Co-Owned Property

If you co-own property with someone, you can transfer your share of the property to your living trust. But whether or not you will want to depends on how you hold title to the property.

IF YOU'RE NOT SURE HOW YOU HOLD TITLE

If you own real estate with someone else but aren't sure how the title is held, look at the deed. It should say how title is held: in joint tenancy, tenancy in common, community property (in community property states) or tenancy by the entirety. In a community property state, if the deed says the property is owned "as husband and wife," that means community property.

If you do decide to transfer just your interest in co-owned property to your living trust, you don't need to specify that your share is one half or some other fraction. For example, if you and your sister own a house together, you need only list "the house at 7989 Lafayette Court, Boston, MA." Your trust document will simply state that you have transferred all your interest in that property to the trust.

If you are married and want to transfer only your share of property you own together with your spouse, see Chapter 6, Creating a Shared Marital Trust, Part 4.

a.   Property Held in Joint Tenancy

Property owned in joint tenancy does not go through probate. When one co-owner (joint tenant) dies, his or her share goes directly to the surviving co-owners, without probate. So if avoiding probate is your only concern, you don't need to transfer joint tenancy property to your living trust.

A living trust does, however, offer more flexibility than joint tenancy.

Beneficiaries. If you do transfer your share of joint tenancy property to a living trust, the joint tenancy is destroyed, and you can leave your share of the property to anyone you choose—it won't automatically go to the surviving co-owners.

Simultaneous death. Joint tenancy doesn't avoid probate if the joint owners die simultaneously. If that happens, each co-owner's half-interest in the property is passed to the beneficiaries named in the residuary clauses of their wills. If there's no will, the property passes to the closest relatives under the state "intestate succession" law.

If you transfer the property to your living trust, you can name an alternate beneficiary to receive your share of the property. It's a bit more paperwork, but you're assured that probate will be avoided even in the (statistically very unlikely) event of simultaneous death.

b. Property Held in Tenancy by the Entirety

"Tenancy by the entirety" is, basically, a kind of joint tenancy that's only for married couples. It is available only in the states listed below.

STATES IN WHICH TENANCY BY THE ENTIRETY IS AVAILABLE

Alaska*	Indiana*	Missouri	Oregon*
Arkansas	Kentucky	New Jersey*	Pennsylvania
Delaware	Maryland	New York*	Tennessee
District of Columbia	Massachusetts	North Carolina*	Vermont
Florida	Michigan*	Ohio	Virginia*
Hawaii	Mississippi	Oklahoma	Wyoming*

*allowed only for real estate

If you own property with your spouse in tenancy by the entirety, you cannot transfer your half-interest in the property to an individual living trust. Neither spouse can transfer his or her half of the property alone, either while alive or by will or trust. It must go to the surviving spouse. (This is different from joint tenancy; a joint tenant is free to transfer his or her share to someone else during his life.)

c. Community Property

Arizona	Louisiana	New Mexico	Washington
California	Nevada	Texas	Wisconsin
Idaho			

Community property is another form of ownership that's only for married couples, in the states listed above. If you and your spouse together own community property, you should probably create a shared living trust. See Chapter 4, What Kind of Living Trust Do You Need?

For more about putting community property into a living trust, see Chapter 6, Creating a Shared Marital Trust, Part 4.

C. How to Describe Trust Property

When *Living Trust Maker* asks you to list the property you want to put in your trust, describe each item clearly enough so that the successor trustee can identify the property and transfer it to the right person. No magic legal words are required.

Think about whom the property will ultimately go to. If you're leaving everything to one person, or a few major items will be divided among a few people, there's less need to go into great detail. But if there will be a number of trust beneficiaries, and objects could be confused, be more specific about each one. When in doubt, err on the side of including more information.

RULES FOR ENTERING DESCRIPTIONS OF TRUST PROPERTY

- Don't use "my" or "our" in a description. Don't, for example, enter "my books" or "my stereo system." That's because once the property is in the living trust, technically it doesn't belong to you anymore—it belongs to the living trust.
- Don't begin a description with a capital letter (unless it must begin with a proper name, like "Steinway"). That's because the descriptions will be inserted into a sentence in the trust document, and it would look odd to see a capital letter in the middle of a sentence.
- Don't end a description with a period. Again, this is because the descriptions will be inserted into a sentence in the trust document.

You may want to identify some items by their location—for example, "the books kept at 335 Forest Way, Denver, CO." But if the property you're describing is valuable—expensive jewelry or artworks, for example—be more specific. Describe the item in detail, in much the same way you would describe it if you were listing it on an insurance policy.

Here are some sample descriptions:

Real estate

- "the house at 321 Glen St., Omaha, NE"
- "the house at 4444 Casey Road, Fandon, Illinois and the 20-acre parcel on which it is located."

Legal Manual

Usually, the street address is enough. It's not necessary to use the "legal description" found on the deed, which gives a subdivision plat number or a metes-and-bounds description. If the property has no street address—for example, if it is undeveloped land out in the country—you will need to carefully copy the full legal description, word for word, from the deed.

If you own a house and several adjacent lots, it's a good idea to indicate that you are transferring the entire parcel to your living trust by describing the land as well as the house.

If you own the property with someone else and are transferring only your share, you don't need to specify the share you own. Just describe the property. The trust document will show that you are transferring all your interest in the property, whatever share that is, to the living trust.

Bank and retirement accounts

- "Savings Account No. 9384-387, Arlington Bank, Arlington, MN"
- "Money Market Account 47-223 at Charles Schwab & Co., Inc., San Francisco, CA"
- "IRA Account No. 990-66-221, Working Assets Money Fund, San Francisco, CA"

Household items

- "all the furniture normally kept in the house at 44123 Derby Ave., Ross, KY"
- "the antique brass bed in the master bedroom in the house at 33 Walker Ave., Fort Lee, New Jersey"
- "all furniture and household items normally kept in the house at 869 Hopkins St., Great Falls, Montana"

Sole proprietorship business property

- "Mulligan's Fish Market"
- "Fourth Street Records and CDs"
- "all accounts receivable of the business known as Garcia's Restaurant, 988 17th St., Atlanta, GA"
- "all food preparation and storage equipment, including refrigerator, freezer, hand mixers and slicer used at Garcia's Restaurant, 988 17th St., Atlanta, GA"

As explained in Section B, above, you should both list the name of the business and separately list items of business property.

Partnership interest

- "all interest in the Don and Dan's Bait Shop Partnership owned by the grantor before being transferred to this living trust"

    Because a partnership is a legal entity that can own property, you don't need to list items of property owned by the partnership.

Shares in a closely-held corporation

- "The stock of ABC Hardware, Inc"

Shares in a solely-owned corporation

- "all shares in the XYZ Corporation"
- "all stock in Fern's Olde Antique Shoppe, Inc., 23 Turnbridge Court, Danbury, Connecticut"

Securities

- "all securities in account No. 3999-34-33 at Smith Brokerage, 33 Lowell Place, New York, NY"
- "200 shares of General Industries, Inc. stock"
- "Good Investment Co. mutual fund account No. 888-09-09"

Life insurance proceeds

- "the proceeds of Acme Co. Life Insurance Policy #9992A"

Miscellaneous items

- "the Macintosh SE30 computer (serial number 129311) with keyboard (serial number 165895)"
- "the medical textbooks in the office at 1702 Parker Towers, San Francisco, CA"
- "the stamp collection usually kept at 321 Glen St., Omaha, NE"
- "the collection of European stamps, including [describe particularly valuable stamps], usually kept at 440 Loma Prieta Blvd., #450, San Jose, CA"
- "the Martin D-35 acoustic guitar, serial number 477597"
- "the signed 1960 Ernie Banks baseball card kept in safe deposit box 234, First National Bank of Augusta, Augusta, IL"
- "the Baldwin upright piano kept at 985 Dawson Court, South Brenly, Massachusetts"

Legal Manual

> **IMPORTANT REMINDER: TRANSFERRING PROPERTY TO THE TRUST**
>
> If an item has a title (ownership) document, such as a deed or title slip, its ownership is not transferred to the trust just by listing it in the program. You *must* also change the title document to show that you, as trustee, are the legal owner of the property.
>
> *You should transfer ownership as soon as possible after you print out and sign your Declaration of Trust.*
>
> Instructions are in Chapter 8, Transferring Property to the Trust.

Part 5: Beneficiaries of Trust Property

Once you've entered a list of the property you're transferring to your living trust, the next step is to say who you want to inherit that property. *Living Trust Maker* lets you name a beneficiary for each item of trust property separately, or name one beneficiary to receive all the trust property.

The beneficiaries you name in your trust document are not entitled to anything while you are alive. Just as with a will, you can amend your trust document and change the beneficiaries any time you wish.

⚠ DISINHERITING A SPOUSE OR CHILD

If you are married and don't plan to leave at least half of what you own to your spouse, consult a lawyer experienced in estate planning. State law may entitle your spouse to some of your estate, including the property in your living trust.

In most circumstances, you don't have to leave anything to your children. But if you want to disinherit a child, you should make a back-up will and specifically mention the child in it. (See Chapter 2, About Living Trusts.)

A. How Do You Want Your Property Distributed?

Living Trust Maker asks you first whether you want to leave all your trust property to one beneficiary (or more than one, to share it all) or leave different items to different beneficiaries.

The simplest approach is to leave all your trust property to one person, or to one or more person to share. If you choose that option, all you have to do is name each beneficiary and then name an alternate beneficiary for each, who will inherit the trust property if a primary beneficary does not survive you by five days. (Alternates are discussed in Section C, below.)

If you choose to leave different items to different beneficiaries, you will be taken to a screen that displays a list of all the property items you listed earlier. You can choose any number of the items and name beneficiaries for them.

1. Minors or Young Adults

If a beneficiary you name is a minor or a young adult who can't yet manage property without adult help, you can arrange for an adult to manage the trust property for the beneficiary. *Living Trust Maker* lets you do this after you have named all your beneficiaries. (See Part 7, below.)

2. Your Successor Trustee

It's very common and perfectly legal to make the person you named to be successor trustee (the person who will distribute trust property after your death) a beneficiary as well.

> **EXAMPLE:** Nora names her son Liam as successor trustee of her living trust. She also names him as sole beneficiary of her trust property. When Nora dies, Liam, acting as trustee, will transfer ownership of the trust property from the trust to himself.

3. Co-Beneficiaries

You can name more than one beneficiary to share any item of trust property. Simply list their names in the box provided on the screen. Type the names one per line; don't join the names with an "and." (See the Users' Guide for examples.)

Always use the beneficiaries' actual names; don't use collective terms such as "my children." It's not always clear who is included in such descriptions. And there can be serious confusion if one of the people originally included as a beneficiary dies before you do.

Obviously, if you name co-beneficiaries for a piece of property that can't be physically divided—a cabin, for example—give some thought to whether or not the beneficiaries are likely to get along. If they are incompatible, disagreements could arise over taking care of property or deciding whether or not to sell it. If they can't settle their differences, any co-owner could go to court and demand a partition—a court-ordered division and sale—of the property.

Co-beneficiaries will share the property equally unless you state otherwise. You will be asked, after you enter the names, whether or not you want this item of trust property to be shared equally among the beneficiaries.

> **EXAMPLE:** Georgia wants to leave her house to her two children, Ross and Ryan, but wants Ross to have a 75% share of it. She enters their names and then, on a later screen, enters their interests, in fractions: 3/4 for Ross and 1/4 for Ryan.
>
> When the children inherit the property, they own it together. But Ross will be liable for 75% of the taxes and upkeep cost, and entitled to 75% of any income the house produces. If they sell it, Ross will be entitled to 75% of the proceeds.

4. Beneficiaries for Your Share of Co-Owned Trust Property

If you own property together with someone else, you will name beneficiaries for your share of the property. At your death, only your interest in the property will go to the beneficiary you name.

As with naming co-beneficiaries (Section 3, above), pay attention to who will end up as co-owners of the property after your death. If, for example, you and your brother own a house together, and you leave your share to your daughter—who detests her uncle—problems are likely.

B. Entering Beneficiaries' Names

When you enter a beneficiary's name, use the name by which the beneficiary is known for purposes such as a bank account or driver's license. Generally, if the name you use clearly and unambiguously identifies the person, it is sufficient.

The name you use doesn't have to be the one that appears on the person's birth certificate. And you don't need to include all the nicknames ("Chuck" for someone whose real name is Charles, for example) a beneficiary is known by.

If you name an institution (charitable or not) to inherit the property in your trust, enter its complete name. It may be commonly known by a shortened version, which could cause confusion if there are similarly named organizations. Call to ask if you're unsure. (An institution that stands to inherit some of your money will be more than happy to help you.) Also be sure to specify if you want a specific branch or part of a national organization to receive your gift—for example, a local chapter of the Sierra Club.

Legal Manual

C. Alternate Beneficiaries

Living Trust Maker allows you to name an alternate for every person you name as a primary beneficiary. The alternate will get the property left to the primary beneficiary if your first choice does not live for more than 120 hours (five days) after your death. This "survivorship" period ensures that if you and a primary beneficiary die simultaneously or almost so, the property will go to the alternate beneficiary you chose, not to the primary beneficiary's heirs.

> **EXAMPLE:** Laura leaves all her trust property to her sister Jean, and names her daughter as alternate beneficiary. Laura and Jean are seriously injured in a car accident; Jean dies a day after Laura does. Because Jean did not survive Laura by at least five days, the trust property she would have inherited from Laura goes to Laura's daughter instead.
>
> If there had been no survivorship requirement, the trust property would have gone to Jean; when she died a day later, it would have gone to the beneficiaries she had named (or, if she had made no will, to the heirs according to state law).

You don't have to name an alternate for a charitable (or other) institution you name as a beneficiary. If the institution is well established, it is probably safe to assume that it will still exist at your death.

With other beneficiaries, however, there is always the chance that the primary beneficiary may not survive you. If you don't name an alternate, the property that beneficiary would have received will be distributed to the person or institution you name, in the next part of the program, as your "residuary beneficiary." (See Part 6, below.)

You can name more than one person or institution as alternate beneficiaries. If you do, these "co-alternate beneficiaries" will share the property equally.

> **EXAMPLE:** Sherry transfers her half-interest in a house to her living trust. She names her brother, the co-owner, as beneficiary. As alternate beneficiaries, she names her three children, Sean, Colleen and Tim.
>
> Sherry's brother dies shortly before she does, leaving his half of the house to Sherry. She transfers her new half-interest in the house to the trust. At Sherry's death, the house goes to the three children equally. All three own equal shares in all of it. If they sell the property, each will be entitled to a third of the proceeds.

Part 6: Residuary Beneficiaries

You must name a residuary beneficiary for your living trust. The residuary beneficiary of your living trust is the person or organization who will receive:

- any trust property for which both the primary and alternate beneficiaries you named die before you do
- any trust property that you didn't leave to a named beneficiary (this could include property you transferred to the trust later but didn't name a beneficiary for)
- any property you leave to your living trust through your will. (Because property left through a pour-over will doesn't avoid probate, there's usually no reason to use one. See Chapter 3, A Living Trust as Part of Your Estate Plan.)
- any property that you actually transferred to your living trust but didn't list in the trust document.

Often, the residuary beneficiary of a living trust doesn't inherit anything from the trust. Usually, naming a residuary beneficiary is just a back-up measure, to guard against the extremely small chance that both a primary and alternate trust beneficiary do not survive you.

You may, however, deliberately leave the residuary beneficiary trust property by:

- Adding property to the trust later and not naming a specific beneficiary to receive it after your death.
- Using a pour-over will to leave property to your living trust.

If you name more than one person or institution as residuary beneficiary, they will each get an equal share of any trust property they receive.

EXAMPLE: You name your two children, Anne and Alice, as your residuary beneficiaries. If they end up receiving trust property, they will own it together, and both will own an equal share of it.

Part 7: Property Management for Young Beneficiaries

If any of your beneficiaries (including alternate and residuary beneficiaries) might inherit trust property before they are ready to manage it without an adult's help, you should arrange for someone else to manage it for them for a while. There are several ways to go about it:

- Leave the property to an adult to use for the child. Many people don't leave property directly to a child. Instead, they leave it to the child's parent or to the person they expect to have care and custody of the child if neither parent is available. There's no formal legal arrangement, but they trust the adult to use the property for the child's benefit.
- Create a child's subtrust. You can use *Living Trust Maker* to establish a "child's subtrust" in your living trust. If you do, your successor trustee will manage the property you left the child and dole it out for education, health and other needs. The subtrust ends at whatever age you designate (up to 35), and any remaining property is turned over to the child outright.

- Name a custodian under the Uniform Transfers to Minors Act (UTMA). In many states, you can name a "custodian" to manage property you leave a child until the child reaches 18 or 21, depending on state law (up to 25 in Alaska, California and Nevada). If you don't need management to last beyond that age, a custodianship is probably preferable.

  Subtrusts and custodianships are explained below.

CHILDREN WITH SPECIAL NEEDS

These property management options are not designed to provide long-term property management for a child with serious disabilities. You should see a lawyer and make arrangements geared to your particular situation.

A. Should You Arrange for Management?

It's up to you whether or not to make arrangements, in the trust document, to have someone manage trust property if it is inherited by young beneficiaries.

The consequences of forgoing management for trust property inherited by a young beneficiary depend on whether the beneficiary is over or under age 18 at your death.

1. Children Under 18 Years Old

Minors—children under 18—cannot, legally, own or manage significant amounts of property. An adult must be in charge if the minor acquires more than a few thousand dollars' worth of property. (The exact amount depends on state law.)

If your minor beneficiaries won't inherit anything of great value—if you're leaving them objects that have more sentimental than monetary value—you don't need to arrange for an adult to manage the property.

But if a beneficiary inherits valuable trust property while still a minor, and you have not arranged for the property to be managed by an adult, the beneficiary will have to have a court-appointed guardian to manage the property. Contrary to what you might expect, a child's parent does not automatically have legal authority to manage any property the child inherits. So even if one or both of the beneficiary's parents are alive, they will not automatically have authority to manage the property. They will have to ask the court to grant them that authority, and will be subject to the court's supervision. If neither of the beneficiary's parents are alive, there may be no obvious person for the court to appoint as property guardian. In that case, it may be even more important for you to name someone in your living trust.

2. Young Adults 18 to 35 Years Old

If a living trust beneficiary is over 18 when he or she inherits trust property, you do not need, legally, to have anyone manage the property on the beneficiary's behalf. And if you don't make any arrangements, the beneficiary will get the property with no strings attached. But you can arrange for property management to last until a beneficiary turns any age up to 35.

There is no legal requirement that management for a trust beneficiary's property must end at 35, but we think 35 is a reasonable cutoff. If you don't want to let a beneficiary get his or her hands on trust property by the time he or she reaches 35, you probably need to see a lawyer and tailor a plan to the beneficiary's needs.

B. Which Method Is Best: Subtrust or Custodianship?

Using *Living Trust Maker*, you can create either a child's subtrust or a custodianship under the Uniform Transfer to Minors Act (if it's available in your state). Both are safe, efficient ways of managing trust property that a young person inherits. Under either system, the person in charge of the young beneficiary's property has the same responsibility to use the property for the beneficiary's support, education and health.

The most significant difference is that a child's subtrust can last longer than a custodianship, which must end at age 18 to 21 (up to 25 in Alaska, Nevada and California) in most states. For that reason, a child's subtrust is a good choice when a child could conceivably inherit a large amount of property.

Because an UTMA custodianship is easier to administer, it is usually preferable if the beneficiary will inherit no more than about $50,000 worth of trust property ($100,000 or more if the child is quite young). That amount is likely to be used up for living and education expenses by the time the beneficiary is 18 to

21, so there's no need to create a child's subtrust that can continue beyond that age.

A custodianship has other advantages as well:

- Handling a beneficiary's property can be easier with a custodianship than with a trust. A custodian's powers are written into state law, and most institutions, such as banks and insurance companies, are familiar with the rules. Trusts, on the other hand, vary in their terms. So before a bank lets a trustee act on behalf of a beneficiary, it may demand to see and analyze a copy of the Declaration of Trust.

- You can name whomever you wish to be a custodian, and you can name different custodians for different beneficiaries. So if you want to arrange custodianships for grandchildren, for example, you could name each child's parent as custodian. A child's subtrust is not quite so flexible: the successor trustee will be the trustee of all children's subtrusts created for your young beneficiaries.

- If the property in a subtrust earns income, and that income isn't distributed quickly to the beneficiary, the trust will have to pay tax on it. The federal tax rate on such retained income may be higher than it would be if the young beneficiary were taxed on it.

STATES THAT HAVE ADOPTED THE UNIFORM TRANSFERS TO MINORS ACT

State	Age at which minor gets property	State	Age at which minor gets property
Alabama	21	Missouri	21
Alaska	18-25	Montana	21
Arizona	21	Nebraska	21
Arkansas	18-21	Nevada	18-25
California	18-25	New Hampshire	21
Colorado	21	New Jersey	18-21
District of Columbia	18	New Mexico	21
Florida	21	North Carolina	18-21
Georgia	21	North Dakota	21
Hawaii	21	Ohio	21
Idaho	21	Oklahoma	18
Illinois	21	Oregon	21
Indiana	21	Rhode Island	18
Iowa	21	South Dakota	18
Kansas	21	Tennessee	21
Kentucky	18	Utah	21
Maine	18-21	Virginia	18-21
Maryland	21	Washington	21
Massachusetts	21	West Virginia	21
Minnesota	21	Wisconsin	21
Mississippi	21	Wyoming	21

C. Children's Subtrusts

Living Trust Maker allows you to set up a separate "child's subtrust" for each young beneficiary.

1. How a Child's Subtrust Works

In your trust document, you state the age at which the beneficiary should receive trust property outright. If at your death the beneficiary is younger than the age you specified, a subtrust will be created for that beneficiary. (If the beneficiary is older, he or she gets the trust property with no strings attached, and no subtrust is created.) Each beneficiary gets a separate child's subtrust.

Living Trust Maker is set up so that the successor trustee will serve as trustee of any children's subtrusts. If you want different people to manage property inherited by different beneficiaries, you may want to use a custodianship instead of a child's subtrust. (To appoint someone else to be trustee of a child's subtrust, the trust document would have to be changed significantly; see a lawyer.)

Whatever trust property the beneficiary is entitled to receive upon your death will go into the child's subtrust, if the child is still under the age set for termination of the subtrust. The trustee will manage the subtrust property and use it as necessary for the beneficiary's health, education and support. After your death, the subtrust cannot be revoked or amended. (Until then, you are free to change your mind about having a subtrust set up for a particular beneficiary.)

The child's subtrust will end when the beneficiary reaches the age you designated in your Declaration of Trust. This can be any age up to and including 35. The trustee will then give the beneficiary what remains of the subtrust property.

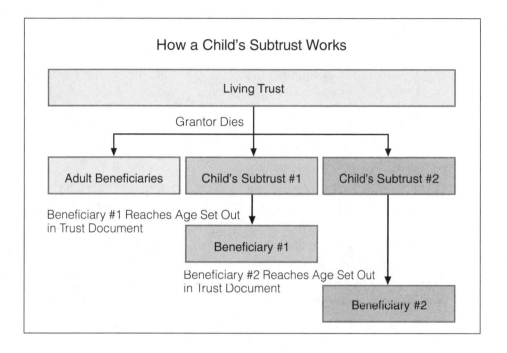

EXAMPLE 1: In his trust document, Stanley names his 14-year-old son Michael as beneficiary of $25,000 worth of stock. He specifies that any stock Michael becomes entitled to when Stanley dies should be kept in a subtrust until Michael is 25, subject to the trustee's right to spend it on Michael's behalf.

Stanley dies when Michael is 19. The stock goes into a subtrust for him, managed by the successor trustee of Stanley's living trust. The trustee is free to use the stock (or the income it produces) to pay for Michael's education and support. Michael will receive what's left of the stock when he turns 25.

EXAMPLE 2: Victoria creates a living trust and leaves her trust property to her daughters, who are 22 and 25. She specifies that any trust property they inherit should stay in children's subtrusts until each daughter reaches 30. Victoria names her sister, Antoinette, as successor trustee.

Victoria dies in a car accident when one daughter is 28 and the other is 31. The 28-year-old's half of the trust property stays in a subtrust, managed by Antoinette, until she turns 30. The 31-year-old gets her half outright; no subtrust is created for her.

2. The Trustee's Duties

The subtrust trustee must:

- Manage subtrust property until the beneficiary reaches the age set out in the trust document—which can take years.
- Use subtrust property or income to pay for expenses such as the beneficiary's support, education and healthcare.
- Keep separate records of subtrust transactions and file income tax returns for the subtrust.

The trustee's powers and responsibilities are spelled out in the trust document. If the subtrust trustee needs to hire an accountant, tax lawyer or other expert, he or she can use subtrust assets to pay a reasonable amount for the help.

The trust document also provides that the trustee of a subtrust is entitled to reasonable compensation for his or her work as trustee. The trustee decides what is a reasonable amount; the compensation is paid from the subtrust assets.

For more on the trustee's responsibilities, see Chapter 10, After a Grantor Dies.

D. Custodianships

A custodianship is the preferable alternative for many people. Here's how it works.

1. How a Custodianship Works

In the trust document, the grantor names someone to serve as custodian for a particular beneficiary. That person manages any trust property the young beneficiary inherits until the beneficiary reaches the age at which state law says the custodianship must end. (See table in Section B, above.)

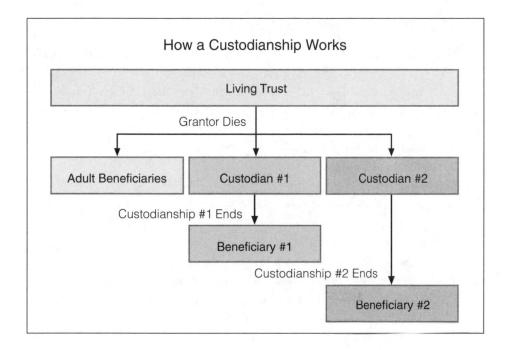

EXAMPLE: In her living trust, Sandra leaves 100 shares of General Motors stock to her niece, Jennifer. She names Hazel, Jennifer's mother, as custodian under the Illinois Uniform Transfers to Minors Act.

After Sandra's death, her successor trustee gives the stock to the custodian, Hazel. She will manage it for Jennifer until Jennifer turns 21, the age Illinois law says she must be given the property outright.

In some states, you can specify—within limits—at what age the custodianship will end. If your state allows this, the program will ask you to enter an age at which you want the custodianship to end.

EXAMPLE: Jonathan, a divorced father who lives in New Jersey, makes a living trust. He leaves a substantial amount of trust property to his young children, Ian and Noel. He specifies, in the trust document, that any trust property the children inherit should be managed by his ex-wife, Elizabeth, as custodian under the New Jersey Uniform Transfers to Minors Act, until the boys turn 21.

When Jonathan dies, Elizabeth takes over management of the trust property for her children. When each boy turns 21, he will receive whatever of the property hasn't been used for his support or education.

2. The Custodian's Responsibilities

A custodian has roughly the same responsibility as the trustee of a child's subtrust: to manage the beneficiary's property wisely and honestly. The custodian's authority and duties are clearly set out by state law (the Uniform Transfers to Minors Act, as enacted by your state. The UTMA is a model law written by a national panel of experts, but legislatures may make minor modifications in it when they adopt it for their states). No court directly supervises the custodian.

The custodian must:

- Manage the property until the beneficiary reaches the age at which, by law, he or she gets the property outright. If the child is a minor at your death, this can be a number of years.
- Use the property or income to pay for expenses such as the young beneficiary's support, education and healthcare.
- Keep the property separate from his or her own property.
- Keep separate records of trust transactions. The custodian does not have to file a separate income tax return; income from the property can be reported on the young beneficiary's return. (By comparison, the trustee of a child's subtrust must file a separate tax return for the subtrust.)

A custodian who needs to hire an accountant, tax lawyer or other expert can use the property to pay a reasonable amount for the help.

If state law allows it, the custodian is entitled to reasonable compensation and reimbursement for reasonable expenses. The payment, if any is taken, comes from the property the custodian manages for the beneficiary.

3. Choosing a Custodian

You can name a different custodian for each young beneficiary, if you wish.

In most cases, you should name the person who will have physical custody of the minor child. That's almost always one of the child's parents. If the beneficiary is your child, name the child's other parent unless you have serious reservations about that person's ability to handle the property for the child.

Only one person can be named as custodian for one beneficiary. You can, however, name an alternate custodian to take over if your first choice is unable to serve.

Sample Individual Trust

Signing, Storing and Registering the Trust Document

Before You Sign

Before you sign the trust document, make sure it says exactly what you want it to say and that you understand it all. If you want to make changes, use the program and print out another trust document. (If you need help, see the Users' Guide.) Don't write any changes on the document.

Get Your Signature Notarized

Sign your living trust document in front of a notary public for your state.

Making Copies

If you need copies of the trust document, use a photocopy of the original trust document—the one you signed and had notarized. Do not just print out and sign another copy.

Registering the Trust

Some states (Alaska, Colorado, Florida, Hawaii, Idaho, Maine, Michigan, Missouri, Nebraska, and North Dakota) require that you register your living trust document with the local court. But there are no legal consequences or penalties if you don't. See Chapter 7 of the Legal Manual for instructions on how to register.

Storing the Trust Document

Store your living trust document and the Living Trust Maker disk where you keep important papers. Make sure your successor trustee knows where the original trust document is and can get hold of it soon after your death.

Important Reminder: Transferring Property to the Trust

If an item has a title (ownership) document, such as a deed or title slip, its ownership is not transferred to the trust just by listing it in the program. You must also change the title document to show the that you, as trustee of your living trust, are the legal owner of the property. *You should transfer ownership as soon as possible after you print out and sign your Declaration of Trust.* Instructions are in Chapter 8 of the Legal Manual.

Keep Up to Date

Fill out the Living Trust Maker registration card included in the package and send it to Nolo Press at the address below. As a registered user, you will receive product updates and notice of

Signing Instructions — Page 1

significant law changes that affect living trusts. And we
promise never to give your name to any other organization. If
you do not have the full Living Trust Maker package, include
$79.95 and we will send it to you.

Nolo Press
950 Parker Street, Berkeley, CA 94710
(510) 549-1976

Living Trust Maker 2.0
Date: Friday, July 22, 1994 Time: 10:25:25

Declaration of Trust

Part 1. Trust Name
This revocable living trust shall be known as The Judith M. Avery Revocable Living Trust.

Part 2. Declaration of Trust
Judith M. Avery, called the grantor, declares that she has transferred and delivered to the trustee all her interest in the property described in Schedule A attached to this Declaration of Trust. All of that property is called the "trust property." The trustee hereby acknowledges receipt of the trust property and agrees to hold the trust property in trust, according to this Declaration of Trust.

The grantor may add property to the trust.

Part 3. Terminology
The term "this Declaration of Trust" includes any provisions added by valid amendment.

Part 4. Amendment and Revocation

A. Amendment or Revocation by Grantor
The grantor may amend or revoke this trust at any time, without notifying any beneficiary. An amendment must be made in writing and signed by the grantor. Revocation may be in writing or any manner allowed by law.

B. Amendment or Revocation by Other Person
The power to revoke or amend this trust is personal to the grantor. A conservator, guardian or other person shall not exercise it on behalf of the grantor, unless the grantor specifically grants a power to revoke or amend this trust in a Durable Power of Attorney.

Part 5. Payments From Trust During Grantor's Lifetime
The trustee shall pay to or use for the benefit of the grantor as much of the net income and principal of the trust property as the grantor requests. Income shall be paid to the grantor at least annually.

Part 6. Trustees

A. Trustee
Judith M. Avery shall be trustee of this trust.

B. Trustee's Responsibility
The trustee in office shall serve as trustee of all trusts created under this Declaration of Trust, including children's subtrusts.

C. Terminology

In this Declaration of Trust, the term "trustee" includes successor trustees or alternate successor trustees serving as trustee of this trust. The singular "trustee" also includes the plural.

D. Successor Trustee

Upon the death or incapacity of Judith M. Avery, the trustee of this trust and of any children's subtrusts created by it shall be Robert S. Avery and Anne Avery Puckett. If Robert S. Avery and Anne Avery Puckett are both unable or unwilling to serve as successor trustee, David R. Puckett shall be the trustee.

E. Resignation of Trustee

Any trustee in office may resign at any time by signing a notice of resignation. The resignation must be delivered to the person or institution who is either named in this Declaration of Trust, or appointed by the trustee under Part 6, Section F, to next serve as the trustee.

F. Power to Appoint Successor Trustee

If no one named in this Declaration of Trust as a successor trustee or alternate successor trustee is willing or able to serve as trustee, the last acting trustee may appoint a successor trustee and may require the posting of a reasonable bond, to be paid from the trust property. The appointment must be made in writing, signed by the trustee and notarized.

G. Bond

No bond shall be required for any trustee named in this Declaration of Trust.

H. Compensation

No trustee shall receive any compensation for serving as trustee, unless the trustee serves as a trustee of a child's subtrust created by this Declaration of Trust.

I. Liability of Trustee

With respect to the exercise or non-exercise of discretionary powers granted by this Declaration of Trust, the trustee shall not be liable for actions taken in good faith. Such actions shall be binding on all persons interested in the trust property.

Part 7. Trustee's Management Powers and Duties

A. Powers Under State Law

The trustee shall have all authority and powers allowed or conferred on a trustee under Illinois law, subject to the trustee's fiduciary duty to the grantor and the beneficiaries.

B. Specified Powers

The trustee's powers shall also include:

1. The power to borrow money and to encumber trust property, including trust real estate, by mortgage, deed of trust or other method.

2. The power to manage trust real estate as if the trustee were the absolute owner of it, including the power to lease (even if the lease term may extend beyond the period of any trust) or grant options to lease the property, to make repairs or alterations and to insure against loss.

3. The power to sell or grant options for the sale or exchange of any trust property, including stocks, bonds, debentures and any other form of security or security account, at public or private sale for cash or on credit.

4. The power to invest trust property in property of any kind, including but not limited to bonds, debentures, notes, mortgages and stocks.

5. The power to receive additional property from any source and add to any trust created by this Declaration of Trust.

6. The power to employ and pay reasonable fees to accountants, lawyers or investment experts for information or advice relating to the trust.

7. The power to deposit and hold trust funds in both interest-bearing and non-interest-bearing accounts.

8. The power to deposit funds in bank or other accounts uninsured by FDIC coverage.

9. The power to enter into electronic fund transfer or safe deposit arrangements with financial institutions.

Part 8. Incapacity of Grantor

If the grantor becomes physically or mentally incapacitated, whether or not a court has declared the grantor incompetent or in need of a conservator, the successor trustee named in Part 6 shall be trustee. Incapacity must be certified in writing by a licensed physician.

In that event, the trustee shall manage the trust property. The trustee shall use any amount of trust income or trust property necessary for the grantor's proper healthcare, support, maintenance, comfort and welfare, in accordance with the grantor's accustomed manner of living. Any income not spent for the benefit of the grantor shall be accumulated and added to the trust property.

The successor trustee shall manage the trust until a licensed physician certifies in writing that the grantor is no longer physically or mentally incompetent.

Part 9. Death of Grantor

When the grantor dies, this trust shall become irrevocable. It may not be amended or altered except as provided for by this

Declaration of Trust. It may be terminated only by the distributions authorized by this Declaration of Trust.

The trustee may pay out of trust property such amounts as necessary for payment of debts, estate taxes and expenses of the last illness and funeral.

Part 10. Beneficiaries

At the death of the grantor, the trustee shall distribute the trust property as follows, subject to provisions in this Declaration of Trust that create children's subtrusts or create custodianships under the Uniform Transfers to Minors Act:

1. Robert S. Avery shall be given all the grantor's interest in 200 shares of General Industries stock. If Robert S. Avery does not survive the grantor by 120 hours that property shall be given to Cheryl Avery.

2. Anne Avery Puckett shall be given all the grantor's interest in Account No. 3999-34-3 at Smith Brokerage, 33 Lowell Place, New York, NY. If Anne Avery Puckett does not survive the grantor by 120 hours that property shall be given to David R. Puckett.

3. David R. Puckett shall be given all the grantor's interest in the two $100 United States Saving Bonds kept in safe deposit box 3351 at Crystal Lake Savings and Loan, Crystal Lake, Illinois.

4. Anne Avery Puckett and Robert S. Avery shall be given all the grantor's interest in all household furnishings in the house at 88823 Lakeview Dr., Crystal Lake, Illinois and the house at 88823 Lakeview Dr., Crystal Lake, Illinois in equal shares. If Anne Avery Puckett does not survive the grantor by 120 hours, his or her interest in this property shall be given to David R. Puckett. If Robert S. Avery does not survive the grantor by 120 hours, his or her interest in this property shall be given to Cheryl Avery.

5. Anne Avery Puckett and Robert S. Avery shall be given all trust property not otherwise specifically and validly disposed of by this Part.

Part 11. Custodianships Under the Uniform Transfers to Minors Act

1. Any property David R. Puckett becomes entitled to under Part 10 of this Declaration of Trust shall be given to Anne Avery Puckett, as custodian for David R. Puckett under the Illinois Uniform Transfers to Minors Act, until David R. Puckett reaches the age of 21. If Anne Avery Puckett is unable or ceases to serve as custodian, Anthony B. Puckett shall serve as custodian.

/////
/////
/////
/////

Part 12. Severability of Clauses

If any provision of this Declaration of Trust is ruled unenforceable, the remaining provisions shall stay in effect.

Certification of Grantor

I certify that I have read this Declaration of Trust and that it correctly states the terms and conditions under which the trust property is to be held, managed and disposed of by the trustees, and I approve the Declaration of Trust.

_____   Dated: _____
Judith M. Avery, Grantor and Trustee

State of _____

County of _____

On _____, before me, _____, a notary public for said state, personally appeared Judith M. Avery, personally known to me (or proved to me on the basis of satisfactory evidence) to be the person whose name is subscribed to the within instrument, and acknowledged to me that she executed the same in her authorized capacity and that by her signature on the instrument the person, or the entity upon behalf of which the person acted, executed the instrument.

Witness my hand and official seal.

_____
NOTARY PUBLIC for the State of _____
My commission expires _____.

Legal Manual

Schedule A

1. 200 shares of General Industries stock.
2. Account No. 3999-34-3 at Smith Brokerage, 33 Lowell Place, New York, NY.
3. All household furnishings in the house at 88823 Lakeview Dr., Crystal Lake, Illinois.
4. The house at 88823 Lakeview Dr., Crystal Lake, Illinois.
5. The two $100 United States Saving Bonds kept in safe deposit box 3351 at Crystal Lake Savings and Loan, Crystal Lake, Illinois.

Creating a Shared Marital Trust

Legal Manual

W hen you create your living trust document with *Living Trust Maker*, you have only a few choices to make. Basically, you must decide five things:

- Whether to make an individual living trust or a shared living trust with your spouse.
- What property you want to put in your living trust.
- Who you want to receive trust property at your death. These people or organizations are the beneficiaries of your living trust.
- Who is to be the successor trustee—the person or institution who, after both spouses have died, will distribute the surviving spouse's trust property.
- How you should arrange for someone to manage trust property inherited by beneficiaries who are too young to handle it without supervision.

You may already have a good idea of how you want to decide these issues. This chapter discusses the factors you should think about as you make each decision. It is organized the same way as the program is (Parts 1 through 7), so that you can easily refer to it while you're actually running *Living Trust Maker*. It's a good idea, though, to read through this chapter before you sit down at the computer—it will make the whole process clearer and easier.

Checklist for Creating a Valid Living Trust

√ Prepare the trust document with *Living Trust Maker*.

√ Print out the trust document and sign it in front of a notary public.

√ Transfer ownership of the property listed in the trust document into the trust.

√ Update your trust document when needed.

An Overview:
How a Shared Marital Trust Works

Here, in brief, are the important points about how a shared trust works:

Control of trust property. You and your spouse will both be trustees of your living trust, so you'll both have control over the property in the trust. Either spouse can act on behalf of the trust—sell or give away trust property, for example. (As a practical matter, the consent of both spouses may be necessary—see Part 3, below.)

Amendments or revocation. Either spouse can revoke the trust or add separately owned property to it at any time. Both spouses, however, must consent to change any terms of the trust document—who gets what property, or who is named as successor trustee, for example.

This way either spouse can, by revoking the trust, return the situation to exactly what it was before the trust was formed. (Co-owned property is returned to both spouses, and separately owned property to the owner-spouse.) But while both spouses are living, neither can alone change what they've decided on in the trust—who should get what property when each spouse dies.

Death of the first spouse. When the first spouse dies, the shared living trust is automatically split into two trusts.

- Trust #1 contains the deceased spouse's share of trust property, except any trust property left to the surviving spouse.
- Trust #2 contains the surviving spouse's share, including any trust property left by the deceased spouse to the survivor.

The surviving spouse is sole trustee of both trusts. The survivor must distribute the deceased spouse's property (what's in Trust #1) exactly as he or she instructed in the trust document, with no modifications. The surviving spouse is also responsible for managing any Trust #1 property left to a young beneficiary in a child's subtrust (explained later in the chapter). When all the property in Trust #1 is distributed to the beneficiaries, Trust #1 ceases to exist.

Continuation of the living trust. Trust #2 (the survivor's) goes on as before, with the addition of any trust property the survivor inherited from the deceased spouse. The surviving spouse is free to change the trust document as he or she wishes. For example, the surviving spouse might name someone else as successor trustee, or name a new beneficiary for property that was to have gone to the deceased spouse.

Death of the second spouse. When the second spouse dies, the person named in the trust document as successor trustee takes over. He or she is responsible for distributing trust property to the beneficiaries and managing any trust property left to a young beneficiary in a child's subtrust (explained later).

To see how a shared living trust works, read the example below. You may want to refer it later as you're using the program.

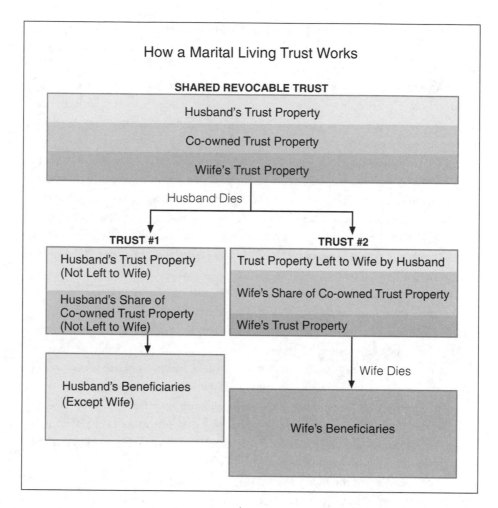

How a Marital Living Trust Works

SHARED REVOCABLE TRUST

Husband's Trust Property

Co-owned Trust Property

Wiife's Trust Property

Husband Dies

TRUST #1

Husband's Trust Property (Not Left to Wife)

Husband's Share of Co-owned Trust Property (Not Left to Wife)

Husband's Beneficiaries (Except Wife)

TRUST #2

Trust Property Left to Wife by Husband

Wife's Share of Co-owned Trust Property

Wife's Trust Property

Wife Dies

Wife's Beneficiaries

EXAMPLE: Harry and Maude, a married couple, set up a shared revocable living trust to avoid probate. In the trust document, they make themselves co-trustees, and appoint their niece Emily as successor trustee, to take over as trustee after they have both died. They transfer much of their co-owned property—their house, savings accounts and stocks—to the living trust. Maude also puts some of her family heirlooms, which are her separate property, in the trust.

The trust document states that Maude's brother is to receive the heirlooms when she dies; everything else goes to Harry. Harry leaves all his trust property to Maude.

Maude dies first. The trust splits into Trust #1, which contains Maude's heirlooms, and Trust #2, which contains everything else—Harry's trust property and the trust property he inherits from Maude. Harry becomes the sole trustee of both trusts.

Following the terms of the trust document, Harry distributes Maude's heirlooms (Trust #1) to her brother, without probate. When the property is distributed, Trust #1 ceases to exist. Harry doesn't have to do anything with the trust property Maude left him; it's already in Trust #2.

After Maude's death, Harry decides to make a couple of changes in his living trust document. He names his nephew, Burt, as successor trustee. And he names his 12-year-old granddaughter, Cecile, to receive some trust property. In the trust document, he provides that if Cecile is not yet 25 when he dies, the trust property she inherits will stay in a child's subtrust, managed by the successor trustee, Burt.

When Harry dies, Burt becomes trustee and distributes the trust property following Harry's instructions in the trust document. He also manages the property inherited by Cecile, who is 21 at Harry's death, until her 25th birthday. When all the property is given to Harry's beneficiaries, the trust ends.

Part 1: Your State

In this part of the program, you choose the state that is your legal residence, also called your "domicile." That's the state where you and your spouse live now and intend to keep living.

Your choice affects many aspects of your living trust, including the ways you can set up management for any trust property young beneficiaries may inherit and what property belongs to each spouse.

(You may notice that the list of states on the screen doesn't include Louisiana. We didn't forget it—but because Louisiana law is different from all other states, you can't use this program if you live there.)

Legal Manual

A. If You Live in More Than One State

If during the course of a year you live in more than one state, your residence is the state with which you have the most significant contacts—where you vote, register vehicles, own valuable property, have bank accounts or run a business.

If you might be justified in claiming more than one state as your legal residence, you may want to arrange your affairs so that your legal residence is in the state with the most advantageous state estate tax laws. Some states (such as New York) impose stiff inheritance taxes; others (California and Florida, for example) have essentially no inheritance tax. If you have significant contacts with more than one state and a substantial estate, it may pay to have a lawyer with tax and estate planning experience advise you.

> **EXAMPLE:** Ben and Geraldine, a couple in their 60s, spend about half the year in Florida and the other half in New York. They have bank accounts and other real estate in both states.
>
> To take advantage of Florida's lack of a state inheritance tax, they register their car in Florida, vote there and move their bank accounts there. This leaves them owning nothing in New York but a condominium near where their son lives. They decide to sell him the condo and lease it back six months of every year, severing their last important property ownership contact with New York.

B. If You Live Outside the United States

If you are living outside the U.S., your residence is the state you still have contacts with and expect to return to. If you don't maintain ties with a particular state and have a large estate, see a lawyer to discuss what state you should declare as your residence.

If you are in the Armed Forces and living out of the country temporarily, your legal residence is the state you declared as your Home of Record—the state you lived in before going overseas, or where your spouse or parents live.

Part 2: Your Names

The next piece of information the program asks you for is easy: your names. The names you enter in this part of the program will form part of the name of your trust. For example, if you enter "William S. Jorgensen" and "Helga M. Jorgensen," your trust will be named "The William S. Jorgensen and Helga M. Jorgensen Revocable Living Trust." Your names will also appear as the original trustees of your living trust (see Part 3, below).

Enter your name the way it appears on other formal business documents, such as your driver's license or bank accounts. This may or may not be the name on your birth certificate.

Use only one name per person; don't enter various versions of your name joined by "aka" (also known as).

If you go by more than one name, be sure that the name you use for your living trust is the one that appears on the ownership documents for property you plan to transfer to the trust. If it isn't, it could cause confusion later, and you should change the name on your ownership documents before you transfer the property to the trust.

EXAMPLE: You use the name William Dix for your trust, but own real estate in your former name of William Geicherwitz. You should prepare and sign a new deed, changing the name of the owner to William Dix, before you prepare another deed to transfer the property to your living trust.

Part 3: Trustees

To be legally valid, every living trust must have a trustee—someone to manage the property owned by the trust. When you create a revocable living trust with this program, you and your spouse are the trustees while you are alive. Someone else, who you named in the trust document to be the successor trustee, takes over after both you and your spouse have died.

A. The Original Trustees

You and your spouse will be the original trustees of your living trust. As trustees, both of you will have complete control over the property that will technically be owned by the trust.

As a day-to-day, practical matter, it makes little difference that your property is now owned by your living trust. You won't have any special duties as trustees of your trust. You do not even need to file a separate income tax return for the living trust. Any income the property generates must be reported on your personal income tax return, as if the trust did not exist.

You have the same freedom to sell, give away or mortgage trust property as you did before you put the property into the living trust. The only difference is that you must now sign documents in your capacities as trustees. It's that easy.

EXAMPLE: Celeste and Robert want to sell a piece of land that is owned in the name of their living trust. They prepare a deed transferring ownership of the land from the trust to the new owner, and sign the deed as "Celeste Tornetti and Robert Tornetti, trustees of the Celeste Tornetti and Robert Tornetti Revocable Living Trust dated February 4, 1994."

It's important to realize that once the property belongs to the trust, either trustee (spouse) has authority over it. That means that either spouse can sell or give away any of the trust property—including the property that was co-owned or was the separate property of the other spouse before it was transferred to the trust. In practice, however, both spouses will probably have to consent to transfer real estate out of the living trust. Especially in community property states, buyers and title insurance companies usually insist on both spouses' signatures on transfer documents.

If you don't want to give your spouse legal authority over your separately owned property, it's best to make separate living trusts. (See Chapter 4, What Kind of Living Trust Do You Need?)

NAMING SOMEONE ELSE AS TRUSTEE

In the unlikely event you and your spouse don't want to be the trustees, or want only one of you to be trustee, you cannot use *Living Trust Maker;* you need to see an estate planning lawyer to draw up a more specialized living trust. If only one spouse is a trustee, the other loses legal control over his or her trust property. And if you name someone else as trustee, there are important tax consequences.

B. The Trustee After One Spouse's Death or Incapacity

When one spouse dies or becomes incapacitated and unable to manage his or her affairs, the other becomes sole trustee.

A spouse's physical or mental incapacity must be certified in writing by a physician. The other spouse, as sole trustee, takes over management of trust property. That's the extent of his or her authority; he or she has no power over property not owned by the living trust, and no authority to make healthcare decisions for the incapacitated spouse. For this reason, it's also wise for each spouse to create documents called Durable Powers of Attorney, giving the other spouse authority to manage property not owned in the name of the trust and to make healthcare decisions. (See Chapter 3, A Living Trust as Part of Your Estate Plan, Section F.)

After one spouse's death, the surviving spouse, as trustee, is responsible for distributing trust property of the deceased spouse that is not left to the surviving spouse. The surviving spouse must follow the deceased spouse's wishes as they are set out in the trust document. The surviving spouse has no legal power to modify the deceased spouse's intentions in any way. (See Chapter 10, After a Grantor Dies.)

Usually, the process takes only a few weeks. The surviving spouse may, however, have long-term duties if the trust document creates a child's subtrust for trust property inherited by a young beneficiary. It falls to the surviving spouse to manage trust property left to a young beneficiary in this way, possibly for many years (this is explained in Part 7, below).

C. The Successor Trustee

You and your spouse must also choose a successor trustee—someone to act as trustee after both of you have died or become incapacitated. (Incapacity is the inability to manage your affairs. The trust document created by *Living Trust Maker* requires that incapacity be documented in writing by a physician before your spouse or the successor trustee can take over management of the trust property.)

The successor trustee has no power or responsibility if at least one spouse is alive and capable of managing the trust.

1. The Successor Trustee's Duties After Both Spouses' Deaths

After both spouses have died, the successor trustee named in the trust document takes over as trustee. The successor trustee's primary responsibility is to distribute trust property to the beneficiaries named in the trust document. That is usually a straightforward process that can be completed in a few weeks. (How to transfer certain common kinds of property is explained in Chapter 10, After a Grantor Dies.)

The successor trustee may, however, have long-term duties if the trust document creates a "child's subtrust" for trust property inherited by a young beneficiary (this is explained in Part 7, below).

2. The Successor Trustee's Duties If You or Your Spouse Is Incapacitated

The successor trustee will take over as trustee before both spouses have died if neither spouse is able to manage his or her affairs. A spouse's incapacity must be documented in writing by a physician. In this situation, the successor trustee has broad authority to manage the property in the living trust and use it for both spouses' healthcare, support and welfare. The law requires him or her to act honestly and prudently in managing the property. And because the grantors are no longer the trustees, the new trustee must file an income tax return for the trust.

3. Choosing a Successor Trustee

The person or institution you choose as successor trustee will have a crucial role: to manage trust property (if you and your spouse become incapacitated, or if the successor trustee must manage a child's subtrust) or distribute it to your beneficiaries (after you and your spouse have died).

If the successor trustee is in charge of managing property over the long term, the trust document produced by *Living Trust Maker* gives him or her very broad authority, so that the trustee will be able to do whatever is necessary to respond to the demands of the circumstances. For example, the trustee has the power to invest trust funds in accounts, such as money market accounts, that are not federally insured. The trustee is also free to spend trust income or property for the health and welfare of the incapacitated spouses or beneficiary of a child's subtrust.

Obviously, when you are giving someone this much power and discretion, you should choose someone with good common sense whom you trust completely, such as an adult son or daughter, other relative or close friend. If you don't know anyone who fits this description, think twice about establishing a living trust.

Keep in mind that the successor trustee does not take over until both spouses have died (or become incapacitated). That means that after one spouse's death, the surviving spouse will probably have plenty of time to amend the trust document and name a different successor trustee if he or she wishes.

In most situations, the successor trustee will not need extensive experience in financial management; common sense, dependability and complete honesty are usually enough. A successor trustee who may have long-term responsibility over a young beneficiary's trust property needs more management and financial skills than a successor trustee whose only job is to distribute trust property. The successor trustee does have authority, under the terms of the trust document, to get any reasonably necessary professional help—from an accountant, lawyer or tax preparer, perhaps—and pay for it out of trust assets.

Usually, it makes sense to name just one person as successor trustee, to avoid any possibility of conflicts. But it's legal and may be desirable to name more than one person. For example, you might name two or more of your children, if you don't expect any disagreements between them and you think one of them might feel hurt and left out if not named.

Carefully consider the issue of conflicts, however. If you name more than one person as successor trustee, all of them must agree before they can act on behalf of the trust. If they can't agree, it could hold up the distribution of trust property to your beneficiaries. In extreme situations, the other trustees might even have to go to court to get the recalcitrant trustee removed, so that your instructions can be carried out. The result might be more bad feeling than if you had just picked one person to be trustee in the first place.

Having more than one successor trustee is especially likely to cause serious problems if the successor trustees are in charge of the property you have left to a young beneficiary in a child's subtrust. The trustees may have to manage a young beneficiary's property for many years, and will have many decisions to make about how to spend the money—greatly increasing the potential for conflict. (Children's subtrusts are discussed in Part 7, below.)

If you name more than one successor trustee, and one of them can't serve, the others will serve. If none of them can serve, the alternate you name (in the next section of the program) will take over.

It's perfectly legal to name a beneficiary of the trust (someone who will receive trust property after your death) as successor trustee. In fact, it's common.

EXAMPLE: Mildred and James name their only child, Allison, to be successor trustee of their living trust. They name each other as trust beneficiaries, and Allison as alternate beneficiary. When James dies, his share of the trust property goes to Mildred. When Mildred dies, Allison uses her authority as trustee to transfer the remaining trust property to herself, the beneficiary.

INSTITUTIONS AS SUCCESSOR TRUSTEES

Normally, your first choice as successor trustee should be a flesh-and-blood person, not the trust department of a bank or other institution. Institutional trustees charge hefty fees, which come out of the trust property and leave less for your family and friends. And they probably won't even be interested in "small" living trusts—ones that contain less than several hundred thousand dollars worth of property.

But if there's no close relative or friend you think is capable of serving as your successor trustee, probably your best bet is to consider naming a private trust services company as successor trustee. Typically, their fees are pricey, but as a rule they charge less than a bank, and your affairs will probably receive more personal attention.

For a very large living trust, another possibility is to name a person and an institution as co-successor trustees. The bank or trust services company can do most of the paperwork, and the person can keep an eye on things and approve all transactions.

The successor trustee does not have to live in the same state as you do. But if you are choosing between someone local and someone far away, think about how convenient it will be for the person you choose to distribute the living trust property after your death. Someone close by will probably have an easier job, especially with real estate transfers. But for transfers of property such as securities and bank accounts, it usually won't make much difference where the successor trustee lives.

Obviously, before you and your spouse finalize your living trust, you must check with the person you've chosen to be your successor trustee. You want to be sure your choice is willing to serve. If you don't, you may well create problems down the line. The person you've chosen may not want to serve, for a variety of reasons. And even if the person would be willing, if he or she doesn't know of his or her responsibilities, transfer of trust property after your death could be delayed.

If you choose an institution, you must check out the minimum size of trust it will accept and the fees it charges for management, and make arrangements for how the institution will take over as trustee at the second spouse's death.

AVOIDING CONFLICTS WITH YOUR WILL AND OTHER DOCUMENTS

Your living trust gives your spouse the authority to manage trust property if you become incapacitated. To avoid conflicts, you should also give your spouse authority to make other decisions if you can't:

- In your will, appoint your spouse to be executor, to be responsible for distributing your property (except living trust property) after your death.
- In your Durable Power of Attorney for Finances, appoint your spouse to be your "attorney-in-fact," to have authority to make financial and management decisions for property (except property owned in the name of the living trust) if you become incapacitated.

If you do choose different people to be your attorney-in-fact and successor trustee, each will have a role after your death or incapacity. The successor trustee will be in charge of all trust property, and the attorney-in-fact will have authority, granted in the Power of Attorney, to control property not owned by the living trust.

Legal Manual

4. Payment of the Successor Trustee

Typically, the successor trustee of a simple probate-avoidance living trust isn't paid. This is because in most cases, the successor trustee's only job is to distribute the trust property to beneficiaries soon after the grantor's death—and often, the successor trustee inherits most of the trust property anyway.

An exception is a successor trustee who manages the property in a child's subtrust. In that case, the successor trustee is entitled, under the terms of the trust document, to "reasonable compensation." The successor trustee decides what is reasonable and takes it from the trust property left to the young beneficiary.

Allowing the successor trustee to set the amount of the payment can work well, as long as your successor trustee is completely trustworthy. If the young beneficiary feels the trustee's fees are much too high, he or she will have to go to court to challenge them. If you want to restrict the successor trustee's freedom to decide on payment, see a lawyer.

The trust document created by *Living Trust Maker* does not require the successor trustee to post a bond (a kind of insurance policy) to guarantee conscientious fulfillment of his or her duties.

5. Naming an Alternate Successor Trustee

Living Trust Maker asks you to name an alternate successor trustee, in case your first choice is unable to serve.

If you named two or more successor trustees, the alternate won't become trustee unless none of your original choices can serve.

> **EXAMPLE:** Caroline and Oscar name their two grown children, Eugene and Vanessa, as successor trustees. They name a close friend, Nicole, as alternate successor trustee. After Caroline and Oscar have died, Vanessa is ill and can't serve as trustee. Eugene acts as sole successor trustee. If he were unable to serve or had died, Nicole would take over.

If no one you named in the trust document can serve, the last trustee to serve has the power to appoint, in writing, another successor trustee. (See Chapter 10, After a Grantor Dies.)

> **EXAMPLE:** To continue the previous example, if Nicole were ill and didn't have the energy to serve as successor trustee, she could appoint someone else to serve as trustee.

Part 4: Property to Be Put in Trust

Now you're getting to the heart of the program. In this part, you and your spouse must list each item of property—both jointly owned and separately owned—you want to transfer to your living trust. It will take some thought to decide what property to include and how to list it in the trust document. (Later in the program, you will name beneficiaries to receive each item of trust property at your death.)

This is a crucial step. Any property you don't list will not go into your living trust and will not pass under the terms of the trust. It may instead have to go through probate.

Adding property to the trust later. If you mistakenly leave something out or acquire more valuable property after you create your trust, you will be able to add it to your living trust. Chapter 9, Living With Your Living Trust, explains how.

A. Inventory Your Valuable Property

Before you begin to list your property in the program, sort out what you have and who owns it—you, your spouse, or both of you. You need to label each item this way because each spouse names beneficiaries for his or her share of the trust property separately.

After you've made an inventory, the next section will help you decide which items you want to transfer to your living trust so they don't have to go through probate after your death.

1. Take Inventory

First, get out a pencil or your word processor and make a list all the valuable items of property you own. The categories below should jog your memory.

Even if you plan to leave everything to your spouse or children, you must make a list. That's because every item (or group of items, in some circumstances) must be specifically described and listed in the trust document.

When you list your property in the program, you can group items, if you're leaving them all to one beneficiary. For example, if you want to leave all your books to your daughter, there's no need to describe each one individually—unless your collection includes some particularly valuable or important books that you want to make extra sure get to the beneficiary.

Legal Manual

GETTING ORGANIZED

While you're taking stock of all your valuable property, it might be a good time to go a step further and gather the information your family will need at your death.

You can use your computer to get organized by using *Nolo's Personal RecordKeeper* database program. It can keep track of all the important information in your family's life, including securities data, investments, real estate records, medical information, insurance records, credit card information and more.

(Ordering information is in the back of the manual.)

VALUABLE PROPERTY

Animals	Computers	Retirement accounts
Antiques	Copyrights, patents, trademarks	–401(k) plans
Appliances	Electronic equipment	–IRAs
Art	Furniture	–Keogh plans
Books	Furs	Royalties
Business interests	Jewelry	Securities
–Sole proprietorship	Limited partnership	–Bonds
–Partnership	Precious metals	–Commodities
–Corporation	Real estate	–Mutual funds
Business property (if you	–Agricultural land	–Stocks
own a sole proprietorship)	–Boat/Marina dock space	–U.S. bills, notes and bonds
Cameras & photographic	–Co-op	Tools
equipment	–Condo	Vehicles
Cash accounts	–Duplex	–Cars
–Certificates of deposit	–House	–Motorcycles
–Checking	–Mobile home	–Bicycles
–Money market funds	–Rental property	–Boats
–Savings	–Time-share	–Motor homes/RVs
China, crystal, silver	–Undeveloped land	–Planes
Coins, stamps	–Vacation house	
Collectibles		

Valuable Property Inventory

Item	His	Hers	Ours
_____	☐	☐	☐
_____	☐	☐	☐
_____	☐	☐	☐
_____	☐	☐	☐
_____	☐	☐	☐
_____	☐	☐	☐
_____	☐	☐	☐
_____	☐	☐	☐

2. Who Owns It?

You'll need to label each item as "his, hers or ours" when you enter it in the program. This is because only your share of the trust property is distributed at your death.

For many couples, especially if they've been married a long time, nearly everything is owned together. But if you haven't been married long, or have been married before, you may own a sizeable amount of property separately. If you're unsure about who owns what, this section explains the ownership rules for community property and non-community property states.

a. Community property states

Arizona	Louisiana	New Mexico	Washington
California	Nevada	Texas	Wisconsin
Idaho			

If you live in a community property state and you aren't sure who owns what, don't rely on whose name is on the title document. For example, if while you were married you bought a house with money you earned, your spouse legally owns a share of that property—even if only your name is on the deed.

Generally, any property that either spouse earns or acquires during the marriage (before permanent separation) is community property. Both spouses (the "community") own it together. The main exception to this shared ownership rule is that property one spouse acquires by gift or inheritance belongs to that spouse alone. Property acquired before marriage also belongs to each spouse separately.

Even separate property may, however, turn into community property if it is mixed ("commingled") with community property. For example, if you deposit separate property funds into a joint bank account and then make more deposits and withdrawals, making it impossible to tell what part of the account is separate money, it's all considered community property.

In most community property states, there are restrictions on one spouse's freedom to transfer community property. Especially in the case of real estate, the consent of both spouses is necessary for either to sell or give away his or her half-interest in the property. Each spouse can, however, leave his or her half-interest in the property through a will or living trust.

Married couples don't have to accept the property ownership rules established by their states' community property laws. They can sign a written agreement that makes some or all community property the separate property of one spouse, or vice versa. If you and your spouse have such an agreement about who owns what, you may want to prepare individual living trusts. (See Chapter 4, What Kind of Living Trust Do You Need?)

WHAT HAPPENS TO COMMUNITY PROPERTY PUT IN A LIVING TRUST

If you live in a community property state and you and your spouse create a living trust together, transferring property to the trust won't change its legal character.

Community property (owned by both spouses equally) transferred to your living trust will stay community property, even though it is technically owned by the living trust. Separately owned property (property of only one spouse) will remain the separate property of the spouse. That means that the community property transferred to a living trust is still eligible for the favorable tax treatment given community property at one spouse's death. (Both halves of community property left to the surviving spouse get a "stepped-up basis" for income tax purposes; see Chapter 3, A Living Trust as Part of Your Estate Plan.)

It also means that if either spouse revokes the living trust, ownership of the property will go back to the spouses as it was before the property was transferred to the living trust. Community property goes back to both spouses equally, and separate property goes to the spouse who owned it before ownership was transferred to the trust.

Legal Manual

b. Non-community property states

Alabama	Indiana	Montana	Pennsylvania
Alaska	Iowa	Nebraska	Rhode Island
Arkansas	Kansas	New Hampshire	South Carolina
Colorado	Kentucky	New Jersey	South Dakota
Connecticut	Maine	New York	Tennessee
Delaware	Maryland	North Carolina	Utah
District of Columbia	Massachusetts	North Dakota	Vermont
Florida	Michigan	Ohio	Virginia
Georgia	Minnesota	Oklahoma	West Virginia
Hawaii	Mississippi	Oregon	Wyoming
Illinois	Missouri		

In these states, it is usually fairly simple to figure out who owns what. If the property has a title document—for example, a deed to real estate or a car title slip—then the spouse whose name is on the title is the owner. If the property doesn't have a title document, it belongs to the spouse who paid for it or received it as a gift. (It's possible, though, that if there were a dispute between spouses, a judge could determine, based on the circumstances, that a spouse whose name is not on the title document might own an interest in the property.)

If the trust is revoked, the property will be returned to each spouse based on the same ownership rights they had before the property was transferred to the trust.

B. Decide What Property to Put in Your Living Trust

Now that you've got a list of what you and your spouse own, you're ready to decide what items you want to transfer to your living trust. You're creating a revocable living trust primarily to avoid probate fees. As a general rule, the more an item is worth, the more it will cost to probate it. That means you should transfer at least your most valuable property items to your living trust (or use some other probate-avoidance device to leave them at your death). Think about including:

- houses and other real estate
- jewelry, antiques, furs and valuable furniture
- stock in a closely-held corporation
- stock, bond and other security accounts held by brokerages
- small business interests
- money market and bank accounts
- other financial accounts
- patents and copyrights
- precious metals
- valuable works of art
- valuable collections of stamps, coins or other objects.

ADDING PROPERTY TO YOUR LIVING TRUST

You and your spouse will be able to add property to your living trust at any time. As trustees, you can always sell or give away property in the trust. You can also take it out of the living trust and put it back in your name as individuals. Chapter 9, Living With Your Living Trust, explains how to make these changes.

You don't need to put everything you own into a living trust to save money on probate. For some assets, you may decide to use other probate-avoidance devices instead of a living trust. Property that is of relatively low value (the amount depends on state law) may be exempt from probate or qualify for a streamlined probate procedure that's relatively fast and cheap. And at least some of the property left to a surviving spouse can probably be transferred without a full-blown probate court proceeding. (See Chapter 3, A Living Trust as Part of Your Estate Plan.)

Even if the non-trust property does have to go through regular probate, attorney and appraisal fees are generally based on the value of the probated property, so they'll be relatively low.

This section discusses how to decide whether or not to transfer various kinds of property to your living trust.

---

1. Real Estate

The most valuable thing most people own is their real estate: their house, condominium or land. You and your spouse can probably save your family substantial probate costs by transferring your real estate through a living trust.

In some situations, however, you and your spouse may not want to transfer your real estate to your living trust. See:

- Section 8, Property Held in Joint Tenancy
- Section 9, Property Held in Tenancy by the Entirety
- Section 10, Community Property

IF YOU'RE NOT SURE HOW YOU HOLD TITLE

If you own real estate with someone else but aren't sure how the title is held, look at the deed. It should say how title is held: in joint tenancy, tenancy in common, community property (in community property states) or tenancy by the entirety. In a community property state, if the deed says the property is owned "as husband and wife," that means community property.

If you or your spouse owns real estate with someone else, you can transfer just your interest in it to your living trust. You won't need to specify that your share is one half or some other fraction. For example, if you and your sister own a house together, you need only list "the house at 7989 Lafayette Court, Boston, MA." Your trust document will state that you have transferred all your interest in that property to the trust. The share of the property owned by your sister, obviously, is not included.

Co-op apartments. If you own shares in a co-op corporation that owns your apartment, you'll have to transfer your shares to your living trust. You may run into difficulties with the corporation; some are reluctant to let a trust, even a revocable trust completely controlled by the grantor, own shares. Check the co-op corporation's rules to see if the transfer is allowed.

2. Small Business Interests

The delay, expense and court intrusion of probate can be especially detrimental to an ongoing small business. Using your living trust to transfer business interests to beneficiaries quickly and after your death is almost essential if you want the beneficiaries to be able to keep the business running.

If you want to control the long-term management of your business, however, a revocable living trust is not the right vehicle. See an estate planning lawyer to draft a different kind of trust, with provisions tailored to your situation.

Different kinds of business organizations present different issues when you want to transfer your interest to your living trust:

Sole proprietorships. If you operate your business as a sole proprietorship, with all business assets held in your own name, you can simply transfer your business property to your living trust like you would any other property. You should also transfer the business's name itself: that transfers the customer goodwill associated with the name.

Partnership interests. If you operate your business as a partnership with other people, you can probably transfer your partnership share to your living trust. If there is a partnership certificate, it must be changed to include the trust as owner of your share.

Some partnership agreements require the people who inherit a deceased partner's share of the business to offer that share to the other partners before taking it. But that happens after death, so it shouldn't affect your ability to transfer the property through a living trust.

It's not common, but a partnership agreement may limit or forbid transfers to a living trust. If yours does, you and your partners may want to see a lawyer before you make any changes.

Solely owned corporations. If you own all the stock of a corporation, you should have no difficulty transferring it to your living trust.

Closely-held corporations. A closely-held corporation is a corporation that doesn't sell shares to the public. All its shares are owned by a few people who are usually actively involved in running the business. Normally, you can use a living trust to transfer shares in a closely-held corporation by listing the stock in the trust document and then having the stock certificates reissued in the trust's name.

You'll want to check the corporation's bylaws and articles of incorporation to be sure that if you transfer the shares to a living trust, you will still have voting rights in your capacity as trustee of the living trust; usually, this is not a problem. If it is, you and the other shareholders should be able to amend the corporation's bylaws to allow it.

There may, however, be legal restrictions on your freedom to transfer your shares to a living trust. Check the corporation's bylaws and articles of incorporation, as well as any separate shareholders' agreements.

One fairly common rule is that surviving shareholders (or the corporation itself) have the right to buy the shares of a deceased shareholder. In that case, you can still use a living trust to transfer the shares, but the people who inherit them may have to sell them to the other shareholders.

Legal Manual

3. Bank and Retirement Accounts

It's not difficult to transfer bank or retirement accounts (IRAs, or Keogh or 401k accounts) to your living trust. But you may well decide that you don't need to.

You can directly designate a beneficiary for the funds in a bank or retirement account. If you name a beneficiary to receive whatever is in your account at your death, you don't need to transfer those accounts to a living trust just to avoid probate. Their contents won't need to go through probate in the first place.

This option can be especially useful for personal checking accounts, which you may not want to transfer to your living trust—it can be difficult to cash checks that say the account is owned by a revocable living trust.

A living trust, however, offers one advantage that most pay-on-death arrangements do not: If you transfer an account to a living trust, you can always name an alternate beneficiary to receive the account if your first choice as beneficiary isn't alive at your death. The lack of an alternate may not be a problem if you use a pay-on-death account and name more than one beneficiary to inherit the funds, however; if one of the beneficiaries isn't alive, the other(s) will inherit the money.

Pay-on-death accounts are discussed in Chapter 3, A Living Trust as Part of Your Estate Plan.

4. Vehicles and Property That Is Often Sold

Some kinds of property are cumbersome to keep in a living trust. It's not a legal problem, just a practical one. Two common examples are:

- **Cars or other vehicles you use.** Having registration and insurance in the trust's name could be confusing, and some insurance companies balk at insuring cars that technically are owned by living trusts. If you have valuable antique autos, or a mobile home that is permanently attached to land and considered real estate under your state's law, however, you may want to go ahead and transfer ownership to your living trust. You should be able to find an insurance company that will cooperate.

- **Property you buy or sell frequently.** If you don't expect to own the property at your death, there's no compelling reason to transfer it to your living trust. (Remember, the probate process you want to avoid doesn't happen until after your death.) On the other hand, if you're buying property, it's no more trouble to acquire it in the name of the trust.

⚠️ **OTHER ARRANGEMENTS FOR PROPERTY NOT IN YOUR LIVING TRUST.** If you choose not to put valuable items in your living trust, you may want to make arrangements to have them avoid probate in some other way. If you don't, they will pass to the residuary beneficiary of your back-up will. (See Chapter 3, A Living Trust as Part of Your Estate Plan.)

5. Life Insurance

If you own a life insurance policy at your death, the proceeds given to the named beneficiary do not go through probate. (They are, however, considered part of your estate for federal estate tax purposes.)

If you have named a minor or young adult as the beneficiary of an insurance policy, however, you may want to name your living trust as the beneficiary of the policy. Then, in the trust document, you name the child as beneficiary of any insurance proceeds paid to the trust and arrange for an adult to manage the policy proceeds if the beneficiary is still young when you die. If you don't arrange for management of the money, and the beneficiary is still a minor (under 18) when you die, a court will have to appoint a financial guardian after your death. (Young beneficiaries are discussed in Part 7, below.)

Passing the proceeds of a life insurance policy through your living trust is a bit more complicated than leaving other property this way. You must take two steps:

1. Name the living trust as the beneficiary of your life insurance policy. (Your insurance agent will have a form that lets you change the beneficiary of the policy.)
2. When you list property items in the living trust document, list the proceeds of the policy, not the policy itself. (Section C, below, contains sample descriptions.)

6. Securities

If you buy and sell stocks regularly, you may not want to go to the trouble of acquiring them in the living trust's name and selling them using your authority as trustee of the trust.

Legal Manual

Fortunately, there's an easier way to do it: hold your stocks in a brokerage account that is owned in the living trust's name. All securities in the account are then owned by your living trust, which means that you can use your living trust to leave all the contents of the account to a specific beneficiary. If you want to leave stock to different beneficiaries, you can either establish more than one brokerage account or leave one account to more than one beneficiary to own together.

AN ALTERNATIVE: PAY-ON-DEATH REGISTRATION

Some states allow ownership of securities to be registered in a "transfer-on-death" form. (These state have adopted the Uniform Transfer-on-Death Security Registration Act.) In those states, you can designate someone to receive the securities, including mutual funds and brokerage accounts, after your death. No probate will be necessary. Ask your broker about the forms you need to fill out to name a beneficiary for your securities. States that allow transfer-on-death securities registration are Arkansas, Colorado, Kansas, Minnesota, Missouri, Montana, Nebraska, New Mexico, North Dakota, Ohio, Oregon, Virginia, Washington, West Virginia, Wisconsin and Wyoming.

Stock in closely-held corporations. See Section 2, Small Business Interests, above.

7. Cash

It's common for people to want to leave cash to beneficiaries—for example, to leave $5,000 to a relative, friend or charity. Don't, however, just type in "$5,000 cash" when you list the property you want to transfer to the living trust. There's no way to transfer cash to a living trust.

You can, however, easily accomplish the same goal by transferring ownership of a cash account—savings account, money market account or certificate of deposit, for example—to your living trust. You can then name a beneficiary to receive the contents of the account. So if you want to leave $5,000 to cousin Fred, all you have to do is put the money in a bank or money market account, transfer it to your living trust and name Fred, in the trust document, as the beneficiary.

If you don't want to set up a separate account to leave a modest amount of cash to a beneficiary, think about buying a savings bond and leaving it to the beneficiary, or leaving one larger account to several beneficiaries.

EXAMPLE: Michael would like to leave some modest cash gifts to his two grown nephews, Warren and Brian, whom he's always been fond of. He puts $5,000 into a money market account and then transfers the account into his living trust. In his trust document, he names Warren and Brian as beneficiaries of the account. After Michael's death, the two nephews will inherit the account together, and each will be entitled to half of the funds.

8. Property Held in Joint Tenancy

Property owned in joint tenancy does not go through probate. When one co-owner (joint tenant) dies, his or her share goes directly to the surviving co-owners, without probate. So if avoiding probate is your only concern, you and your spouse don't need to transfer your joint tenancy property to your living trust.

Joint tenancy doesn't avoid probate, however, if the joint owners die simultaneously—there is no survivor to inherit the other's share. If spouses die at the same time, each spouse's half interest in the joint tenancy property is passed to the beneficiaries named in the residuary clauses of their wills. If a spouse didn't make a will, the property passes to the closest relatives under the state "intestate succession" law.

If you're concerned about what would happen to the property in the (statistically very unlikely) event that you and your spouse died simultaneously, you have two choices.

- You can name a beneficiary, who would inherit the property in the event of simultaneous death, in your back-up will. If the property passes under your will, however, it will probably go through probate.
- You can transfer the property to your living trust, and each spouse can name the other as primary beneficiary and name an alternate beneficiary to receive his or her share of the property in case of simultaneous death. It's a bit more paperwork, but you're assured that probate will be avoided even in the event of simultaneous death.

There's another reason to use a living trust for joint tenancy property: If you want to leave your share of the property to someone besides the other joint tenant(s). Joint tenancy property automatically goes to the surviving co-owners when one co-owner dies. But if you transfer joint tenancy property to a living trust, the joint tenancy is destroyed, and you can leave your share to anyone you please.

9. Property Held in Tenancy by the Entirety

STATES THAT ALLOW TENANCY BY THE ENTIRETY			
Alaska*	Indiana*	Missouri	Oregon*
Arkansas	Kentucky	New Jersey*	Pennsylvania
Delaware	Maryland	New York*	Tennessee
District of Columbia	Massachusetts	North Carolina*	Vermont
Florida	Michigan*	Ohio	Virginia*
Hawaii	Mississippi	Oklahoma	Wyoming*

*allowed only for real estate

You and your spouse may hold title to property in "tenancy by the entirety"—basically, a kind of joint tenancy that's only for married couples. Not all states have this form of ownership.

Like joint tenancy, tenancy by the entirety property does not go through probate when one spouse dies; it automatically goes to the surviving spouse. So if avoiding probate is your only concern, you and your spouse don't need to transfer your tenancy by the entirety property to your living trust.

Tenancy by the entirety property doesn't avoid probate, however, if the spouses die simultaneously. If spouses die at the same time, each spouse's half-interest in the property is passed to the beneficiaries named in the residuary clauses of their wills. If a spouse didn't make a will, the property passes to the closest relatives under the state "intestate succession" law.

If you're concerned about what would happen to the property in the (statistically very unlikely) event you and your spouse died simultaneously, you have two choices.

- You can name a beneficiary, who would inherit the property in the event of simultaneous death, in your back-up will. If the property passes under your will, however, it will probably go through probate.

- You can transfer the property to your living trust, and each spouse can name an alternate beneficiary to receive his or her share of the property. It's a bit more paperwork, but you're assured that probate will be avoided even in the event of simultaneous death.

10. Community Property

Arizona	Louisiana	New Mexico	Washington
California	Nevada	Texas	Wisconsin
Idaho			

Most community property states have tried to make it easier on surviving spouses who inherit the couple's community property, by letting at least some community property bypass formal probate. In Nevada, for example, the surviving spouse is presumed to inherit community property real estate; he or she only has to fill out and file (with the county recorder) an affidavit (sworn statement) to get ownership of the property transferred to his or her name. (Nev. Rev. State. § 111.365.) So if avoiding probate is your only concern, and you and your spouse each want to leave your community property to the survivor, you may not need to transfer community property to your living trust.

But be aware that although community property may avoid probate when the first spouse dies, if the property is left to the survivor, it's of no help when the second spouse dies. To avoid probate then, the property must be transferred to inheritors via a living trust or other probate-avoidance device.

Community property doesn't avoid probate if both spouses die simultaneously. If you're concerned about what would happen to the property if you and your spouse died simultaneously, you have two choices.

- You can name a beneficiary, who would inherit the property in the event of simultaneous death, in your back-up will. If the property passes under your will, however, it will probably go through probate.
- You can transfer the property to your living trust, and each spouse can name the other as primary beneficiary and name an alternate beneficiary to receive his or her share of the property in case of simultaneous death. It's a bit more paperwork, but you're assured that probate will be avoided even in the event of simultaneous death.

C. How to Describe Trust Property

When *Living Trust Maker* asks you to list the property you want to put in your trust, describe each item clearly enough so that the surviving spouse or successor trustee can identify the property and transfer it to the right person. No magic legal words are required.

Think about whom the property will ultimately go to. If you're leaving everything to one person, or a few major items will be divided among a few people, there's less need to go into great detail. But if there will be a number of trust beneficiaries, and objects could be confused, be more specific about each one. When in doubt, err on the side of including more information.

RULES FOR ENTERING DESCRIPTIONS OF TRUST PROPERTY

- Don't use "my" or "our" in a description. Don't, for example, enter "my books" or "my stereo system." That's because once the property is in the living trust, technically it doesn't belong to you anymore—it belongs to the living trust.
- Don't begin a description with a capital letter (unless it must begin with a proper name, like "Steinway"). That's because the descriptions will be inserted into a sentence in the trust document, and it would look odd to see a capital letter in the middle of a sentence.
- Don't end a description with a period. Again, this is because the descriptions will be inserted into a sentence in the trust document.

You may want to identify some items by their location—for example, "the books kept at 335 Forest Way, Denver, CO." But if the property you're describing is valuable—expensive jewelry or artworks, for example—be more specific. Describe the item in detail, in much the same way you would describe it if you were listing it on an insurance policy.

Here are some sample descriptions:

Real estate

- "the house at 321 Glen St., Omaha, NE"

- "the house at 4444 Casey Road, Fandon, Illinois and the 20-acre parcel on which it is located."

Usually, the street address is enough. It's not necessary to use the "legal description" found on the deed, which gives a subdivision plat number or a metes-and-bounds description. If the property has no street address—for example, if it is undeveloped land out in the country—you will need to carefully copy the full legal description, word for word, from the deed.

If you own a house and several adjacent lots, it's a good idea to indicate that you are transferring the entire parcel to your living trust by describing the land as well as the house.

If you own the property with someone else and are transferring only your share, you don't need to specify the share you own. Just describe the property. The trust document will show that you are transferring all your interest in the property, whatever share that is, to the living trust.

Bank and retirement accounts

- "Savings Account No. 9384-387, Arlington Bank, Arlington, MN"
- "Money Market Account 47-223 at Charles Schwab & Co., Inc., San Francisco, CA"
- "IRA Account No. 990-66-221, Working Assets Money Fund, San Francisco, CA"

Household items

- "all the furniture normally kept in the house at 44123 Derby Ave., Ross, KY"
- "the antique brass bed in the master bedroom in the house at 33 Walker Ave., Fort Lee, New Jersey"
- "all furniture and household items normally kept in the house at 869 Hopkins St., Great Falls, Montana"

Sole proprietorship business property

- "Mulligan's Fish Market"
- "Fourth Street Records and CDs"
- "all accounts receivable of the business known as Garcia's Restaurant, 988 17th St., Atlanta, GA"
- "all food preparation and storage equipment, including refrigerator, freezer, hand mixers and slicer used at Garcia's Restaurant, 988 17th St., Atlanta, GA"

As explained in Section B, above, you should both list the name of the business and separately list items of business property.

Partnership interest

- "all interest in the Don and Dan's Bait Shop Partnership owned by the grantor before being transferred to this living trust"

Because a partnership is a legal entity that can own property, you don't need to list items of property owned by the partnership.

Shares in a closely-held corporation

- "the stock of ABC Hardware, Inc"

Shares in a solely-owned corporation

- "all shares in the XYZ Corporation"
- "all stock in Fern's Olde Antique Shoppe, Inc., 23 Turnbridge Court, Danbury, Connecticut"

Securities

- "all securities in account No. 3999-34-33 at Smith Brokerage, 33 Lowell Place, New York, NY"
- "200 shares of General Industries, Inc. stock"
- "Good Investment Co. mutual fund account No. 888-09-09"

Life insurance proceeds

- "the proceeds of Acme Co. Life Insurance Policy #9992A"

Miscellaneous items

- "the Macintosh SE30 computer (serial number 129311) with keyboard (serial number 165895)"
- "the medical textbooks in the office at 1702 Parker Towers, San Francisco, CA"
- "the stamp collection usually kept at 321 Glen St., Omaha, NE"
- "the collection of European stamps, including [describe particularly valuable stamps], usually kept at 440 Loma Prieta Blvd., #450, San Jose, CA"
- "the Martin D-35 acoustic guitar, serial number 477597"
- "the signed 1960 Ernie Banks baseball card kept in safe deposit box 234, First National Bank of Augusta, Augusta, IL"

- "the Baldwin upright piano kept at 985 Dawson Court, South Brenly, Massachusetts"

IMPORTANT REMINDER: TRANSFERRING PROPERTY TO THE TRUST

If an item has a title (ownership) document, such as a deed or title slip, its ownership is not transferred to the trust just by listing it in the program. You *must* also change the title document to show that you, as trustee, are the legal owners of the property.

You should transfer ownership as soon as possible after you print out and sign your Declaration of Trust.

Instructions are in Chapter 8, Transferring Property to the Trust.

Legal Manual

Part 5: Beneficiaries of Trust Property

Once you've entered a list of the property you're transferring to your living trust, the next step is to say who you want to inherit that property. In the trust document, each spouse must name beneficiaries—the family, friends or organizations who will receive his or her share of the trust property.

Each spouse names beneficiaries separately, because each spouse's trust property is distributed when that spouse dies. When the first spouse dies, his or her trust property will be distributed to the beneficiaries he or she named. If it is left to the other spouse, it stays in the trust. When the second spouse dies, the rest of the property in the trust is distributed to his or her beneficiaries.

EXAMPLE: Roger and Marilyn Foster create a shared living trust. Each puts co-owned and separately owned property in the trust. When Roger dies, Marilyn takes over as sole trustee and distributes Roger's trust property to the beneficiaries he named in the trust document. Her property, including the trust property she inherits from Roger, stays in the living trust.

The beneficiaries you name in your trust document are not entitled to any trust property while both spouses are alive. Just as with a will, you can amend your trust document and change the beneficiaries any time you wish.

⚠️ DISINHERITING A SPOUSE OR CHILD

If you don't plan to leave at least half of what you own to your spouse, consult a lawyer experienced in estate planning. State law may entitle your spouse to some of your estate, including the property in your living trust.

In most circumstances, you don't have to leave anything to your children. But if you want to disinherit a child, you should make a back-up will and specifically mention the child in it. (See Chapter 2, About Living Trusts.)

A. How Do You Want Your Property Distributed?

Living Trust Maker asks you first whether you want to leave all your trust property to one beneficiary (or more than one, to share it all) or leave different items to different beneficiaries.

This accommodates the desire of many spouses to leave all trust property to the survivor. If you choose that option, the program inserts your spouse's name (entered earlier) as beneficiary of all your trust property. All you have to do is name an alternate beneficiary, who will inherit your trust property if your spouse does not survive you by five days. (Alternates are discussed in Section D, below.)

If you choose to leave different items to different beneficiaries, you will be taken to a screen that displays a list of all the property items you listed earlier. You can choose any number of the items and name beneficiaries (including your spouse, if you wish) for them.

1. Your Spouse

It's common for spouses to leave each other all or a substantial portion of the property transferred to their shared marital trust. In a shared trust, if one spouse leaves the other trust property, the property stays in the living trust when the first spouse dies.

EXAMPLE: Max and Joan make a shared marital living trust. Each leaves all his or her trust property to the other. Max dies first. All his interest in trust property stays in what is now Joan's living trust. Joan has the right to amend the trust document to name beneficiaries for the trust property that is now hers. (See Chapter 10, After a Grantor Dies.)

2. Children from Prior Marriages

If you or your spouse have children from a prior marriage, you may well want to leave them property in your living trust. A common way to do this is to leave the children specific items—real estate, life insurance policy proceeds, bank accounts or whatever—and leave everything else to your spouse.

Estate planning note. A more complicated way of ensuring that both your spouse and children from an earlier marriage are taken care of is to create a different kind of trust called a "marital life estate trust." Briefly, this type of trust typically gives the surviving spouse the right to use income from (or live in) certain property for his or her life; then the property goes to the children. (These trusts are discussed in Chapter 3, A Living Trust as Part of Your Estate Plan.)

3. Minors or Young Adults

If a beneficiary you name is a minor or a young adult who can't yet manage property without adult help, you can arrange for an adult to manage the trust property for the beneficiary. *Living Trust Maker* lets you do this after you have named all your beneficiaries. (See Part 7, below.)

4. Your Successor Trustee

It's very common and perfectly legal to make the person you named to be successor trustee (the person who will distribute trust property after the second spouse dies) a beneficiary as well.

EXAMPLE: Nora and Sean name their son Liam as successor trustee of their living trust. Each spouse names the other as sole beneficiary of his or her trust property, and both name Liam as alternate beneficiary. When Nora dies, her trust property goes to Sean and stays in the trust. Unless Sean amends the trust document to name someone else as successor trustee, after Sean's death, Liam, acting as trustee, will transfer ownership of the trust property from the trust to himself.

5. Co-Beneficiaries

You can name more than one beneficiary to share any item of trust property. Simply list their names in the box provided on the screen. Type the names one per line; don't join the names with an "and." (See the Users' Guide for examples.)

Always use the beneficiaries' actual names; don't use collective terms such as "my children." It's not always clear who is included in such descriptions. And there can be serious confusion if one of the people originally included as a beneficiary dies before you do.

Obviously, if you name co-beneficiaries for a piece of property that can't be physically divided—a cabin, for example—give some thought to whether or not the beneficiaries are likely to get along. If they are incompatible, disagreements could arise over taking care of property or deciding whether or not to sell it. If they can't settle their differences, any co-owner could go to court and demand a partition—a court-ordered division and sale—of the property.

Co-beneficiaries will share the property equally unless you state otherwise. You will be asked, after you enter the names, whether or not you want this item of trust property to be shared equally among the beneficiaries.

> **EXAMPLE:** Georgia wants to leave her house to her two children, Ross and Ryan, but wants Ross to have a 75% share of it. She enters their names and then, on a later screen, enters their interests, in fractions: 3/4 for Ross and 1/4 for Ryan.
>
> When the children inherit the property, they own it together. But Ross will be liable for 75% of the taxes and upkeep cost, and entitled to 75% of any income the house produces. If they sell it, Ross will be entitled to 75% of the proceeds.

B. Entering Beneficiaries' Names

When you enter a beneficiary's name, use the name by which the beneficiary is known for purposes such as a bank account or driver's license. Generally, if the name you use clearly and unambiguously identifies the person, it is sufficient.

The name you use doesn't have to be the one that appears on the person's birth certificate. And you don't need to include all the nicknames ("Chuck" for someone whose real name is Charles, for example) a beneficiary is known by.

If you name an institution (charitable or not) to inherit the property in your trust, enter its complete name. It may be commonly known by a shortened version, which could cause confusion if there are similarly named organizations. Call to ask if you're unsure. (An institution that stands to inherit some of your money will be more than happy to help you.) Also be sure to specify if you want a specific branch or part of a national organization to receive your gift—for example, a local chapter of the Sierra Club.

C. Beneficiaries for Co-Owned Trust Property

As you name your beneficiaries, remember that when it comes to property you and your spouse co-own, you're naming people to receive only your share. When one spouse dies, only his or her interest in the co-owned property will go to the named beneficiary.

> **EXAMPLE:** Marcia and Perry transfer all the property they own together into their living trust. Marcia names Perry as the beneficiary of all her interest in the trust property. Perry names Marcia to inherit all of his half except his half-interest in their vacation cabin, which he leaves to his son from a previous marriage, Eric. If Perry dies first, Perry's half-interest in the cabin will go to Eric, who will co-own it with Marcia.

D. Alternate Beneficiaries

Living Trust Maker allows you to name an alternate beneficiary for every person you name as a primary beneficiary. The alternate will get the property left to the primary beneficiary if your first choice does not live for more than 120 hours (five days) after your death. This "survivorship" period ensures that if you and a primary beneficiary die simultaneously or almost so, the property will go to the alternate beneficiary you chose, not to the primary beneficiary's heirs.

> **EXAMPLE:** Laura and her husband Juan-Carlos make a shared living trust. Laura leaves all her trust property to Juan-Carlos, and names her daughter from a previous marriage as alternate beneficiary. Laura and Juan-Carlos are seriously injured in a car accident; Juan-Carlos dies a day after Laura does. Because Juan-Carlos did not survive Laura by at least five days, the trust property he would have inherited from Laura goes to Laura's daughter instead.

If there had been no survivorship requirement, the trust property would have gone to Juan-Carlos; when he died a day later, it would have gone to the alternate beneficiaries he had named.

You don't have to name an alternate for a charitable (or other) institution you name as a beneficiary. If the institution is well established, it is probably safe to assume that it will still exist at your death.

With other beneficiaries, however, there is always the chance that the primary beneficiary may not survive you. If you don't name an alternate, the property that beneficiary would have received will be distributed to the person or institution you name, in the next part of the program, as your "residuary beneficiary." (See Part 6, below.)

You can name more than one person or institution as alternate beneficiaries. If you do, these "co-alternate beneficiaries" will share the property equally.

EXAMPLE: Sherry names her husband as beneficiary of her interest in their house, which they have transferred to their living trust. As alternate beneficiaries, she names their three children, Sean, Colleen and Tim.

Sherry's husband dies before she does, leaving his half of the house to Sherry. Under the terms of the trust document, it stays in the living trust. At Sherry's death, the house goes to the three children equally. All three own equal shares in all of it. If they sell the property, each will be entitled to a third of the proceeds.

Part 6: Residuary Beneficiaries

Each spouse must name a residuary beneficiary. The residuary beneficiary of your living trust is the person or organization who will receive:

- any trust property for which both the primary and alternate beneficiaries you named die before you do
- any trust property that you didn't leave to a named beneficiary (this could include property you transferred to the trust later but didn't name a beneficiary for, and trust property that was owned by your spouse, which he or she left you)

- any property you leave to your living trust through your will. (Because property left through a pour-over will doesn't avoid probate, there's usually no reason to use one. See Chapter 3, A Living Trust as Part of Your Estate Plan.)
- any property that you actually transferred to your living trust but didn't list in the trust document.

Often, the residuary beneficiary of a living trust doesn't inherit anything from the trust. Usually, naming a residuary beneficiary is just a back-up measure, to guard against the extremely small chance that both a primary and alternate trust beneficiary do not survive you.

You may, however, deliberately leave the residuary beneficiary trust property by:

- Adding property to the trust later and not naming a specific beneficiary to receive it after your death.
- Using a pour-over will to leave property to your living trust.

If you name more than one person or institution as residuary beneficiary, they will each get an equal share of any trust property they receive.

EXAMPLE: You name your two children, Anne and Alice, as your residuary beneficiaries. If they end up receiving trust property, they will own it together, and both will own an equal share of it.

Part 7: Property Management for Young Beneficiaries

If any of the beneficiaries (including alternate and residuary beneficiaries) named by either spouse might inherit trust property before they are ready to manage it without an adult's help, that spouse should arrange for someone to manage it for them for a while. There are several ways to go about it:

- Leave the property to an adult to use for the child. Many people don't leave property directly to a child. Instead, they leave it to the child's parent or to the person they expect to have care and custody of the child if neither parent is available. There's no formal legal arrangement, but they trust the adult to use the property for the child's benefit.

- Create a child's subtrust. You can use *Living Trust Maker* to establish a "child's subtrust" in your living trust. If you do, your surviving spouse (or the successor trustee, after both spouses' death) will manage the property you left the child and dole it out for education, health and other needs. The subtrust ends at whatever age you designate (up to 35), and any remaining property is turned over to the child outright.
- Name a custodian under the Uniform Transfers to Minors Act (UTMA). In many states, you can name a "custodian" to manage property you leave a child until the child reaches 18 or 21, depending on state law (up to 25 in a few states). If you don't need management to last beyond that age, a custodianship is probably preferable.

Subtrusts and custodianships are explained below.

CHILDREN WITH SPECIAL NEEDS

These property management options are not designed to provide long-term property management for a child with serious disabilities. You should see a lawyer and make arrangements geared to your particular situation.

A. Should You Arrange for Management?

It's left to each spouse whether or not to make arrangements, in the trust document, to have someone manage trust property if it is inherited by young beneficiaries. Each spouse chooses whether or not to arrange for management for his or her beneficiaries.

The consequences of forgoing management for trust property inherited by a young beneficiary depend on whether the beneficiary is over or under age 18 at your death.

1. Children Under 18 Years Old

Minors—children under 18—cannot, legally, own or manage significant amounts of property. An adult must be in charge if the minor acquires more than a few thousand dollars' worth of property. (The exact amount depends on state law.)

If your minor beneficiaries won't inherit anything of great value—if you're leaving them objects that have more sentimental than monetary value—you don't need to arrange for an adult to manage the property.

But if a beneficiary inherits valuable trust property while still a minor, and you have not arranged for the property to be managed by an adult, the beneficiary will have to have a court-appointed guardian to manage the property. Contrary to what you might expect, a child's parent does not automatically have legal authority to manage any property the child inherits. So even if one or both of the beneficiary's parents are alive, they will not automatically have authority to manage the property. They will have to ask the court to grant them that authority, and will be subject to the court's supervision. If neither of the beneficiary's parents are alive, there may be no obvious person for the court to appoint as property guardian. In that case, it may be even more important for you to name someone in your living trust.

2. Young Adults 18 to 35 Years Old

If a living trust beneficiary is over 18 when he or she inherits trust property, you do not need, legally, to have anyone manage the property on the beneficiary's behalf. And if you don't make any arrangements, the beneficiary will get the property with no strings attached. But you can arrange for property management to last until a beneficiary turns any age up to 35.

There is no legal requirement that management for a trust beneficiary's property must end at 35, but we think 35 is a reasonable cutoff. If you don't want to let a beneficiary get his or her hands on trust property by the time he or she reaches 35, you probably need to see a lawyer and tailor a plan to the beneficiary's needs.

B. Which Method Is Best: Subtrust or Custodianship?

Using *Living Trust Maker*, you can create either a child's subtrust or a custodianship under the Uniform Transfer to Minors Act (if it's available in your state). Both are safe, efficient ways of managing trust property that a young person inherits. Under either system, the person in charge of the young beneficiary's property has the same responsibility to use the property for the beneficiary's support, education and health.

The most significant difference is that a child's subtrust can last longer than a custodianship, which must end at age 18 to 21 (up to 25 in Alaska, California, and Nevada) in most states. For that reason, a child's subtrust is a good choice when a child could conceivably inherit a large amount of property.

Because an UTMA custodianship is easier to administer, it is usually preferable if the beneficiary will inherit no more than about $50,000 worth of trust property ($100,000 or more if the child is quite young). That amount is likely to be used up for living and education expenses by the time the beneficiary is 18 to 21, so there's no need to create a child's subtrust that can continue beyond that age.

STATES THAT HAVE ADOPTED THE UNIFORM TRANSFERS TO MINORS ACT

State	Age at which minor gets property	State	Age at which minor gets property
Alabama	21	Missouri	21
Alaska	18-25	Montana	21
Arizona	21	Nebraska	21
Arkansas	18-21	Nevada	18-25
California	18-25	New Hampshire	21
Colorado	21	New Jersey	18-21
District of Columbia	18	New Mexico	21
Florida	21	North Carolina	18-21
Georgia	21	North Dakota	21
Hawaii	21	Ohio	21
Idaho	21	Oklahoma	18
Illinois	21	Oregon	21
Indiana	21	Rhode Island	18
Iowa	21	South Dakota	18
Kansas	21	Tennessee	21
Kentucky	18	Utah	21
Maine	18-21	Virginia	18-21
Maryland	21	Washington	21
Massachusetts	21	West Virginia	21
Minnesota	21	Wisconsin	21
Mississippi	21	Wyoming	21

A custodianship has other advantages as well:

- Handling a beneficiary's property can be easier with a custodianship than with a trust. A custodian's powers are written into state law, and most institutions, such as banks and insurance companies, are familiar with the rules. Trusts, on the other hand, vary in their terms. So before a bank lets a trustee act on behalf of a beneficiary, it may demand to see and analyze a copy of the Declaration of Trust.

- You can name whomever you wish to be a custodian, and you can name different custodians for different beneficiaries. So if you want to arrange custodianships for grandchildren, for example, you could name each child's parent as custodian. A child's subtrust is not quite so flexible: The surviving spouse, or the successor trustee if you are the second spouse to die, will be the trustee of all children's subtrusts created for your young beneficiaries.

- If the property in a subtrust earns income, and that income isn't distributed quickly to the beneficiary, the trust will have to pay tax on it. The federal tax rate on such retained income may be higher than it would be if the young beneficiary were taxed on it.

C. Children's Subtrusts

Living Trust Maker allows you to set up a separate child's subtrust for each young beneficiary.

1. How a Child's Subtrust Works

In your trust document, you state the age at which the beneficiary should receive trust property outright. If at your death the beneficiary is younger than the age you specified, a subtrust will be created for that beneficiary. (If the beneficiary is older, he or she gets the trust property with no strings attached, and no subtrust is created.) Each beneficiary gets a separate child's subtrust.

Living Trust Maker is set up so that the surviving spouse, or the successor trustee after both spouses die, will serve as trustee of all children's subtrusts. If you want different people to manage property inherited by different beneficiaries, you may want to use a custodianship instead of a child's subtrust. (To appoint someone else to be trustee of a child's subtrust, the trust document would have to be changed significantly; see a lawyer.)

Whatever trust property the beneficiary is entitled to receive upon one spouse's death will go into the child's subtrust, if the child is still under the age set for termination of the subtrust. The trustee will manage the subtrust property and use it as necessary for the beneficiary's health, education and support. After the spouse's death, the subtrust cannot be revoked or amended. (Until then, that spouse is free to change his or her mind about having a subtrust set up for a particular beneficiary.)

The child's subtrust will end when the beneficiary reaches the age designated by the spouse in the Declaration of Trust. This can be any age up to and including 35. The trustee will then give the beneficiary what remains of the subtrust property.

EXAMPLE 1: In the trust document that Stanley makes with his wife Natalie, he names his 14-year-old son Michael as beneficiary of $25,000 worth of stock. He specifies that any stock Michael becomes entitled to when Stanley dies should be kept in a subtrust until Michael is 25, subject to the trustee's right to spend it on Michael's behalf.

Stanley dies when Michael is 19. The stock goes into a subtrust for him, managed by Natalie. She is free to use the stock (or the income it produces) to pay for Michael's education and support. Michael will receive what's left of the stock when he turns 25.

EXAMPLE 2: Roger and Victoria create a living trust and leave their trust property to the other. They name their daughters, who are 22 and 25, as alternate beneficiaries, and arrange for any trust property they inherit to stay in children's subtrusts until each daughter reaches 30. They name Victoria's sister, Antoinette, as successor trustee.

Roger and Victoria die in a car accident when one daughter is 28 and the other is 31. The 28-year-old's half of the trust property stays in a subtrust, managed by Antoinette, until she turns 30. The 31-year-old gets her half outright; no subtrust is created for her.

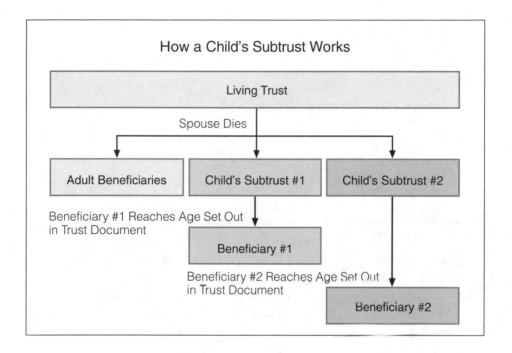

2. The Subtrust Trustee's Duties

The subtrust trustee must:

- Manage subtrust property until the beneficiary reaches the age set out in the trust document—which can take years.
- Use subtrust property or income to pay for expenses such as the beneficiary's support, education and healthcare.
- Keep separate records of subtrust transactions and file income tax returns for the subtrust.

The trustee's powers and responsibilities are spelled out in the trust document. If the subtrust trustee needs to hire an accountant, tax lawyer or other expert, he or she can use subtrust assets to pay a reasonable amount for the help.

The trust document also provides that the trustee of a subtrust is entitled to reasonable compensation for his or her work as trustee. The trustee decides what is a reasonable amount; the compensation is paid from the subtrust assets.

For more on the trustee's responsibilities, see Chapter 10, After a Grantor Dies.

D. Custodianships

A custodianship is the preferable alternative for many people. Here's how it works.

1. How a Custodianship Works

In the trust document, the grantor names someone to serve as custodian for a particular beneficiary. That person manages any trust property the young beneficiary inherits from that spouse until the beneficiary reaches the age at which state law says the custodianship must end. (See table in Section B, above.)

> **EXAMPLE:** Sandra and Don make a living trust. Sandra leaves 100 shares of General Motors stock to her niece, Jennifer Frankel. She names Hazel Frankel, Jennifer's mother, as custodian under the Illinois Uniform Transfers to Minors Act.
>
> After Sandra's death, Don, as trustee, turns the stock over to the custodian, Hazel. She will manage it for Jennifer until Jennifer turns 21, the age Illinois law says she must be given the property outright.

In some states, you can specify—within limits—at what age the custodianship will end. If your state allows this, the program will ask you to enter an age at which you want the custodianship to end.

> **EXAMPLE:** Alexis and Jonathan, who live in New Jersey, make a living trust. They leave each other their trust property and name their young children, Ian and Noel, as alternate beneficiaries. They both specify, in the trust document, that any trust property the children inherit should be managed by Jonathan's mother "as custodian," under the New Jersey Uniform Transfers to Minors Act, until the boys turn 21.
>
> Alexis and Jonathan die simultaneously in an accident. Jonathan's mother takes over management of the trust property for her grandchildren. When each boy turns 21, he will receive whatever of the property hasn't been used for his support or education.

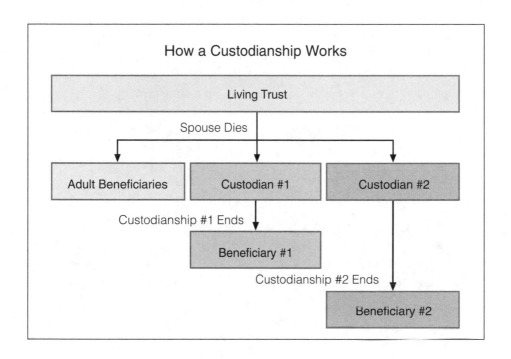

2. The Custodian's Responsibilities

A custodian has roughly the same responsibility as the trustee of a child's subtrust: to manage the beneficiary's property wisely and honestly. The custodian's authority and duties are clearly set out by a law called the Uniform Transfers to Minors Act, as enacted by your state. (The UTMA is a model law written by a national panel of experts, but legislatures may make minor modifications in its when they adopt it for their states.) No court directly supervises the custodian.

The custodian must:

- Manage the property until the beneficiary reaches the age at which, by law, he or she gets the property outright. If the child is a minor at your death, this can be a number of years.
- Use the property or income to pay for expenses such as the young beneficiary's support, education and healthcare.
- Keep the property separate from his or her own property.
- Keep separate records of trust transactions. The custodian does not have to file a separate income tax return; income from the property can be reported

on the young beneficiary's return. (By comparison, the trustee of a child's subtrust must file a separate tax return for the subtrust.)

A custodian who needs to hire an accountant, tax lawyer or other expert can use the property to pay a reasonable amount for the help.

If state law allows it, the custodian is entitled to reasonable compensation and reimbursement for reasonable expenses. The payment, if any is taken, comes from the property the custodian manages for the beneficiary.

3. Choosing a Custodian

You can name a different custodian for each young beneficiary, if you wish.

In most cases, you should name the person who will have physical custody of the minor child. That's almost always one of the child's parents. If the beneficiary is your child, name the child's other parent unless you have serious reservations about that person's ability to handle the property for the child.

Only one person can be named as custodian for one beneficiary. You can, however, name an alternate custodian to take over if your first choice is unable to serve.

Sample Marital Trust

Signing, Storing and Registering the Trust Document

Before You Sign

Before you sign the trust document, make sure it says exactly what you want it to say and that you understand it all. If you want to make changes, use the program and print out another trust document. (If you need help, see the Users' Guide.) Don't write any changes on the document.

Get Your Signature Notarized

Sign your living trust document in front of a notary public for your state. Both you and your spouse need to sign the trust document in front of the notary.

Making Copies

If you need copies of the trust document, use a photocopy of the original trust document—the one you signed and had notarized. Do not just print out and sign another copy.

Registering the Trust

Some states (Alaska, Colorado, Florida, Hawaii, Idaho, Kentucky, Maine, Michigan, Missouri, Nebraska and North Dakota) require that you register your living trust document with the local court. But there are no legal consequences or penalties if you don't. See Chapter 7 of the Legal Manual for instructions on how to register.

Storing the Trust Document

Store your living trust document and the Living Trust Maker disk where you keep important papers. Make sure your successor trustee knows where the original trust document is and can get hold of it soon after your death.

Important Reminder: Transferring Property to the Trust

If an item has a title (ownership) document, such as a deed or title slip, its ownership is not transferred to the trust just by listing it in the program. You must also change the title document to show that you, as trustee of your living trust, are the legal owner of the property.

You should transfer ownership as soon as possible after you print out and sign your Declaration of Trust. Instructions are in Chapter 8 of the Legal Manual.

Keep Up to Date

Fill out the Living Trust Maker registration card included in the package and send it to Nolo Press at the address below. As a registered user, you will receive product updates and notice of

Signing Instructions — Page 1

Legal Manual

significant law changes that affect living trusts. And we
promise never to give your name to any other organization. If
you do not have the full Living Trust Maker package, include
$79.95 and we will send it to you.

                         Nolo Press
            950 Parker Street, Berkeley, CA 94710
                      (510) 549-1976

                  Living Trust Maker 2.0
        Date: Wednesday, August 10, 1994   Time: 13:52:56

Declaration of Trust

Part 1. Trust Name
This revocable living trust shall be known as The Leslie M. Carey and William C. Carey Revocable Living Trust.

Part 2. Declaration of Trust
Leslie M. Carey and William C. Carey, called the grantors, declare that they have transferred and delivered to the trustees all their interest in the property described in Schedules A, B and C attached to this Declaration of Trust. All of that property is called the "trust property." The trustees hereby acknowledge receipt of the trust property and agree to hold the trust property in trust, according to this Declaration of Trust.

Either grantor may add property to the trust.

Part 3. Terminology
The term "this Declaration of Trust" includes any provisions added by valid amendment.

Part 4. Character of Trust Property
While both grantors are alive, property transferred to this trust shall retain its original character as community or separate property, as the case may be.

If the trust is revoked, the trustee shall distribute the trust property listed on Schedule A to the grantors as their community property. The trust property listed in Schedule B shall be distributed to Leslie M. Carey as her separate property, and the trust property listed in Schedule C shall be distributed to William C. Carey as his separate property.

Part 5. Amendment and Revocation

A. Revocation by Grantor
Either grantor may revoke this trust at any time, without notifying any beneficiary. Revocation may be made in writing or any manner allowed by law.

B. Amendment by Grantors
While both grantors are alive, this Declaration of Trust may be amended only by both of them acting together. All amendments must be in writing and signed by both grantors.

C. Amendment or Revocation by Other Person
The power to revoke or amend this trust is personal to the grantors. A conservator, guardian or other person shall not exercise it on behalf of either grantor, unless the grantor specifically grants a power to revoke or amend this trust in a Durable Power of Attorney.

Part 6. Payments from Trust During Grantors' Lifetimes

The trustees shall pay to or use for the benefit of the grantors as much of the net income and principal of the trust property as the grantors request. Income shall be paid to the grantors at least annually.

Part 7. Trustees

A. Original Trustees

Leslie M. Carey and William C. Carey shall be trustees of this trust. Either alone may act for or represent the trust in any transaction.

B. Trustee on Death of Original Trustee

Upon the death or incapacity of Leslie M. Carey or William C. Carey, the surviving trustee shall serve as sole trustee of this trust and of all children's subtrusts created by it.

C. Trustee's Responsibility

The trustee in office shall serve as trustee of all trusts created under this Declaration of Trust, including children's subtrusts.

D. Terminology

In this Declaration of Trust, the term "trustee" includes successor trustees or alternate successor trustees serving as trustee of this trust. The singular "trustee" also includes the plural.

E. Successor Trustee

Upon the death or incapacity of the surviving spouse, or the incapacity of both spouses, Jeffrey R. Carey shall serve as trustee of this trust and of any children's subtrusts created by it. If after the death or incapacity of the surviving spouse, Jeffrey R. Carey is unable or unwilling to serve as successor trustee, Susan DiFlorio shall be the trustee.

F. Resignation of Trustee

Any trustee in office may resign at any time by signing a notice of resignation. The resignation must be delivered to the person or institution who is either named in this Declaration of Trust, or appointed by the trustee under Part 7, Section G, to next serve as the trustee.

G. Power to Appoint Successor Trustee

If no one named in this Declaration of Trust as a successor trustee or alternate successor trustee is willing or able to serve as trustee, the last acting trustee may appoint a successor trustee and may require the posting of a reasonable bond, to be paid from the trust property. The appointment must be made in writing, signed by the trustee and notarized.

H. Bond

No bond shall be required for any trustee named in this Declaration of Trust.

I. Compensation

No trustee shall receive any compensation for serving as trustee, unless the trustee serves as a trustee of a child's subtrust created by this Declaration of Trust.

J. Liability of Trustee

With respect to the exercise or non-exercise of discretionary powers granted by this Declaration of Trust, the trustee shall not be liable for actions taken in good faith. Such actions shall be binding on all persons interested in the trust property.

Part 8. Trustee's Management Powers and Duties

A. Powers Under State Law

The trustee shall have all authority and powers allowed or conferred on a trustee under California law, subject to the trustee's fiduciary duty to the grantors and the beneficiaries.

B. Specified Powers

The trustee's powers shall also include:

1. The power to borrow money and to encumber trust property, including trust real estate, by mortgage, deed of trust or other method.

2. The power to manage trust real estate as if the trustee were the absolute owner of it, including the power to lease (even if the lease term may extend beyond the period of any trust) or grant options to lease the property, to make repairs or alterations and to insure against loss.

3. The power to sell or grant options for the sale or exchange of any trust property, including stocks, bonds, debentures and any other form of security or security account, at public or private sale for cash or on credit.

4. The power to invest trust property in property of any kind, including but not limited to bonds, debentures, notes, mortgages and stocks.

5. The power to receive additional property from any source and add to any trust created by this Declaration of Trust.

6. The power to employ and pay reasonable fees to accountants, lawyers or investment experts for information or advice relating to the trust.

7. The power to deposit and hold trust funds in both interest-bearing and non-interest bearing accounts.

8. The power to deposit funds in bank or other accounts uninsured by FDIC coverage.

9. The power to enter into electronic fund transfer or safe deposit arrangements with financial institutions.

Legal Manual

Part 9. Incapacity of Grantor

If Leslie M. Carey or William C. Carey becomes physically or mentally incapacitated, whether or not a court has declared the grantor incompetent or in need of a conservator, the other spouse shall be sole trustee until a licensed physician certifies in writing that the grantor is again able to manage his or her affairs. Incapacity must be certified in writing by a licensed physician.

If both spouses become incapacitated, the successor trustee named in Part 7, Section E of this Declaration of Trust shall serve as trustee.

The trustee shall manage the trust property and use any amount of trust income or trust principal necessary for the proper healthcare, support, maintenance, comfort and welfare of both grantors, in accordance with their accustomed manner of living. Any income not spent for the benefit of the grantors shall be accumulated and added to the trust property.

Part 10. Death of a Grantor

The first grantor to die shall be called the "deceased spouse." The living grantor shall be called the "surviving spouse."

Upon the deceased spouse's death, the trustee shall divide the property of The Leslie M. Carey and William C. Carey Revocable Living Trust listed on Schedules A, B and C into two separate trusts, Trust #1 and Trust #2. The trustee shall serve as trustee of Trust #1 and Trust #2.

Trust #1 shall contain all the property of The Leslie M. Carey and William C. Carey Revocable Living Trust owned by the deceased spouse before it was transferred to the trust, plus accumulated income, except trust property left by the terms of this trust to the surviving spouse. Trust #1 shall become irrevocable at the death of the deceased spouse.

The trustee shall distribute the property in Trust #1 to the beneficiaries named in Part 11 of this Declaration of Trust.

Trust #2 shall consist of all the property of The Leslie M. Carey and William C. Carey Revocable Living Trust owned by the surviving spouse before it was transferred to the trust, plus accumulated income, and any trust property left by the deceased spouse to the surviving spouse. It shall remain revocable until the death of the surviving spouse.

The trustee may pay out of trust property such amounts as necessary for payment of debts, estate taxes and expenses of the last illness and funeral of the deceased and surviving spouses.

Part 11. Beneficiaries

A. Husband's Beneficiaries

At the death of William C. Carey, the trustee shall distribute the trust property listed on Schedule C, plus accumulated interest; the share of the property on Schedule A owned by William C. Carey before it was transferred to the trust, plus accumulated interest; and if William C. Carey is the second spouse to die, any property listed on Schedule B left to him by the deceased spouse, plus accumulated interest; as follows, subject to provisions in this Declaration of Trust that create children's subtrusts or custodianships under the Uniform Transfers to Minors Act:

1. Leslie M. Carey shall be given all William C. Carey's interest in all the furniture in the house at 3320 Windmill Road, Andersonville, California, the condominium at 19903 Forest Way #43, Wawona, California and the house at 3320 Windmill Road, Andersonville, California. If Leslie M. Carey does not survive William C. Carey by 120 hours, that property shall be given to Claudia A. Carey.

2. Jonathan Goldfarb shall be given all William C. Carey's interest in brokerage account No. 3301-A94 at International Brokers, San Francisco, California. If Jonathan Goldfarb does not survive William C. Carey by 120 hours, that property shall be given to Melissa Goldfarb.

3. Claudia A. Carey shall be given all William C. Carey's interest in trust property not otherwise specifically and validly disposed of by this Part. If Claudia A. Carey does not survive William C. Carey by 120 hours, The Nature Conservancy shall be given all William C. Carey's interest in trust property not otherwise specifically and validly disposed of by this Part.

B. Wife's Beneficiaries

At the death of Leslie M. Carey, the trustee shall distribute the trust property listed on Schedule B, plus accumulated interest; the share of the property on Schedule A owned by Leslie M. Carey before it was transferred to the trust, plus accumulated interest; and if Leslie M. Carey is the second spouse to die, any property listed on Schedule C left to her by the deceased spouse, plus accumulated interest; as follows, subject to provisions in this Declaration of Trust that create children's subtrusts or custodianships under the Uniform Transfers to Minors Act:

1. William C. Carey shall be given all Leslie M. Carey's interest in the trust property. If William C. Carey does not survive Leslie M. Carey by 120 hours, that property shall be given to Claudia A. Carey.

2. Claudia A. Carey shall be given all Leslie M. Carey's interest in trust property not otherwise specifically and validly disposed of by this Part.

C. Property Left to the Surviving Spouse

Any trust property left by the deceased spouse to the surviving spouse shall remain in the surviving spouse's revocable trust, Trust #2.

Part 12. Children's Subtrusts

A. Beneficiaries for Whom Subtrusts May Be Created

1. If Claudia A. Carey has not yet reached the age of 29 when Claudia A. Carey becomes entitled to any trust property under Part 11.A, that trust property shall be kept in a separate child's subtrust, under the provisions of this Part, until Claudia A. Carey reaches the age of 29.

2. If Claudia A. Carey has not yet reached the age of 29 when Claudia A. Carey becomes entitled to any trust property under Part 11.B, that trust property shall be kept in a separate child's subtrust, under the provisions of this Part, until Claudia A. Carey reaches the age of 29.

B. Powers of Subtrust Trustee

The trustee may distribute as much of the net income or principal of the child's subtrust as the trustee deems necessary for the beneficiary's health, support, maintenance or education. Education includes, but is not limited to, college, graduate, postgraduate and vocational studies, and reasonably related living expenses.

In deciding whether or not to make a distribution, the trustee may take into account the beneficiary's other income, resources and sources of support. Any subtrust income not distributed by the trustee shall be accumulated and added to the principal of the subtrust.

C. Assignment of Subtrust Assets

The interests of the beneficiary of a child's subtrust shall not be transferable by voluntary or involuntary assignment or by operation of law before receipt by the beneficiary. They shall be free from the claims of creditors and from attachments, execution, bankruptcy or other legal process to the fullest extent permitted by law.

D. Compensation of Trustee

Any trustee of a child's subtrust created under this Declaration of Trust shall be entitled to reasonable compensation out of the subtrust assets for ordinary and extraordinary services, and for all services in connection with the termination of any subtrust.

E. Termination of Subtrusts

A child's subtrust shall end when any of the following events occurs:

1. The beneficiary dies. If the subtrust ends for this reason, the subtrust property shall pass to the beneficiary's heirs.

2. The beneficiary reaches the age specified in Section A of this Part. If the subtrust ends for this reason, the remaining principal and accumulated income of the subtrust shall be given

outright to the beneficiary.

3. The trustee distributes all subtrust property under the provisions of this Declaration of Trust.

Part 13. Custodianships Under the Uniform Transfers to Minors Act

1. Any property Melissa Goldfarb becomes entitled to under Part 11.A of this Declaration of Trust shall be given to Jane Goldfarb, as custodian for Melissa Goldfarb under the California Uniform Transfers to Minors Act, until Melissa Goldfarb reaches the age of 22. If Jane Goldfarb is unable or ceases to serve as custodian, Leslie M. Carey shall serve as custodian.

Part 14. Severability of Clauses

If any provision of this Declaration of Trust is ruled unenforceable, the remaining provisions shall stay in effect.

Certification of Grantors

We certify that we have read this Declaration of Trust and that it correctly states the terms and conditions under which the trust property is to be held, managed and disposed of by the trustees, and we approve the Declaration of Trust.

_____   Dated: _____
William C. Carey, Grantor and Trustee

_____   Dated: _____
Leslie M. Carey, Grantor and Trustee

State of _____

County of _____

On _____, before me, _____, a notary public for said state, personally appeared Leslie M. Carey and William C. Carey, personally known to me (or proved to me on the basis of satisfactory evidence) to be the persons whose names are subscribed to the within instrument, and acknowledged to me that they executed the same in their authorized capacities and that by their signatures on the instrument the persons, or the entity upon behalf of which the persons acted, executed the instrument.

Witness my hand and official seal.

_____
NOTARY PUBLIC for the State of _____
My commission expires _____.

Schedule A

1. All the furniture in the house at 3320 Windmill Road, Andersonville, California.
2. The condominium at 19903 Forest Way #43, Wawona, California.
3. The house at 3320 Windmill Road, Andersonville, California.

Schedule B

1. Scudder International Fund Account 993-222-1.
2. The 4-volume American stamp collection kept at 3320 Windmill Road, Andersonville, California.

Legal Manual

Schedule C

1. Brokerage account No. 3301-A94 at International Brokers, San Francisco, California.

Signing, Storing and Registering the Trust Document

Y ou don't yet have a valid living trust when you've completed the program and printed out your living trust document. Here's what to do next.

A. Before You Sign

When you've printed out the trust document, take plenty of time to read it. Carefully. Make sure it says what you want it to say. Check to be sure you have:

- included all property you want to leave through the trust
- clearly and accurately identified all property (doublecheck any account and serial numbers, for example)
- included all beneficiaries to whom you want to leave property
- spelled beneficiaries' (including alternate and residuary beneficiaries) names correctly and consistently
- made adequate arrangements for management of trust property that young beneficiaries might inherit.

If you want to make changes, go back to the part of the program you need to change, enter the new data, and print out another trust document. (If you need help, see the Users' Guide.)

Although in most instances it isn't necessary, you may also want to have an experienced estate planning lawyer look over the trust document before you sign it. You may already have consulted a lawyer, if you found yourself in a situation where we recommend that you get expert help—for example, if you haven't left at least half of your estate to your spouse or want to disinherit a minor child.

Now that you have the trust document in your hands, we recommend that you see a lawyer if:

- you're unsure about the legal effect of anything in the trust document, or
- you want to make changes, even if they seem insignificant, to the trust document created by *Living Trust Maker.*

The cost of paying an experienced estate planning attorney to review the trust document should be reasonable—especially compared to the cost of having an attorney do the whole thing from scratch. (Chapter 11, If You Need Expert Help, discusses how to find a lawyer and get the most help for your legal fees.)

A word of caution: Be aware that a lawyer who has a set way of doing things may disparage your self-help efforts and try to sell you expensive services you don't need. Before you sign up, be sure that the work is really necessary and justifies the expense.

B. Signing Your Trust Document in Front of a Notary

To create your living trust, you must sign the trust document. A living trust document, unlike a will, does not need to be signed in front of witnesses (in Florida, two witnesses are not required but are customarily used.) But you do need to sign your living trust document in front of a notary public for your state. If you and your spouse create a living trust together, both of you need to sign the trust document in front of the notary. If anyone challenges the authenticity of your signature after your death, the notarization will serve as evidence that it is genuine. And some institutions (stock brokerage houses, for example) may require that the signature be notarized before they will transfer assets into the trust.

You can usually find a notary public at a bank, title or escrow company, real estate brokerage or library. Or check the yellow pages under "Notaries Public."

Getting a signature notarized is quite simple. You show some evidence of your identity, and then the notary watches you sign the trust document and signs and dates it, too. The notary also stamps a notarial seal on the document.

The living trust document produced by *Living Trust Maker* includes, at the end of the document after the lines for your signature, a place for the notarization. The notarization form should be valid in most places, but if the notary public for your state wants to modify it, that's fine; some states require slightly different wording.

C. Making Copies

You will probably need copies of the trust document to transfer certain kinds of property (stocks, for example) into your living trust. (The details are in Chapter 8, Transferring Property to the Trust.) If a broker, bank or other institution wants to see your trust document, use a photocopy of the original trust document—the one you signed and had notarized. Do not just print out and sign another copy. Each copy you actually sign becomes, legally, an original trust document. Later, if you amend or revoke your living trust, you don't want lots of duplicate original trust documents floating around.

You should give a copy of the trust document to anyone you named to be a custodian of trust property inherited by a young beneficiary. The custodian may need it to show his or her authority to manage the property on behalf the beneficiary.

It's possible, but not usually advisable, to give copies of the trust document to beneficiaries. The problem is that if you later revoke or amend the trust but don't collect all the old copies, there will be outdated copies of your trust document floating around.

D. Registering the Trust

STATES THAT PROVIDE FOR REGISTRATION OF LIVING TRUSTS			
Alaska	Hawaii	Michigan	Nebraska*
Colorado**	Idaho	Missouri*	North Dakota
Florida*	Maine		

* not mandatory.

**registration of a revocable living trust not required until the grantor's death; no registration required required if all trust property is distributed to the beneficiaries then.

Some states require that the trustee of a trust register the trust with the local court. But there are no legal consequences or penalties if you don't.

Registration of a living trust doesn't give the court any power over the administration of the trust, unless there's a dispute. Registration serves to give the court jurisdiction over any disputes involving the trust—for example, if after your death a beneficiary wants to object to the way your successor trustee distributed the trust property. But if you don't register your trust, the result is the same: the court still has jurisdiction if a disgruntled relative or creditor files suit. (The only exception is that if a court demands that a trustee register a trust, and the trustee refuses, the trustee can be removed.)

To register a revocable living trust, the trustee must file a statement with the court where the trustee resides or keeps trust records. The statement must include:

- the name and address of the trustee
- an acknowledgement of the trusteeship
- the name(s) of the grantor(s)
- the name(s) of the original trustee(s)

- the date of the trust document.

A trust can be registered in only one state at a time.

E. Storing the Trust Document

Store your living trust document, a floppy disk with a copy of your trust data file, the *Living Trust Maker* disk and the manual where you keep important papers such as your will or durable power of attorney. A fireproof box in your home or office is fine. If you want to be extra careful, a safe deposit box is a good choice.

Make sure your successor trustee (or spouse, if you made a shared marital trust) knows where the original trust document is and can get hold of it soon after your death. The new trustee will need it to carry out your instructions on how to manage and distribute trust property. The new trustee will also need the information in Chapter 10, After a Grantor Dies, to carry out his or her duties.

The copy of your trust document stored on the disk does not create a valid living trust. The trust document must be printed out and signed to create a trust.

Transferring Property to the Trust

A fter you sign your living trust document, you have a valid living trust. But the trust is of absolutely no use to you until the property you listed in the trust document is actually transferred into the trust's name. Lawyers call this "funding" the trust.

Transferring your property to your living trust is crucial, and takes some time and paperwork, but it's not difficult. You should be able to do it yourself, without a lawyer.

For some types of property, the work is done simply by preparing your trust document. If the property does not have an official title (ownership) document—a deed or title certificate, for example—the trust document itself states that the property is transferred to the trust. That's enough; you don't need another piece of paper that says the same thing. Property that falls into this category includes most furniture, clothing, books, appliances and other household goods.

But for items that have a title document that shows ownership—real estate, bank accounts, securities and much more—you will have to prepare a new document to show that the trust owns the property. This chapter shows you how.

⚠ TAKE CARE OF THIS LAST STEP PROMPTLY

Failing to transfer property to the trust is the most common and serious mistake people make when creating a living trust. If you don't get around to preparing and signing these new documents, the trust document will have no effect on what happens to your property after your death. Instead, the property will go to the "residuary beneficiary" named in your will, if you have one (you should—see Chapter 3, A Living Trust as Part of Your Estate Plan). If you don't have a will, the property will go to certain close relatives, according to state law. Either way, it will probably go through probate.

A. Making a Certification or Abstract of Trust

When you go to transfer property in or out of your living trust, a bank or other institution may ask to see the trust document. The institution wants to know that the trust exists and that you really have the authority you say you do.

If you don't want to show your trust document, in most cases you can use a shorter version of it, called a certification, abstract, certificate or memorandum of trust. This gives institutions the information they need but lets you keep some key provisions private. Notably, you don't have to disclose the names of the beneficiaries to whom you're leaving trust property. A certification or abstract is almost universally accepted in place of an entire trust document.

Some institutions have a form for you to fill out. If not, you can easily make a document whenever you need one, just by taking some of the pieces from your trust document. Draw up and sign a new certification whenever you need one; the institution will want a current signature.

Before you create a certification, ask the institution exactly what it requires. Generally, a certification should include:

- a statement that the trust exists
- the name of the trust
- a statement that the trust is revocable
- the names of the persons who have authority to revoke it
- the date the trust document was signed
- the name of each grantor
- the name of each original trustee
- the name and address of each currently acting trustee
- the powers of the trustee(s)
- if there is more than one trustee, whether or not each has authority to act independently
- how title to trust assets should be taken (for example, you might specify that title should be taken in the name of "Karl and Sophie Loggam, trustees of the Karl Loggam and Sophie Loggam Revocable Living Trust dated March 14, 1993")
- a statement that the trust hasn't been revoked or modified in any way that would contradict anything else you've said in the certification.

State law may, however, require other elements, or even specific words, in the certification. A few states (California and Minnesota, for example) have recently enacted laws allowing certifications of trust to be offered in lieu of the trust document. These laws set out specific requirements for the contents of a certification.

These laws may also help ensure that your certification is accepted in place of the whole trust document. California law, for example, states that someone who refuses to accept the information in the certification and demands to see the whole trust document may be liable for damages suffered by the trust grantor. (Cal. Prob. Code § 18100.5.)

All currently acting trustees should sign the certification in front of a notary public. A sample is shown below.

Sample Abstract of Trust

Abstract of Trust

Existence and Name of Trust

    Judith M. Avery, called the grantor, declares that she created a revocable living trust, known as The Judith M. Avery Revocable Living Trust, by Declaration of Trust dated July 26, 1994, and that this trust has not been amended or revoked since that date.

Amendment and Revocation

Amendment or Revocation by Grantor

    The grantor may amend or revoke this trust at any time, without notifying any beneficiary. An amendment must be made in writing and signed by the grantor. Revocation may be in writing or any manner allowed by law.

Amendment or Revocation by Other Person

    The power to revoke or amend this trust is personal to the grantor. A conservator, guardian or other person shall not exercise it on behalf of the grantor, unless the grantor specifically grants a power to revoke or amend this trust in a Durable Power of Attorney.

Trustees

Trustee

    Judith M. Avery shall be trustee of this trust.

Trustee's Responsibility

    The trustee in office shall serve as trustee of all trusts created under this Declaration of Trust, including children's subtrusts.

Terminology

    In this Declaration of Trust, the term "trustee" includes successor trustees or alternate successor trustees serving as trustee of this trust. The singular "trustee" also includes the plural.

Trustee's Management Powers and Duties

Powers Under State Law

    The trustee shall have all authority and powers allowed or conferred on a trustee under Illinois law, subject to the trustee's fiduciary duty to the grantor and the beneficiaries.

Specified Powers

    The trustee's powers shall also include:

1. The power to borrow money and to encumber trust property, including trust real estate, by mortgage, deed of trust or other method.

2. The power to manage trust real estate as if the trustee were the absolute owner of it, including the power to lease (even if the lease term may extend beyond the period of any trust) or grant options to lease the property, to make repairs or alterations and to insure against loss.

3. The power to sell or grant options for the sale or exchange of any trust property, including stocks, bonds, debentures and any other form of security or security account, at public or private sale for cash or on credit.

4. The power to invest trust property in property of any kind, including but not limited to bonds, debentures, notes, mortgages and stocks.

5. The power to receive additional property from any source and add to any trust created by this Declaration of Trust.

6. The power to employ and pay reasonable fees to accountants, lawyers or investment experts for information or advice relating to the trust.

7. The power to deposit and hold trust funds in both interest-bearing and non-interest-bearing accounts.

8. The power to deposit funds in bank or other accounts uninsured by FDIC coverage.

9. The power to enter into electronic fund transfer or safe deposit arrangements with financial institutions.

_____   _____

Judith M. Avery, Grantor and Trustee   Date

State of _____

County of _____

On _____, before me, _____
_____, a notary public for said state, personally appeared Judith M. Avery, personally known to me (or proved to me on the basis of satisfactory evidence) to be the person whose name is subscribed to the within instrument, and acknowledged to me that she executed the same in her authorized capacity and that by her signature on the instrument the person, or the entity upon behalf of which the person acted, executed the instrument.

Witness my hand and official seal.

_____

NOTARY PUBLIC for the State of _____
My commission expires _____.

STATE LAWS ARE CHANGING
Before drawing up a certification of trust, check to see if your state has jumped on this new bandwagon and adopted a law setting out the contents of a certification.

B. Real Estate

To transfer real estate (also called real property) into the name of your trust, you must prepare and sign a new deed. The deed transfers ownership from you to the trust. You can fill out a new deed yourself; it's not difficult.

Co-op apartments. If you own a co-op apartment, you can't use a deed to transfer your shares in the co-op. You will have to check the co-op corporation's rules to see if the transfer is allowed. Some co-ops resist such transfers because they are afraid a living trust isn't a proper shareholder in the corporation. You can probably overcome any resistance you encounter by reminding the powers that be that for all practical purposes, you and the trust are the same—you have the same tax identification number, for example.

1. Preparing the Deed

First, get a deed form. In many places, you can find blank deed forms in stationery or office supply stores. If you can't find what you need there, try a local law library; look for books on "real property" that have deed forms you can photocopy. You can use a "quitclaim" or "grant" deed form. (The type of deed isn't important when you're transferring property to your own living trust. If you use a grant deed, you are promising the new owner (the trust) that you have good title to the property. If you use a quitclaim deed, you are promising only to transfer whatever interest you own in the property. The distinction isn't important when you control the trust.)

If you're in California, you can find deed forms and instructions for filling them out in *The Deeds Book*, by Mary Randolph (Nolo Press). Much of the information in *The Deeds Book* is valid in other states as well, but it's best to use a deed form that's in common use in your area.

Deed forms vary somewhat, but they all require the same basic information. Using a typewriter, fill out your deed like the sample shown below. Type in:

- The current owners' names. If you are the sole owner, or if you and someone else co-own the property and you are transferring just your share, only your name goes here. If you and your spouse own the property together and are transferring it to a shared marital trust, type in both of your names. Use exactly the same form of your name as is used on the deed that transferred the property to you and you used in your living trust document.

- The new owner's name. Fill in your name(s), as trustee(s) exactly as it appears in the first paragraph of your trust document, and the date you signed the trust document in front of a notary public.

- The "legal description" of the property. Copy the description exactly as it appears on the previous deed.

If you co-own the property with someone and are transferring only your share to the living trust, you must also state, with the legal description, that you are transferring only that share (a one-half interest, for example) or that you are transferring "all your interest in" the property.

> **EXAMPLE:** Amanda, who owns a house with her sister, wants to transfer her half of the property to her living trust. When she fills out a new deed, she can insert either "a one-half interest in" or "all my interest in" before the legal description.

After everything is filled in, sign and date the deed in front of a notary public for the state in which the property is located. Everyone you listed as a current owner, who is transferring his or her interest in the property to the trust, must sign the deed.

2. Recording the Deed

After the deed is signed, you need to "record" it—that is, put a copy of the notarized deed on file in the county office that keeps local property records. In most places, the land records office is called the County Recorder's Office, Land Registry Office or County Clerk's office.

Just take the original, signed deed to the land records office. For a small fee, a clerk will make a copy and put it in the public records. You'll get your original back, stamped with a reference number to show where the copy can be found in the public records.

SAMPLE GRANT DEED

Recording requested by

Rose and Michael Morris
4432 Franklin Avenue
Fresno, CA 96833

and when recorded mail
this deed and tax statements to:

same as above

For recorder's use

GRANT DEED

☒ This transfer is exempt from the documentary transfer tax.
☐ The documentary transfer tax is $_____ and is computed on:
   ☐ the full value of the interest or property conveyed.
   ☐ the full value less the value of liens or encumbrances remaining thereon at the time of sale.
The property is located in ☐ an unincorporated area. ☐ the city of _____.

For a valuable consideration, receipt of which is hereby acknowledged,

Rose Morris and Michael Morris

hereby grant(s) to

Rose Morris and Michael Morris, trustees of the Rose Morris and
Michael Morris Revocable Living Trust dated January 13, 19XX

the following real property in the City of ___Fresno___, County of ___Fresno___,
California:

[legal description exactly as on previous deed]

Date: ___Jan. 15, 19XX___   _Rose Morris_

Date: ___Jan. 15, 19XX___   _Michael Morris_

Date: _____   _____

Date: _____   _____

State of California

County of _Fresno_) ss.

On _January 15 19XX_, before me, _Geraldine A. Fishman_ [insert name
and title of the officer], personally appeared _Rose Morris & Michael Morris_,
personally known to me (or proved to me on the basis of satisfactory evidence) to be the
person(s) whose name(s) is/are subscribed to the within instrument and acknowledged to me
that he/she/they executed the same in his/her/their authorized capacity(ies), and that by
his/her/their signature(s) on the instrument the person(s), or the entity upon behalf of which the
person(s) acted, executed the instrument.

   WITNESS my hand and official seal.

Geraldine A. Fishman   [SEAL]

Signature of Notary

3. Transfer Taxes

In most places, you will not have to pay a state or local transfer tax when you transfer real estate to a revocable living trust. Most real estate transfer taxes are based on the sale price of the property and do not apply when no money changes hands. Others specifically exempt transfers where the real owners don't change—as is the case when you transfer property to a revocable living trust you control.

Before you record your deed, you can get information on transfer tax from the county tax assessor, county recorder or state tax officials.

4. Insurance

After you have transferred ownership of real estate to your living trust, call your insurance agent to report the change. The company will change its records on the policy, but the change won't affect your coverage or the cost of the policy.

5. Due-on-Sale Mortgage Clauses

Many mortgages contain a clause that allows the bank to call ("accelerate") the loan—that is, demand that you pay the whole thing off immediately—if you transfer the mortgaged property. Fortunately, in most instances lenders are forbidden by federal law to invoke a due-on-sale clause when property is transferred to a living trust. The lender can't call the loan if the borrower is a trust beneficiary and the transfer is "unrelated to occupancy" of the premises. (Garn-St. Germain Depository Institutions Act of 1982 (96 Stat. 1505).)

CALIFORNIA PROPERTY TAXES

In California, increases in real estate taxes are limited by constitutional amendment (Proposition 13). The assessed value of the property can't go up more than 2% annually until a piece of property is sold. When the property is sold, however, the house is taxed on its market value. Transferring real property to a revocable living trust—or back to the person who set up the trust—does not trigger a reassessment for property tax purposes. (Cal. Rev. & Tax Code § 62(d).)

You may, however, have to file a form called a Preliminary Change of Title Report with the county tax assessor. Call the assessor to find out.

C. Bank Accounts and Safe Deposit Boxes

It should be simple to re-register ownership of a bank account in the name of your living trust or open a new account in the trust's name. Just ask the bank what paperwork you need to submit.

The bank will be concerned with the authority granted to the trustees to act on behalf of the trust. Depending on the kind of account, the bank may want to know if the trustees have the power to borrow money, put funds in a non-interest-bearing account, or engage in electronic transfers. (The trust document created by *Living Trust Maker* includes all these powers.)

To verify your authority, the bank may want to see a copy of your trust document, or have you fill out its own form, often called a Trust Certification.

If you want to transfer title to a safe deposit box to your trust, you'll have to re-register its ownership, too. The bank will have a form for you to fill out.

> #### CREDIT UNIONS
>
> If you want to transfer a credit union account to your living trust, you cannot simply change the name on the account. Because credit unions are membership organizations, the trust must qualify as a member of the credit union. Most credit unions accept living trusts as members. Ask your credit union for instructions.

Estate planning note. Instead of transferring a bank account to a living trust, you may want to turn the account into a pay-on-death account (also called an revocable trust account). It's another, even easier, way to avoid probate of the money in the account. (See Chapter 3, A Living Trust as Part of Your Estate Plan.)

D. Vehicles

Most people don't transfer vehicles to a living trust, for reasons discussed in Part 7 of Chapter 5 or 6. Putting title to the vehicle in joint tenancy with a co-owner (or, if your state allows it, designating a beneficiary on the car registration) is usually a simpler way to avoid probate of the vehicle at your death.

But if you want to put a vehicle in trust, you must fill out a change of ownership document and have title to the vehicle reissued in the trust's name. The title certificate to your vehicle may contain instructions. If you have questions, call your state's Motor Vehicles Department.

E. Securities

How you transfer stocks, bonds and other securities to your living trust depends on whether you hold your stocks in a brokerage account or separately.

1. Brokerage Accounts

If you hold your stocks, bonds or other securities in a brokerage account, either change the account to the living trust's name or open a new account in the living trust's name. Simply contact your broker and ask for instructions. The brokerage company will probably have a straightforward form that you can fill out, giving information about the trustees and their authority.

If not, you will probably need to send the broker:

- a copy of the trust document or an "abstract of trust" (see Section A, above), and
- a letter instructing the holder to transfer the brokerage account to the living trust's name (or open a new account in the trust's name).

After you've submitted your request, get written confirmation that the account's ownership has in fact been put in the trust's name.

With some brokerage houses, you may run into a slight glitch. Here's what happens: when you go to transfer your account into your name as trustee, the brokerage house assigns it a new account number. Suddenly your property schedule, where you listed the account, has the wrong account number on it.

What to do? Just amend your property schedule to show the new account number (see Chapter 9). Then replace the old schedule with the new one, and you're all set.

2. Stock Certificates

If you have the stock certificates or bonds in your possession—most people don't—you must get new certificates issued, showing the trust as owner. Ask your broker for help. If the broker is unwilling or unable to help, write to the "transfer agent" of the corporation that issued the stock. You can get the address from your broker or the investor relations office of the corporation. The transfer agent will give you simple instructions.

You will probably have to send in:

- your certificates or bonds
- a form called a "stock or bond power," which you must fill out and sign, and
- a copy of the trust document or an "abstract of trust," which is just the first and last pages of the trust document, showing your notarized signature.

The stock or bond power may be printed on the back of the certificates; if not, you can probably find a copy at a stationery store. Send these documents to the transfer agent with a letter requesting that the certificates be reissued in the living trust's name.

      Stock in closely-held corporations. See Section G, Business Interests, below.

3. Government Securities

To transfer government securities—for example, Treasury bills or U.S. bonds— have your broker contact the issuing government agency, or do it yourself.

F. Mutual Fund Accounts

Ask the company that issues the mutual fund what it requires for you to re-register ownership of your mutual fund account in your living trust's name. Most will send you an easy-to-use form to fill out. In addition, it will usually want a copy of your trust document or an "abstract of trust," which is just the first and last pages of the trust document.

G. Business Interests

How you transfer small business interests to your living trust depends on the way the business is owned.

1. Sole Proprietorships

An unincorporated business that you own by yourself is the easiest to transfer to a trust. First, list the business, by name, as an item of property in the trust document. That transfers the name to your living trust and whatever customer goodwill goes with it.

      Because you own the business assets in your own name (a sole proprietorship, unlike a corporation, is not an entity that can own property), you transfer them to your living trust like you would any other valuable property. (See the Valuable Property Inventory, Chapter 5 or 6.)

If you have a registered trademark or service mark, you must re-register ownership in the living trust's name. For sample forms, see *Trademark: How to Name Your Business and Product,* by Kate McGrath and Steve Elias (Nolo Press).

2. Solely-Owned Corporations

If you own all the stock of a corporation, you shouldn't have any problem transferring it to your living trust. Follow these four steps:

Step 1: Fill out the stock transfer section on the back of the certificate.

Step 2: Mark the certificate "cancelled" and place it in your corporate records book.

Step 3: Resissue a new certificate in the name of the living trust.

Step 4: Show the cancellation of the old certificate and the issuance of the new certificate on the stock ledger pages in your corporate records book.

3. Closely-Held Corporations

Normally, you can transfer your shares in a closely-held corporation to your living trust by following corporate bylaws and having the stock certificates reissued in the living trust's name. But first, check the corporation's bylaws and articles of incorporation, as well as any separate shareholders' agreements, to see if there are any restrictions on such transfers. If an agreement limits or forbids transfers, it will have to be changed before you can put your shares in your living trust.

4. Partnership Interests

To transfer your partnership interest to your living trust, you must notify your business partners and modify the partnership agreement to show that your partnership interest is now owned by your living trust. If there is a partnership certificate, it must be changed to substitute the trust as owner of your share.

Occasionally a partnership agreement limits or forbids transfers to a living trust. If so, you and your partners may want to see a lawyer before you make any changes.

Legal Manual

H. Limited Partnerships

Limited partnerships are a form of investment, governed by securities laws. Contact the partnership's general partner to find out what paperwork is necessary to transfer your interest to a living trust.

I. Copyrights

If you want to transfer your interest in a copyright to your living trust, you should list the copyright in the trust document and then sign and file, with the U.S. Copyright Office, a document transferring all your rights in the copyright to the living trust. Sample transfer forms are in *The Copyright Handbook*, by Steve Fishman (Nolo Press).

J. Patents

If you own a patent and want to transfer it to your living trust, you should prepare a document called an "assignment" and record it with the Patent and Trademark Office in Washington, DC. There is a small fee for recording. Sample assignment forms and instructions are in *Patent It Yourself*, by David Pressman (Nolo Press).

K. Property That Names the Trust as Beneficiary

If you name your living trust as beneficiary of a life insurance policy, individual retirement account (IRA) or Keogh account, you don't need to transfer the policy or account itself to the trust. You, not the living trust, are the owner. The living trust is the beneficiary, which will receive the proceeds at your death. The proceeds will be given to the residuary beneficiary of your living trust unless you named someone else, in the trust document, to receive them.

Living With Your Living Trust

Legal Manual

As a day-to-day, practical matter, it makes little difference that your property is now owned by your revocable living trust. You have no special paperwork to prepare, forms to file or other duties to perform as the trustee of your own trust.

   This chapter discusses what you need to know after your living trust is up and running, and how to change your trust document if you wish.

A. Reporting Income From Trust Property

No separate income tax records or returns are necessary as long as you are the trustee of your own living trust. (I.R.S. Reg. § 1.671-4.) Income from property in the trust must be reported on your personal income tax return.

B. If You Move to Another State

Your living trust is still valid if you prepare it in one state and then move to another. You may, however, need to take some actions after your move:

- Your new state may require you to register your living trust document with the local court. (See Chapter 7, Signing, Storing and Registering the Trust Document.)
- You may want to amend the trust document if the new state's laws differ on matters such as marital property rights or property management for young trust beneficiaries. (See Section D, below.)

C. Selling or Giving Away Trust Property

You have complete control over the property you have transferred to the living trust. If you want to sell or give away any of it, simply go ahead, using your authority as trustee. You (or you and your spouse, if you made a shared marital trust) just sign ownership or transfer documents (the deed, bill of sale or other document) in your capacity as trustee of the living trust.

EXAMPLE: Mel transfers ownership of his house to his living trust, but later decides to sell it. When he transfers the house to the buyer, he signs the new deed as "Melvin Owens, trustee of the Melvin Owens Revocable Living Trust dated June 8, 1991."

If you and your spouse made a shared marital trust, either trustee (spouse) has authority over trust property. That means that either spouse can sell or give away any of the trust property—including the property that was co-owned or was the separate property of the other spouse before it was transferred to the trust. In practice, however, both spouses will probably have to consent to transfer real estate out of the living trust. Especially in community property states, buyers and title insurance companies usually insist on both spouses' signatures on transfer documents.

If for any reason you want to take property out of the trust but keep ownership of it, you can transfer it to yourself. The process is, essentially, the reverse of the process you followed to transfer the property to the trust. (See Chapter 8, Transferring Property to the Trust.)

EXAMPLE: Janice wants to take her house out of her living trust but keep ownership in her own name. She makes the deed out from "Janice Yamaguchi, trustee of the Janice Yamaguchi Revocable Living Trust dated November 24, 1993" to "Janice Yamaguchi."

You will also need to make one or two changes to your trust document:

- Modify the property schedule of your trust document to reflect the change. If you don't, the schedule will still show that the property is owned by the trust, and the discrepancy could be confusing to the people who carry out your wishes after your death.
- If you named a specific beneficiary to receive the item, delete that trust provision, using a trust amendment.

Section F, below, shows how to make these changes using *Living Trust Maker*.

EXAMPLE: Wendy and Brian made a shared marital living trust several years ago. Wendy transferred a valuable antique dresser, which she inherited from her grandfather before she was married, to the living trust. It's listed on Schedule B of the trust document as her separate property. The trust document provides that the dresser will go to her son at her death. But she's changed her mind and wants her daughter to have the dresser right now.

After Wendy gives the dresser to her daughter, she uses *Living Trust Maker* to prepare and print out two documents. First, she prepares a new Schedule B, deleting the dresser from the list of property, and replaces the old Schedule B attached to her trust document. Second, she prepares a trust amendment, stating that the paragraph that left the dresser to her son is deleted from the trust document. After she signs the amendment in front of a notary public, her trust document reflects her wishes.

D. When to Amend Your Trust Document

One of the most attractive features of a revocable living trust is its flexibility: you can change its terms, or end it altogether, at any time. This section discusses several events that should be red flags, alerting you that you may need to amend your living trust. (Instructions for using *Living Trust Maker* to make a trust amendment are in Section F, below.)

In most circumstances, you will want to amend your living trust document, not revoke it. It might seem easier to revoke it and start again, as you might with a will. But if you revoke your living trust and create another one, you must transfer all the trust property out of the old living trust and into the new one. (Section G, below, discusses when it is advisable to revoke your living trust and make another.)

Remember that if you and your spouse made a shared marital trust, you both must consent to any amendments.

1. You Change Your Mind

You may simply change your mind about whom you want to inherit trust property, or whom you want to serve as your successor trustee. To change these or other terms of your living trust, you'll need to make a trust amendment.

2. You Marry or Have a Child

If you get married or have a child, you'll almost certainly want to amend your trust document to provide for your new spouse or offspring. (Your spouse or child may be entitled, under state law, to some of your property; see Chapter 2, About Living Trusts.) If you divorce, you should revoke your trust; see Section H, below.

3. You Add Valuable Property to the Trust

If you add property to your living trust, you may need to amend the trust document (as well as the property schedule) to name a beneficiary to inherit the property. (See Section C, above.)

4. You Move to Another State

Although your living trust is still valid if you move to another state, you may want to change your trust document in response to your new state's laws. Here are several aspects of an estate plan that may be affected by a move.

a. Marital Property Laws: Who Owns What

If you and your spouse move to another state, in most cases, the move does not change who owns what. But everything you and your spouse acquire in the new state is subject to that state's laws regarding ownership.

> **EXAMPLE:** Leah and Ben move from Texas, a community property state, to Illinois, a non-community property state. In Texas, money either earned from working belonged to both spouses equally, which means that the car Leah bought with her salary is jointly owned by Leah and Ben. That doesn't change when they move to Illinois. After they move, however, each spouse's salary is his or her separate property.

If, however, you move from a non-community property state to a community property state, the move may change which spouse owns what. Two community property states, California and Idaho, have rules that treat certain property you bring with you as if you had acquired it in the community property state. Here's the general rule: If the property would have been community property had you acquired it in the new state, it is treated like community property at death or divorce. (The legal term for such property is "quasi-community property.") This means that each spouse owns half of this property and can leave only that share at death.

These rules usually don't apply to real estate.

EXAMPLE: Carlo and Sylvia, a married couple, move from New York to California. Their car, bought in New York with Carlo's earnings and registered in his name, would be considered quasi-community property—which means that once Carlo and Sylvia settle in California, the car legally belongs to both of them.

Obviously, this can be a very complicated subject. The good news is that you need be concerned about this issue only if:

1. You move to California or Idaho from a non-community property state; and
2. You are concerned that because of the move, trust property that was formerly owned by only one spouse might now be considered to be owned by both; and
3. In the trust document, you did not leave at least a half-interest in that property to your spouse.

In this situation, you have two options:

- Make a trust amendment, changing ownership of the property from separate property to community property, and having both spouses name beneficiaries for the property.
- See a lawyer who's knowledgeable about your new state's law. If the property you're concerned about is valuable—a large amount of stock, for example—the cost of an expert will be well worth the peace of mind you get.

b. Property Management for Young Beneficiaries

Your state's law determines the choices you have when it comes to arranging for someone to manage property left to young beneficiaries. In all states, you can use *Living Trust Maker* to create a "child's subtrust" for any beneficiary who might inherit trust property before he or she is 35. But state law determines whether or not you have another option: appointing someone to be the "custodian" of trust property inherited by a young beneficiary. (See Chapter 5 or 6, Part 7.)

If you move from a state that doesn't offer the custodianship option to one that does (most do), you may want to create a trust amendment, changing your trust document to let you take advantage of it.

If you move after you have already created a custodianship, the custodianship will still be valid. You can, however, create a trust amendment that deletes the old custodianship clause and adds a new one that conforms to your new state's law.

Legal Manual

c.   Rights of a Surviving Spouse or Child to Inherit

Different states entitle surviving spouses (and in some cases, children) to different shares of a deceased spouse's estate. If you haven't left much property to your spouse or child and are concerned that either might challenge your estate plan after your death, you'll want to know what your new state's laws say. (See Chapter 2, About Living Trusts.) You may want to amend your trust document to change what you leave to your spouse or child.

5. Your Spouse Dies

If you and your spouse made a shared living trust, when one spouse dies the other will probably inherit some, if not all, of the deceased spouse's trust property. The surviving spouse may need to amend his or her trust to name beneficiaries for that property. (See Chapter 10, After a Grantor Dies.) That spouse may also want to amend the trust document if he or she left property to the now-deceased spouse. (See Section 6, just below.)

6. A Major Beneficiary Dies

If you left much or all of your trust property to one person, and that person dies before you do, you may well want to amend your trust document. If you named an alternate beneficiary for the deceased beneficiary, there's not an urgent need to amend the trust document; the alternate will inherit the property. But amending it makes sense, so that you can name another alternate beneficiary, who will receive the property if the former alternate (now first in line) dies before you do.

> **EXAMPLE:** Marty and Frank make a living trust together. Marty leaves all her trust property to Frank, but he dies before she does. Because she named her daughter Stephanie as alternate beneficiary for her husband, she has already planned for the possibility of Frank's death. But it still makes sense for her to amend her trust document, to name an alternate beneficiary for Stephanie.

Remember that your trust document has another back-up device built into it: the residuary beneficiary. If both the primary and alternate beneficiaries die before you do, the residuary beneficiary will inherit the trust property.

E. Who Can Amend a Living Trust Document

Who can amend the terms of a living trust document depends on whether you created an individual living trust or a shared one with your spouse.

1. Individual Living Trusts

If you created an individual living trust, you (the grantor) can amend the trust document at any time.

2. Shared Marital Living Trusts

While both spouses are alive, both must agree to amend any provision of the living trust document—for example, to change a beneficiary, successor trustee or the property management set up for a young beneficiary

After one spouse dies, the shared living trust is split into two trusts, one of which can no longer be amended. (This is explained in Chapter 10, After a Grantor Dies.) Basically, the surviving spouse is free to amend the terms of the trust document that deal with his or her property, but can't change the parts that determine what happens to the deceased spouse's trust property.

3. Someone Acting on a Grantor's Behalf

The trust document created by *Living Trust Maker* does not allow the trust document to be amended by someone acting on a grantor's behalf, unless the grantor has given that authority in another document.

That means someone who is appointed by a court to handle your affairs (a conservator) or someone you have given authority to act for you in a document called a Power of Attorney (your "attorney-in-fact") cannot amend the trust document absent specific authorization. If you want to give your attorney-in-fact authority to amend your living trust, you must specifically grant this authority in your Power of Attorney.

Who Will Handle Your Finances If You Can't? by Denis Clifford and Mary Randolph (Nolo Press) contains forms and instructions for creating a durable power of attorney for financial matters.

Legal Manual

F. How to Amend Your Trust Document

Living Trust Maker makes it easy for you to amend certain provisions of your trust document. You can change:

- beneficiaries
- successor trustees
- custodians (people who will manage trust property inherited by young beneficiaries)
- property in the trust.

Just use *Living Trust Maker* to print out a trust amendment or a new property schedule.

You don't need to (and the program won't let you) create a trust amendment until you've printed out and signed a trust document. (Before that point, you can change any of the information you've entered into the program.) After you've printed, when you start the program again, it will ask you whether or not you've signed the trust document, creating a legally valid trust. If you have, you will not be allowed to make changes to that original trust document. Instead, the program will take you to its amendment module, where you can make trust amendments. (See the Users' Guide, Chapter 7.)

After you create and print out the trust amendment, sign it in front of a notary public and attach it to the signed original trust document. Both spouses must sign a trust amendment to amend a shared marital living trust. Then give a copy of the trust amendment to anyone who already has a copy of the original trust document.

CHANGING YOUR CHANGES

Every time you make a trust amendment and indicate that you have signed it, the program "freezes" the data. You can no longer make changes in that amendment, which is now legally part of your trust document. You can, however, make another trust amendment, changing a previous amendment.

⚠️ Do not change any part of the trust document except with the amendment module of *Living Trust Maker*. Any other changes could create serious problems for your heirs or even invalidate your trust.

1. Changing a Successor Trustee

You can use *Living Trust Maker* to amend your trust document if you change your mind about who you want to serve as:

- **Successor trustee** (the person who handles the trust, and any children's subtrusts, after your death or after the surviving spouse's death if a shared trust was created)
- **Alternate successor trustee** (the person who takes over as trustee if your first choice can't serve).

A sample amendment is shown below.

2. Adding or Deleting Property

If you acquire valuable items of property after you create your living trust, you should promptly add them to the trust so that they won't have to go through probate at your death. You may also want to remove some items.

There are four steps:

Step 1: Use the amendment module of *Living Trust Maker* to create a revised Property Schedule A, B or C of your trust document, adding new items or deleting old ones. (See Users' Guide, Chapter 7.) If you made an individual trust, you have only one schedule, Schedule A. If you and your spouse made a shared marital trust, Schedule A lists your co-owned property, Schedule B lists the wife's property, and Schedule C lists the husband's property.

Step 2: Print out the new schedule and replace the old one on your signed original trust document. That's all you have to do; schedules don't have to be signed.

Step 3: If you added property, transfer ownership of the property to the trust, if the property has a title document. If you removed an item, transfer it out of the trust's name. (See Chapter 8, Transferring Property to the Trust.)

Step 4: If you need to name a beneficiary for property you've added, create a trust amendment. (See Section F3, below.) You won't need to create a trust

SAMPLE TRUST AMENDMENT: CHANGING THE SUCCESSOR TRUSTEE

Amendment to the Judith M. Avery Revocable Living Trust

Under the power reserved to the grantor by Part 4 of the Declaration of Trust creating the Judith M. Avery Revocable Living Trust dated August 10, 1994, the grantor hereby amends the Declaration of Trust as follows:

The following is deleted from Part 6 of the trust document:

Upon the death or incapacity of Judith M. Avery, the trustee of this trust and of any children's subtrusts created by it shall be Robert S. Avery and Anne Avery Puckett. If Robert S. Avery and Anne Avery Puckett are both unable or unwilling to serve as successor trustee, David R. Puckett shall be the trustee.

The following is added to Part 6 of the trust document:

Upon the death or incapacity of Judith M. Avery, the trustee of this trust and of any children's subtrusts created by it shall be Anne Avery Puckett. If Anne Avery Puckett is unable or unwilling to serve as successor trustee, David R. Puckett shall be the trustee.

_____ Dated: _____
Judith M. Avery, Grantor and Trustee

State of _____

County of _____

On _____, before me, _____
_____, a notary public for said state, personally appeared Judith M. Avery, personally known to me (or proved to me on the basis of satisfactory evidence) to be the person whose name is subscribed to the within instrument, and acknowledged to me that she executed the same in her authorized capacity and that by her signature on the instrument the person, or the entity upon behalf of which the person acted, executed the instrument.

Witness my hand and official seal.

_____
NOTARY PUBLIC for the State of _____
My commission expires _____ .

amendment if your trust document leaves all your trust property to one person or if you want the new property to go to the residuary beneficiary of the trust.

EXAMPLE: Rose and her husband Michael created a trust several years ago. When they buy a house, they take title as "Rose and Michael Morris, Trustees of the Rose Morris and Michael Morris Revocable Living Trust dated January 13, 1991." They then prepare a revised Schedule A (which lists co-owned property) of their trust document, print it out and replace the old Schedule A.

Because their trust document leaves all their property to each other, they do not need to prepare a trust amendment.

3. Adding a Beneficiary

If you've added property to the trust by amending a property schedule (Section 1, above), and you want to name a beneficiary to receive the property, you should use the amendment module of *Living Trust Maker* to create a trust amendment. Two samples are shown below.

4. Changing a Beneficiary

You may change your mind about leaving certain trust property to a beneficiary you named in the trust document, or a beneficiary may die before you do. If so, you'll need to prepare a trust amendment.

EXAMPLE: Jim and Toni created their living trust three years ago and named Jim's sister Eileen as beneficiary of some stock that Jim transferred to the trust. But since then Jim and his sister have had a falling out. He wants to amend the trust document to leave the stock to his son, Aaron.

All Jim and Toni need to do is use *Living Trust Maker to* prepare an amendment. The amendment shown below deletes the paragraph in the Declaration of Trust that left the stock to Eileen. It also adds a paragraph leaving the stock to Aaron and stating that if Aaron doesn't survive him, that it should go to his nephew David.

(If they eliminated the gift to Eileen but didn't name a new beneficiary for the property, it would go the residuary beneficiary of the trust.)

A sample amendment is shown below.

SAMPLE TRUST AMENDMENT: ADDING A BENEFICIARY

Amendment to the Judith M. Avery Revocable Living Trust

Under the power reserved to the grantor by Part 4 of the Declaration of Trust creating the Judith M. Avery Revocable Living Trust dated August 10, 1994, the grantor hereby amends the Declaration of Trust as follows:

The following is added to Part 10 of the trust document:

6. Rosemary Warkowsky shall be given all the grantor's interest in the first edition of Roughing It, by Mark Twain. If Rosemary Warkowsky does not survive the grantor by 120 hours that property shall be given to Kasimira Warkowsky.

_____ Dated: _____
Judith M. Avery, Grantor and Trustee

State of _____

County of _____

On _____, before me, _____
_____, a notary public for said state, personally appeared Judith M. Avery, personally known to me (or proved to me on the basis of satisfactory evidence) to be the person whose name is subscribed to the within instrument, and acknowledged to me that she executed the same in her authorized capacity and that by her signature on the instrument the person, or the entity upon behalf of which the person acted, executed the instrument.

Witness my hand and official seal.

_____

NOTARY PUBLIC for the State of _____
My commission expires _____ .

SAMPLE TRUST AMENDMENT: CHANGING A BENEFICIARY

Amendment to the Judith M. Avery Revocable Living Trust

Under the power reserved to the grantor by Part 4 of the Declaration of Trust creating the Judith M. Avery Revocable Living Trust dated August 10, 1994, the grantor hereby amends the Declaration of Trust as follows:

The following is deleted from Part 10 of the trust document:

1. Robert S. Avery shall be given all the grantor's interest in 200 shares of General Industries stock. If Robert S. Avery does not survive the grantor by 120 hours that property shall be given to Cheryl Avery.

The following is added to Part 10 of the trust document:

1. Lucille N. McGuire shall be given all the grantor's interest in 200 shares of General Industries stock. If Lucille N. McGuire does not survive the grantor by 120 hours that property shall be given to Colin Tiernan.

_____ _____ Dated: _____
Judith M. Avery, Grantor and Trustee

State of _____

County of _____

On _____, before me, _____ _____, a notary public for said state, personally appeared Judith M. Avery, personally known to me (or proved to me on the basis of satisfactory evidence) to be the person whose name is subscribed to the within instrument, and acknowledged to me that she executed the same in her authorized capacity and that by her signature on the instrument the person, or the entity upon behalf of which the person acted, executed the instrument.

Witness my hand and official seal.

_____

NOTARY PUBLIC for the State of _____
My commission expires _____ .

5. Changing Property Management for a Young Beneficiary

You can make any number of changes to the provisions of your trust document that arrange for someone to manage trust property inherited by a young beneficiary. You can:

- Add a child's subtrust to your trust document, whether or not your original trust document created any subtrusts.
- Change the age at which a subtrust ends. (A sample amendment is shown below.)
- Add a child's custodianship to your trust document, whether or not your original trust document created any custodianships, if your state's law allows custodianships. (See Chapter 5 or 6, Part 7.) (A sample amendment is shown below.)
- Change the custodian or alternate custodian you named earlier. (A sample amendment is shown below.)
- Change the age at which the custodianship ends, if your state law allows it. Be sure to read the restrictions on your choices in Part 7 of Chapter 5 or 6.

SAMPLE TRUST AMENDMENT: CHANGING WHEN SUBTRUST ENDS

Amendment to the William C. Carey and Leslie M. Carey Revocable Living Trust

Under the power reserved to the grantors by Part 5 of the Declaration of Trust creating the William C. Carey and Leslie M. Carey Revocable Living Trust dated August 10, 1994, the grantors hereby amend the Declaration of Trust as follows:

The following is deleted from Part 12 of the trust document:

2. If Claudia A. Carey has not yet reached the age of 29 when Claudia A. Carey becomes entitled to any trust property under Part 11.B, that trust property shall be kept in a separate child's subtrust, under the provisions of this Part, until Claudia A. Carey reaches the age of 29.

The following is added to Part 12 of the trust document:

2. If Claudia A. Carey has not yet reached the age of 33 when Claudia A. Carey becomes entitled to any trust property under Part 11.B, that trust property shall be kept in a separate child's subtrust, under the provisions of this Part, until Claudia A. Carey reaches the age of 33.

_____ Dated: _____
William C. Carey, Grantor and Trustee

_____ Dated: _____
Leslie M. Carey, Grantor and Trustee

State of _____

County of _____

On _____, before me, _____
_____, a notary public for said state, personally appeared Judith M. Avery, personally known to me (or proved to me on the basis of satisfactory evidence) to be the person whose name is subscribed to the within instrument, and acknowledged to me that she executed the same in her authorized capacity and that by her signature on the instrument the person, or the entity upon behalf of which the person acted, executed the instrument.

Witness my hand and official seal.

_____
NOTARY PUBLIC for the State of _____
My commission expires _____ .

Legal Manual

SAMPLE TRUST AMENDMENT: ADDING CUSTODIANSHIP

Amendment to the Judith M. Avery Revocable Living Trust

Under the power reserved to the grantor by Part 4 of the Declaration of Trust creating the Judith M. Avery Revocable Living Trust dated August 10, 1994, the grantor hereby amends the Declaration of Trust as follows:

The following is added to Part 11 of the trust document:

2. Any property Cheryl Avery becomes entitled to under Part 10 of this Declaration of Trust shall be given to Ramona V. Marcus, as custodian for Cheryl Avery under the Illinois Uniform Transfers to Minors Act, until Cheryl Avery reaches the age of 21. If Ramona V. Marcus is unable or ceases to serve as custodian, Henry Luce Marcus shall serve as custodian.

_____ Dated: _____
Judith M. Avery, Grantor and Trustee

State of _____

County of _____

On _____, before me, _____
_____, a notary public for said state, personally appeared Judith M. Avery, personally known to me (or proved to me on the basis of satisfactory evidence) to be the person whose name is subscribed to the within instrument, and acknowledged to me that she executed the same in her authorized capacity and that by her signature on the instrument the person, or the entity upon behalf of which the person acted, executed the instrument.

Witness my hand and official seal.

_____

NOTARY PUBLIC for the State of _____
My commission expires _____ .

SAMPLE TRUST AMENDMENT: CHANGING CUSTODIANSHIP

Amendment to the Judith M. Avery Revocable Living Trust

Under the power reserved to the grantor by Part 4 of the Declaration of Trust creating the Judith M. Avery Revocable Living Trust dated July 26, 1994, the grantor hereby amends the Declaration of Trust as follows:

The following is deleted from Part 11 of the trust document:

1. Any property David R. Puckett becomes entitled to under Part 10 of this Declaration of Trust shall be given to Anne Avery Puckett, as custodian for David R. Puckett under the Illinois Uniform Transfers to Minors Act, until David R. Puckett reaches the age of 21. If Anne Avery Puckett is unable or ceases to serve as custodian, Anthony B. Puckett shall serve as custodian.

The following is added to Part 11 of the trust document:

1. Any property David R. Puckett becomes entitled to under Part 10 of this Declaration of Trust shall be given to Lucille N. McGuire, as custodian for David R. Puckett under the Illinois Uniform Transfers to Minors Act, until David R. Puckett reaches the age of 21. If Lucille N. McGuire is unable or ceases to serve as custodian, Anthony B. Puckett shall serve as custodian.

_____ Dated: _____
Judith M. Avery, Grantor and Trustee

State of _____

County of _____

On _____, before me, _____
_____, a notary public for said state, personally appeared Judith M. Avery, personally known to me (or proved to me on the basis of satisfactory evidence) to be the person whose name is subscribed to the within instrument, and acknowledged to me that she executed the same in her authorized capacity and that by her signature on the instrument the person, or the entity upon behalf of which the person acted, executed the instrument.

Witness my hand and official seal.

_____

NOTARY PUBLIC for the State of _____
My commission expires _____ .
_____ .

G. Revoking Your Living Trust

You can revoke your living trust at any time. Revoking a living trust (unlike revoking a will) requires some work: You must transfer ownership of all the trust property out of the living trust.

1. Who Can Revoke a Living Trust

If you create an individual living trust, you can revoke it at any time.

Either spouse can revoke a shared living trust, wiping out all terms of the trust. The trust property is returned to each spouse according to how they owned it before transferring it to the trust.

> **EXAMPLE:** Yvonne and André make a shared marital living trust. Each transfers separately owned property to the trust. They also transfer ownership of their house, which they own together, to the trust. Later Yvonne, anticipating a divorce, revokes the living trust. She transfers the property she owned back to herself, and the property her husband owned back to him. The co-owned property goes back to both of them.

The trust document cannot be revoked by someone acting on your behalf unless you have specifically granted that authority. (See Section E, above.)

2. When to Revoke Your Living Trust

If you're like most people, amending your living trust will take care of your changing circumstances over the years, and you will never need to revoke your trust. But there are, of course, a few exceptions to that rule.

a. You Want to Make Extensive Revisions

If you want to make very extensive revisions to the terms of the trust document, you should revoke it and start fresh with a new trust document. If you don't, you risk creating inconsistencies and confusion.

b. You Get Divorced

If you divorce, you should revoke your living trust. In several states, provisions of your living trust that affect your spouse are automatically revoked by divorce, but you shouldn't rely on these laws. Better to have it in writing.

3. How to Revoke Your Living Trust

To revoke your living trust, follow these steps:

Step 1: Transfer ownership of trust property from the living trust back to yourself. Basically, you must reverse the process you followed when you transferred ownership of the property to yourself as trustee. (See Chapter 8, Transferring Property to the Trust.) You can make the transfer because of your authority as trustee of the trust.

Step 2: Use *Living Trust Maker* to prepare a document called a Revocation of Trust. After you've printed your trust document, when you start the program again, it will ask you whether or not you've signed the trust document, creating a legally valid trust. If you have, the program will take you to a screen that lets you choose "Revoke Trust."

Step 3: Print out the Revocation of Trust and sign it in front of a notary public.

Step 4: If you registered your trust with the local court (a procedure authorized in certain states; see Chapter 7, Signing, Storing and Registering the Trust Document), notify the court that the trust has been terminated.

A sample is shown below.

SAMPLE REVOCATION

Revocation of
The Judith M. Avery Revocable Living Trust

I, Judith M. Avery, hereby revoke The Judith M. Avery Revocable Living Trust, created by Declaration of Trust signed August 10, 1994, according to the power reserved to the grantor by Part 4 of the Declaration of Trust.

All property owned by the trust shall be returned to the grantor.

_____ Dated: _____
Judith M. Avery, Grantor and Trustee

State of _____

County of _____

On _____, before me, _____
_____, a notary public for said state, personally appeared Judith M. Avery, personally known to me (or proved to me on the basis of satisfactory evidence) to be the person whose name is subscribed to the within instrument, and acknowledged to me that she executed the same in her authorized capacity and that by her signature on the instrument the person, or the entity upon behalf of which the person acted, executed the instrument.

Witness my hand and official seal.

_____

NOTARY PUBLIC for the State of _____
My commission expires _____ .

After A Grantor Dies

T he benefit of a revocable living trust doesn't come until after the grantor's death, when the trust property is transferred to beneficiaries without probate. The all-important responsibility of handling that transfer falls to your surviving spouse, if you made a shared living trust, or your successor trustee, if you made an individual living trust.

A. What Happens When a Grantor Dies

The process works differently depending on whether you made an individual living trust or a shared trust with your spouse.

1. Individual Trust

When the grantor, who is also the trustee, dies, the successor trustee named in the Declaration of Trust takes over as trustee. The new trustee is responsible for distributing the trust property to the beneficiaries named in the trust document.

The trust continues to exist only as long as it takes the successor trustee to distribute trust property to the beneficiaries. In many cases, a living trust can be wound up in only a few weeks after a grantor's death.

The successor trustee is also in charge of managing any property left to a young beneficiary in a child's subtrust. A subtrust will exist until the beneficiary reaches the age specified in the trust document, so if there's a subtrust the successor trustee may have years of work ahead. (See Section F, below.)

If trust property inherited by a young beneficiary is to be managed by a custodian under the Uniform Transfers to Minors Act, instead of in a child's subtrust, the person named as custodian will be responsible for that property. The successor trustee may also have been named as the custodian for a young beneficiary's property.

THE SUCCESSOR TRUSTEE'S DUTIES

- Distribute trust property to beneficiaries named in the trust document.
- Manage trust property left in a child's subtrust, if any.
- File federal and state estate tax returns, if necessary (this is the responsibility of the executor of the estate, if there was a will).

---

2. Shared Marital Trust

When a married couple creates a shared living trust with *Living Trust Maker*, both spouses are the original trustees. When the first spouse dies, the surviving spouse becomes sole trustee.

The trust itself is automatically split into two trusts:

- Trust #1 contains the deceased spouse's share of trust property, excluding any trust property left to the surviving spouse. Its terms cannot be changed, and it cannot be revoked.

- Trust #2 contains the surviving spouse's share, including any of the deceased spouse's share of the trust property that is left to the surviving spouse. (The Declaration of Trust created by *Living Trust Maker* provides that trust property left to the survivor does not go to the surviving spouse outright but instead stays in the living trust. If it did not contain such a provision, the property would go to the surviving spouse outright. It would have to be transferred from the living trust to the spouse and then, if the surviving spouse wanted it to avoid probate, back to the living trust again.) The surviving spouse is still free to revoke it or amend its terms.

The survivor is sole trustee of Trust #1, Trust #2 and any children's subtrusts set up for the deceased spouse's young beneficiaries.

It's the surviving spouse's job to distribute the property in Trust #1 to the beneficiaries the deceased spouse named in the trust document. If, as is common, much of the trust property is left to the surviving spouse, that spouse will have little to do—the trust property he or she inherits is already in the living trust and does not need to be transferred.

Trust #2 goes on as before, as a revocable living trust. It contains only the surviving spouse's property, and the surviving spouse is free to change it as he or she wishes.

When the second spouse dies, the successor trustee named in the trust document takes over as trustee. The process of winding up the living trust is the same as that for an individual trust (Section 1, above).

EXAMPLE: Harry and Maude, a married couple, set up a revocable living trust to avoid probate. They appoint Maude's cousin Emily as successor trustee, to take over as trustee after they have both died. They transfer ownership of much of their co-owned property—their house, savings accounts and stocks—to the trust. Maude also puts some of her family heirlooms, which are her separate property, in the living trust.

In the trust document, Maude leaves her heirlooms to her younger sister. She leaves her half of the trust property she and Harry own together to Harry.

When Maude dies, Harry becomes the sole trustee. Following the terms of the trust document, he distributes Maude's heirlooms (Trust #1) to her sister, without probate. Maude's half of the property they had owned together stays in the trust (Trust #2); no transfer is necessary. After Maude's death, he decides to amend the trust document to name his nephew, Burt, as successor trustee instead of Maude's cousin Emily. When Harry dies, Burt will become trustee and distribute the trust property following Harry's instructions in the trust document. When all the property is given to Harry's beneficiaries, the trust ends.

THE SURVIVING SPOUSE'S DUTIES

- Distribute the deceased spouse's share of the trust property to beneficiaries named in the trust document.
- Manage property left in a child's subtrust, if any.
- File federal and state estate tax returns, if necessary (this is the executor's responsibility, if a will named someone else as executor of the estate).
- Amend living trust to reflect changed circumstances, if necessary.

Section C, below, has more about transferring property to the surviving spouse.

B. Who Serves as Trustee

With a shared marital trust, it's simple: The surviving spouse serves as trustee after one spouse's death. With an individual trust, or when the surviving spouse dies, the successor trustee is in charge.

WHO SERVES AS TRUSTEE	
Individual trust	**Shared Marital Trust**
1. Successor trustee(s)	1. Surviving spouse
2. Alternate successor trustee(s)	2. Successor trustee(s)
	3. Alternate successor trustee(s)

1. More Than One Successor Trustee

If more than one person is named in the trust document as successor trustee, they all serve together. Each must agree on any action taken with regard to the living trust property.

    If one of the trustees cannot serve, the others remain as trustees. The person named as alternate successor trustee does not take over unless all the people named as successor trustees cannot serve.

2. If a Trustee Resigns

A trustee can resign at any time by preparing and signing a resignation statement like the own shown below. The ex-trustee should deliver the notice to the person who is next in line to serve as trustee (see list above).

Notice of Resignation

I, Lucia Freni, current Trustee of The Robert Ambruzzi Revocable Living Trust dated March 3, 1990, resign my position as trustee, effective immediately.

Date: November 19, 1991

_____

Lucia Freni, Trustee

State of _____)
)
County of _____)

On _____, before me, _____
_____, a notary public in and for said state, personally appeared _____,
personally known to me (or proved to me on the basis of satisfactory evidence) to be the person(s) whose name(s) is/are subscribed to the within instrument, and acknowledged to me that he/she/they executed the same in his/her/their authorized capacity(ies) and that by his/her/their signature(s) on the instrument the person(s), or the entity upon behalf of which the person(s) acted, executed the instrument.

Witness my hand and official seal.

_____

NOTARY PUBLIC for the State of _____
My commission expires _____ .

If no one named in the trust document can serve, the last acting trustee can appoint someone else to take over. The appointment must be in writing, signed and notarized. The trustee can prepare a simple document like the one shown below.

Appointment of Trustee

I, Lucia Freni, Trustee of The Robert Ambruzzi Revocable Living Trust dated March 3, 1990, appoint Clarence Ryan as trustee, effective immediately. This appointment is made under the authority granted in Part 7 of the Declaration of Trust.

Date: November 19, 1991

_____
Lucia Freni, Trustee

State of _____)
)
County of _____)

On _____, before me, _____
_____, a notary public in and for said state, personally appeared _____ ,
personally known to me (or proved to me on the basis of satisfactory evidence) to be the person(s) whose name(s) is/are subscribed to the within instrument, and acknowledged to me that he/she/they executed the same in his/her/their authorized capacity(ies) and that by his/her/their signature(s) on the instrument the person(s), or the entity upon behalf of which the person(s) acted, executed the instrument.

Witness my hand and official seal.

_____
NOTARY PUBLIC for the State of _____
My commission expires _____ .

---

3. Removing a Trustee

Very rarely, a beneficiary becomes seriously unhappy with the way a trustee handles trust property. For example, the beneficiary of a child's subtrust might complain that the trustee isn't spending enough of the trust property's income on the beneficiary's education. If the dispute can't be worked out, the beneficiary can file a lawsuit to try to force the removal of the trustee.

C. Transferring Property to the Surviving Spouse

As mentioned in Section A, above, a surviving spouse who inherits trust property doesn't need to transfer the property. The property is already owned by the living trust, and the surviving spouse now has sole and complete control over all property in the trust.

The surviving spouse may, however, want to amend the trust document to name beneficiaries for the property.

> **EXAMPLE:** Edith and Jacques create a shared living trust. They transfer their house, which they own together, into the trust, and name each other as beneficiaries. Edith names her son as alternate beneficiary.
>
> When Jacques dies, Edith inherits his half-interest in the house. Because of the way the trust document is worded, she doesn't have to change the trust document to name a beneficiary for the other half-interest in the house, which she inherited from her husband. Both halves will go to her son at her death. She may, however, want to amend the trust to make her son the primary beneficiary and name someone else to be alternate beneficiary.
>
> For instructions on how to make a Trust Amendment, see Chapter 9, Living With Your Living Trust.

D. Transferring Property to Other Beneficiaries

The procedure for transferring trust property to the beneficiaries who inherit it depends on the kind of property you're dealing with. Generally, a copy of the grantor's death certificate (both grantors' death certificates, if the trust property was originally co-owned) and a copy of the trust document are necessary. In some cases, the trustee will need to prepare some other paperwork.

Specific requirements for transferring property vary slightly from place to place, and the trustee may have to make inquiries to banks, stock brokerages and other institutions about current procedures, but here are the general rules. (For California residents, *How to Probate an Estate*, by Julia Nissley (Nolo Press) contains instructions on transferring the property of a decedent, including living trust property.) A trustee who runs into difficulties has the authority to get help— from a lawyer, accountant or other expert—and pay for it from trust assets.

Terminology note. This section refers to whoever takes over as trustee after a grantor's death as the "trustee." If you made an individual trust, the trustee is the person you named as successor trustee. If you made a shared marital trust, the trustee is the surviving spouse or, after both spouses have died, the successor trustee. (See Section B, above.)

1. Property Without Title Documents

For trust property that doesn't have a title document—furniture, for example—the task of the trustee is quite simple. The trustee must promptly distribute the property to the beneficiaries named in the trust. If the trustee thinks it's a good idea, it's appropriate to have the recipient sign a receipt.

2. Bank Accounts

It should be simple for the trustee to transfer the funds in a bank or savings and loan account, already held in the name of the living trust, to the beneficiary. Financial institutions are familiar with living trusts and how they work, and the particular bank probably has the trust document (or a bank form with information about the trust) already on file.

The trustee will need to show the bank or savings and loan:

- a certified copy of the trust grantor's death certificate
- a copy of the living trust document, if the bank doesn't already have one, and
- proof of his or her own identity.

3. Real Estate

The trustee need only prepare and sign a deed to transfer ownership of real estate from the trust to the beneficiary. The signed and notarized deed should also be filed (recorded) with the county land records office. In most places, recording costs no more than a few dollars per page. It's unlikely, but depending on local and state law, there may be a transfer tax to pay. (Recording documents and transfer taxes are discussed in Chapter 8, Transferring Property to the Trust.)

EXAMPLE: The deed to Evelyn Crocker's house shows that it is owned by her living trust. The living trust document states that Evelyn's daughter, Amanda,

Legal Manual

is to inherit the house when Evelyn dies. Amanda is also the successor trustee of the trust.

After Evelyn's death, Amanda prepares and signs a new deed, transferring ownership of the house from the trust to herself. She signs the deed in her capacity as trustee of the trust, and records the deed in the county records office.

A title company, before it will issue title insurance to the new owners, will probably want a copy of the trust document and a certified copy of the death certificate of the trust grantor.

4. Stocks and Bonds

How to transfer stocks or bonds from a trust to the beneficiary depends on whether they were held in a brokerage account or separately.

Stock in closely-held corporations. See Section 6, Small Business Interests, below.

a. Brokerage Accounts

The trustee should contact the broker and ask for instructions. The brokerage company will almost surely already have either a copy of the living trust document or a form that includes relevant information about the trust. (These are necessary to transfer the account to the living trust in the first place.)

If not, the trustee will probably need to send the broker:

- a copy of the trust document or an "abstract of trust" (the first, last and other relevant pages of the trust document, showing the notarized signature), and
- a letter instructing the holder to transfer the brokerage account to the beneficiary's name.

b. Stock Certificates

If the deceased grantor kept the stock certificates or bonds in his or her possession—most people don't—the trustee must get new certificates issued, showing the beneficiary as owner.

The trustee will have to send the securities' transfer agent several documents. It's a good idea to write the transfer agent and ask exactly what is needed. Usually, the name and address of the transfer agent appear on the face of the stock or bond certificate. But because transfer agents change occasionally, the first thing the trustee should do is write or call (or check with a stock brokerage firm) to verify the name and address of the current transfer agent.

The trustee will probably have to send in:

- A certified copy of the grantor's death certificate.
- The certificates or bonds.
- A document called a "stock or bond power," which the trustee must fill out and sign, with the signature guaranteed by an officer of a bank or brokerage firm. The stock or bond power may be printed on the back of the certificates; if not, stationery stores carry them.
- A copy of the trust document or an "abstract of trust," (which is just the first, last and other relevant pages of the trust document, showing the notarized signature) if the transfer agent did not receive one when the securities were transferred into the trust.
- An Affidavit of Domicile (a form available from banks and stock brokers) signed by the trustee, showing what the trust grantor's state of residence was.
- A letter of instructions requesting that the certificates be reissued in the beneficiary's name.

c. Government Securities

To transfer government securities—Treasury bills or U.S. bonds, for example—the trustee should ask the broker to contact the issuing government agency, or contact the government directly.

5. Mutual Fund Accounts

The trustee should ask the company what it requires to re-register ownership of a mutual fund account in the beneficiary's name. Generally, the trustee must send the company the grantor's death certificate, a letter of instructions (or a form that the company provides) and a copy of the trust document.

6. Small Business Interests

How a trustee transfers small business interests owned by a living trust depends on the way the business was organized.

a. Sole Proprietorships

The trustee must transfer business assets to the beneficiary like he or she would transfer any other trust property. The name of the business itself, if owned by the living trust, does not have a title document, so the trustee doesn't need to do anything to transfer it to the beneficiary.

A registered trademark or service mark must be re-registered in the name of the beneficiary. See *Trademark: How to Name Your Business and Product,* by Kate McGrath and Steve Elias (Nolo Press).

b. Solely-Owned Corporations

Corporation officers must prepare the appropriate corporate records to show ownership transferred to the beneficiary, and then have the stock certificates reissued in the beneficiary's name.

c. Closely-Held Corporations

The stock certificates owned by the trust will have to be reissued in the beneficiary's name. The trustee should contact the officers of the corporation; the other shareholders may have the right, under the corporation's bylaws or a separate shareholders' agreement, to buy back the shares.

d. Partnership Interests

The trustee should contact the deceased grantor's partners, who may have the right to buy out the grantor's share. If the beneficiary wants to enter into the partnership, the partnership agreement must be changed to add the beneficiary.

7. Copyrights

To transfer an interest in a copyright to a beneficiary, the trustee should sign and file, with the U.S. Copyright Office, a document transferring all the trust's rights in the copyright to the beneficiary. Sample transfer forms are in *The Copyright Handbook,* by Steve Fishman (Nolo Press).

8. Patents

To transfer a patent from a living trust, the trustee should prepare a document called an "assignment" and record it with the Patent and Trademark Office in Washington, DC. There is a small fee for recording. Sample assignment forms and instructions are in *Patent It Yourself,* by David Pressman (Nolo Press).

9. Other Property With Title Documents

If an item of trust property has a title document that shows ownership in the name of the trust, the trustee must prepare and sign a new title document transferring ownership to the beneficiary. Usually, the trustee will need a copy of the trust document and of the trust grantor's death certificate if the property is in someone else's possession.

    If a vehicle was owned by the trust, the trustee should contact the state Department of Motor Vehicles to get the forms required to transfer it to the beneficiary.

E. Preparing and Filing Tax Returns

If a state death tax or federal estate tax return must be filed for the grantor, it is the responsibility of the executor named in the decedent's will; usually, the same person is both executor and trustee.

    A federal estate tax return must be filed if the decedent's gross estate was worth more than $600,000. It is due nine months after the decedent's death. The successor trustee can get a helpful 20-page set of instructions, "Instructions for Form 706," from the Internal Revenue Service. Another useful IRS publication is called "Federal Estate and Gift Taxes" (Publication 448). And again, the trustee is entitled to pay for professional help out of the trust assets.

F. Administering a Child's Subtrust

If, in the trust document, the deceased grantor set up a child's subtrust, the trustee will have to manage that property until the beneficiary is old enough to receive it. A child's subtrust comes into being only if the beneficiary has not yet reached the age the grantor specified.

> **EXAMPLE:** Carl sets up a living trust and names his two young children as beneficiaries. He specifies that if the children are younger than 30 when he dies, the property they are to receive from the trust should be kept in a separate children's subtrust for each child.
>
> When Carl dies, one child is 30; the other is 25. The 30-year-old will receive her trust property with no strings attached. But a child's subtrust will be created for the 25-year-old. The successor trustee named in the trust document is responsible for managing the property and turning it over to the child when he turns 30.

The trustee must:

- Take good care of the subtrust property. The trustee must always act honestly and in the best interests of the beneficiary. For example, the trustee must not make risky investments with subtrust property.

- Use the income from subtrust property, or the subtrust property itself, to pay for the beneficiary's needs. The living trust document created with *Living Trust Maker* gives the trustee broad authority to use subtrust assets for the beneficiary's health, support, maintenance or education.

- File an annual trust income tax return. The subtrust may also have to pay estimated income taxes.

- Give the remaining subtrust property to the beneficiary when he or she reaches the age designated in the trust document.

The trustee can use subtrust assets to get professional assistance if necessary. For example, the trustee might want to pay a tax preparer for help with the subtrust's income tax return, or consult a financial planner for investment advice.

The trust document also provides that the trustee of a subtrust is entitled to reasonable compensation for his or her work as trustee. The trustee decides what is a reasonable amount; the compensation is paid from the subtrust assets. A beneficiary who disagrees with the trustee's decisions about payment—or other decisions about management or distribution of the subtrust property—must go to court to challenge the trustee's decisions.

G. Administering a Custodianship

Someone who is is appointed, in the trust document, to be the custodian of trust property inherited by a young beneficiary has about the same management responsibilities as the trustee of a child's subtrust. (See Section F, above.) The specifics are set out in the Uniform Transfers to Minors Act, as adopted by the particular state's legislature.

A custodian, however, does not have to file a separate income tax return. Any income from the beneficiary's property is reported on the beneficiary's own return.

If You Need Expert Help

Y ou probably won't need a lawyer's help to make a living trust with *Living Trust Maker.*

Many other methods of avoiding probate—joint tenancy and pay-on-death bank accounts, for example—are also safe and straightforward enough to use yourself without consulting an expert. To understand how to draw up a complete estate plan making use of a living trust and other devices, we recommend Nolo's *Plan Your Estate* , by Denis Clifford and Cora Jordan.

But you may come up with questions about your particular situation that should be answered by an expert. This is especially likely if you have a very large estate, must plan for an incapacitated minor or have to deal with the assets of a good-sized small business. These and other "red flags" that should alert you to the need for professional advice are highlighted throughout the manual and program.

A. What Kind of Expert Do You Need?

If you have questions, the first thing to decide is what type of expert you should seek out. Questions about estate taxes may be better (and less expensively) answered by an experienced accountant than a lawyer. Or if you're wondering what type of life insurance to buy, you may be better off talking to a financial planner.

Consult a lawyer if you have specific questions about a provision of your living trust or other estate planning device. Also see a lawyer if you want to get into sophisticated estate planning—for instance, if you want to establish a marital life estate trust to save on federal estate taxes or a long-term trust for a disabled child.

B. How to Choose a Lawyer

Finding a competent estate planning lawyer who charges a reasonable fee and respects your efforts to prepare your own living trust may not be easy. Here are some suggestions on how to go about the task.

1. Look Into a Group Legal Plan

Some unions, employers and consumer action organizations offer group legal plans to their members or employees, who can obtain comprehensive legal assistance free or for low rates. If you are a member of such a plan, check with it first. Your problem may be covered free of charge. If it is, and you are satisfied that the lawyer you are referred to is knowledgeable in estate planning, this route is probably a good choice.

Some plans give you only a slight reduction in a lawyer's fee. In that case, you may be referred to a lawyer whose main virtue is the willingness to reduce fees in exchange for a high volume of referrals.

2. Check Out a Prepaid Legal Plan

For basic advice, you may want to consider joining a prepaid legal plan that offers advice, by phone or in person, at no extra charge. (Some of these plans throw in a free simple will, too.) Your initial membership fee may be reasonable, compared to the cost of hiring a lawyer by the hour, but there's no guarantee that the lawyers available through these plans are of the best caliber.

Most plans have renewal fees; you can join a plan for a specific service and then not renew. The plans are sold by companies such as Montgomery Ward and Amway, and are often offered to credit card holders or sold door-to-door.

You should realize that the lawyer you see probably receives at most $2 or $3 a month for dealing with you. Why do lawyers agree to this minimal amount? They hope to find clients who will pay for extra legal services not covered by the monthly premium. The low basic fee means the lawyers have an incentive to complicate, rather than simplify, your problem. So if a plan lawyer recommends an expensive legal procedure, get a second opinion.

3. Ask Businesspeople and Friends

Anyone who owns a small business probably has a relationship with a lawyer. Ask around to find someone you know who is a satisfied client. If that lawyer does not handle estate planning, he or she will likely know someone who does. And because of the continuing relationship with your friend, the lawyer has an incentive to recommend someone who is competent.

Also ask people you know in any social or other organization in which you are involved. They may well know of a good lawyer whose attitudes are similar to yours. Senior citizens' centers and other groups that advise and assist older people may have a list of local lawyers who specialize in wills and estate planning and are well regarded.

4. Consult a Legal Clinic

Law firms with lots of small offices across the country, such as Hyatt Legal Services and Jacoby & Meyers, trumpet their low initial consultation fees. It's true that a basic consultation is cheap, often about $20; anything beyond that isn't cheap at all. Generally, the rates average about the same as those charged by other lawyers in general practice.

If you do consult a legal clinic, often the trick is to quickly extract the information you need and resist attempts to convince you that you need more services. If the lawyer you talk to is experienced in estate planning, however, and you're comfortable with the person and the service, it may be worthwhile. Unfortunately, most of these offices have extremely high lawyer turnover, so you may see a different one every time you visit.

5. Call an Attorney Referral Service

A lawyer referral service will give you the name of an attorney who practices in your area. Usually, you can get a referral to an attorney who claims to specialize in estate planning and will give you an initial consultation for a low fee.

Most county bar associations have referral services. In some states, independent referral services, run by or for groups of lawyers, also operate.

Unfortunately, few referral services screen the attorneys they list, which means those who participate may not be the most experienced or competent. Often, the lawyers who sign up with referral services are just starting out and need clients. It may be possible to find a skilled estate planning specialist through a referral service, but be sure to take the time to check out the credentials and experience of the person to whom you're referred.

LIVING TRUST SEMINARS

Newspapers, radio and TV are full of ads for free "seminars" on living trusts. Usually, these events are nothing more than elaborate pitches for paying a lawyer $1,000 to $1,500 to write a living trust. Is it worth it? Probably not.

For a relatively small estate, *Living Trust Maker* will probably be all you need. For more complicated estate planning, you will almost surely get better, less expensive and more personal advice from a local estate planning specialist.

C. Dealing With a Lawyer

If you decide to speak to a lawyer, find one who specializes in estate planning. Most general practice lawyers are simply not sufficiently educated in this field to competently address complicated problems.

Many lawyers, however, have recently discovered living trusts—or, more accurately, discovered their profit-making potential. Lawyers who know almost nothing about living trusts (it's easy to go through law school without ever hearing of one) have found that they can charge huge fees—$900 to $1500 is common—for a simple document. Some use computer programs to churn out trusts and may or may not take into account your specific needs.

The fee of an experienced specialist may be 10 to 30% higher than that of a general practitioner, but the specialist will probably produce results more efficiently and save you money in the long run.

Lawyer fees usually range from $100 to $350 or more per hour. But price is not always related to quality. It depends on the area of the county you live in, but generally, fees of $100 to $200 per hour are reasonable in urban areas, given the lawyer's overhead. In rural areas and smaller cities, $80 to $150 is more like it.

Be sure you've settled your fee arrangement—preferably in writing—at the start of your relationship. In addition to the hourly fee, you should get a clear, written commitment from the lawyer about how many hours your problem should take to handle.

Before you talk to the lawyer, decide what kind of help you really need. Do you want someone to advise you on a complete estate plan, or just to review your living trust to make sure it looks all right? If you don't clearly tell the lawyer what you want, you may find yourself agreeing to turn over all your estate planning work.

One good strategy is to do some background research and write down your questions as specifically as you can. If the lawyer doesn't give you clear, concise answers, try someone else. If the lawyer acts wise but says little except to ask that the problem be placed in his or her hands—with a substantial fee, of course—watch out. You're either dealing with someone who doesn't know the answer and won't admit it (common) or someone who finds it impossible to let go of the "me expert, you plebeian" philosophy (even more common).

Users' Guide

Index

Legal Manual

Index

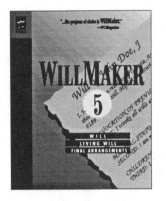

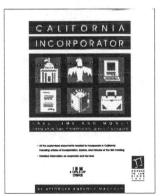

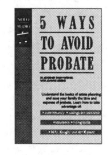

NOLO PRESS CATALOG

ESTATE PLANNING & PROBATE

Make Your Own Living Trust, Denis Clifford	1st Ed	$19.95	LITR
The Conservatorship Book (California), Goldoftas & Farren	2nd Ed	$29.95	CNSV
How to Probate an Estate (California), Nissley	8th Ed	$34.95	PAE

GOING TO COURT

Represent Yourself in Court, Bergman & Berman-Barrett	1st Ed	$29.95	RYC
Everybody's Guide to Municipal Court (California), Duncan	1st Ed	$29.95	MUNI
Everybody's Guide to Small Claims Court (California), Warner	11th Ed	$18.95	CSCC
Everybody's Guide to Small Claims Court (National), Warner	5th Ed	$18.95	NSCC
Fight Your Ticket (California), Brown	5th Ed	$18.95	FYT
Collect Your Court Judgment (California), Scott, Elias & Goldoftas	2nd Ed	$19.95	JUDG
How to Change Your Name (California), Loeb & Brown	6th Ed	$24.95	NAME
The Criminal Records Book (California), Siegel	3rd Ed	$19.95	CRIM
Winning in Small Claims Court, Warner & Greene (audio cassette)	1st Ed	$14.95	TWIN

LEGAL REFORM

Fed Up with the Legal System, Nolo Press	2nd Ed	$9.95	LEG

BUSINESS & WORKPLACE

💾 Software Development: A Legal Guide, Fishman	1st Ed	$44.95	SFT
The Legal Guide for Starting & Running a Small Business, Steingold	1st Ed	$22.95	RUNS
Sexual Harassment on the Job, Petrocelli & Repa	2nd Ed	$18.95	HARS
Your Rights in the Workplace, Repa	2nd Ed	$15.95	YRW
How to Write a Business Plan, McKeever	4th Ed	$21.95	SBS
Marketing Without Advertising, Phillips & Rasberry	1st Ed	$14.00	MWAD
The Partnership Book, Clifford & Warner	4th Ed	$24.95	PART
The California Nonprofit Corporation Handbook, Mancuso	6th Ed	$29.95	NON
💾 The California Nonprofit Corporation Handbook, Mancuso (DOS & MAC)	6th Ed	$39.95	NPI
💾 How to Form a Nonprofit Corporation (National), Mancuso (DOS)	2nd Ed	$39.95	NNP
How to Form Your Own California Corporation, Mancuso	7th Ed	$29.95	CCOR

💾 = **BOOKS WITH DISK**

TO ORDER CALL 1-800-992-6656

NOLO PRESS CATALOG

MONEY MATTERS

Stand Up to the IRS, Daily	2nd Ed	$21.95	SIRS
Money Troubles: Legal Strategies to Cope With Your Debts, Leonard	2nd Ed	$16.95	MT
How to File for Bankruptcy, Elias, Renauer & Leonard	4th Ed	$25.95	HFB
Simple Contracts for Personal Use, Elias & Stewart	2nd Ed	$16.95	CONT
Nolo's Law Form Kit: Power of Attorney,Clifford, Randolph & Goldoftas	1st Ed	$14.95	KPA
Nolo's Law Form Kit: Personal Bankruptcy, Elias, Renauer, Leonard & Goldoftas	1st Ed	$14.95	KBNK
Nolo's Law Form Kit: Rebuild Your Credit, Leonard & Goldoftas	1st Ed	$14.95	KCRD
Nolo's Law Form Kit: Loan Agreements, Stewart & Goldoftas	1st Ed	$14.95	KLOAN
Nolo's Law Form Kit: Buy & Sell Contracts, Elias, Stewart & Goldoftas	1st Ed	$9.95	KCONT

JUST FOR FUN

29 Reasons Not to Go to Law School, Warner & Ihara	4th Ed	$9.95	29R
Devil's Advocates, Roth & Roth	1st Ed	$12.95	DA
Poetic Justice, Roth & Roth	1st Ed	$9.95	PJ
Nolo's Favorite Lawyer Jokes on Disk	DOS	$9.95	JODI
	MAC	$9.95	JODM

PATENT, COPYRIGHT & TRADEMARK

Trademark: How To Name Your Business & Product, McGrath & Elias, with Shena	1st Ed	$29.95	TRD
Patent It Yourself, Pressman	3rd Ed	$39.95	PAT
The Inventor's Notebook, Grissom & Pressman	1st Ed	$19.95	INOT
The Copyright Handbook, Fishman	2nd Ed	$24.95	COHA

LANDLORDS & TENANTS

The Landlord's Law Book, Vol. 1: Rights & Responsibilities (California), Brown & Warner	4th Ed	$32.95	LBRT
The Landlord's Law Book, Vol. 2: Evictions (California), Brown	4th Ed	$32.95	LBEV
Tenants' Rights (California), Moskovitz & Warner	12th Ed	$18.95	CTEN
Nolo's Law Form Kit: Leases & Rental Agreements (California), Warner & Stewart	1st Ed	$14.95	KLEAS

HOMEOWNERS

How to Buy a House in California, Warner, Serkes & Devine	3rd Ed	$24.95	BHCA
For Sale By Owner, Devine	2nd Ed	$24.95	FSBO
Homestead Your House, Warner, Sherman & Ihara	8th Ed	$9.95	HOME
The Deeds Book, Randolph	3rd Ed	$16.95	DEED

OLDER AMERICANS

Beat the Nursing Home Trap: A Consumer's Guide to Choosing & Financing Long Term Care, Matthews	2nd Ed	$18.95	ELD
Social Security, Medicare & Pensions, Matthews with Berman	5th Ed	$18.95	SOA

RESEARCH/REFERENCE

Legal Research, Elias & Levinkind	3rd Ed	$19.95	LRES
Legal Research Made Easy: A Roadmap Through the Law Library Maze (2 1/2 hr videotape & manual), Nolo & Legal Star	1st Ed	$89.95	LRME

CONSUMER

How to Win Your Personal Injury Claim, Matthews	1st Ed	$24.95	PICL
Nolo's Pocket Guide to California Law, Guerin & Nolo Press Editors	2nd Ed	$10.95	CLAW
Nolo's Pocket Guide to California Law on Disk	Windows	$24.95	CLWIN
	MAC	$24.95	CLM
Nolo's Law Form Kit: Hiring Child Care & Household Help, Elias	1st Ed	$14.95	KCHLD
Nolo's Pocket Guide to Consumer Rights, Kaufman	2nd Ed	$12.95	CAG

IMMIGRATION

How to Get a Green Card: Legal Ways to Stay in the U.S.A., Lewis with Madlanscay	1st Ed	$22.95	GRN
Como Obtener La Tarjeta-Verde, Lewis with Madlanscay	1st Ed	$24.95	VERDE

Visit Our Store

If you live in the Bay Area, be sure to visit the Nolo Press Bookstore on the corner of 9th & Parker Streets in west Berkeley. You'll find our complete line of books and software—all at a discount.
CALL 1-510-704-2248 for hours.

Get 25% Off Your Next Purchase

Recycle your out-of-date books

It's important to have the most current legal information. Because laws and legal procedures change often, we update our books regularly. To help keep you up-to-date we are extending this special offer. Cut out and mail the title portion of the cover of any old Nolo book with your next order and we'll give you a 25% discount off the retail price of ANY new Nolo book you purchase directly from us. For current prices and editions call us at 1-800-992-6656. This offer is to individuals only.

ORDER FORM

Code	Quantity	Title	Unit price	Total

Subtotal	
California residents add Sales Tax	
Shipping & Handling ($4 for 1st item; $1 each additional)	
2nd day UPS (additional $5; $8 in Alaska and Hawaii)	
TOTAL	

Name

Address

(UPS to street address, Priority Mail to P.O. boxes)

FOR FASTER SERVICE, USE YOUR CREDIT CARD AND OUR TOLL-FREE NUMBERS

Monday-Friday, 7 a.m. to 6 p.m. Pacific Time

Order Line   1 (800) 992-6656 (in the 510 area code, call 549-4648)
General Information 1 (510) 549-1976
Fax your order   1 (800) 645-0895 (in the 510 area code, call 548-5902)

METHOD OF PAYMENT

☐ Check enclosed
☐ VISA   ☐ Mastercard   ☐ Discover Card   ☐ American Express

Account #   Expiration Date

Authorizing Signature

Daytime Phone

Allow 2-3 weeks for delivery. Prices subject to change.

NOLO PRESS, 950 PARKER ST., BERKELEY, CA 94710

LTWI2

TO ORDER CALL 1-800-992-6656